TESOL Teacher Educatic

M000119346

TESOL Teacher Education
A Reflective Approach

Thomas S. C. Farrell

EDINBURGH
University Press

Edinburgh University Press is one of the leading university presses in the UK. We publish academic books and journals in our selected subject areas across the humanities and social sciences, combining cutting-edge scholarship with high editorial and production values to produce academic works of lasting importance. For more information visit our website: edinburghuniversitypress.com

© Thomas S. C. Farrell, 2021

Edinburgh University Press Ltd
The Tun – Holyrood Road, 12(2f) Jackson's Entry, Edinburgh EH8 8PJ

Typeset in 10/12 Minion by
Servis Filmsetting Ltd, Stockport, Cheshire

A CIP record for this book is available from the British Library

ISBN 978-1-4744-7442-9 (hardback)
ISBN 978-1-4744-7444-3 (webready PDF)
ISBN 978-1-4744-7443-6 (paperback)
ISBN 978-1-4744-7445-0 (epub)

The right of Thomas S. C. Farrell to be identified as the author of this work has been asserted in accordance with the Copyright, Designs and Patents Act 1988, and the Copyright and Related Rights Regulations 2003 (SI No. 2498).

CONTENTS

SERIES EDITORS' PREFACE

Editors Fiona Farr, University of Limerick, and Bróna Murphy, University of Edinburgh

This series of textbooks addresses a range of topics taught within **TESOL programs** around the world. Each volume is designed to match a taught 'core' or 'option' course (identified by a survey of TESOL programs worldwide) and could be adopted as a prescribed text. Other series and books have been aimed at Applied Linguistics students or language teachers in general, but this aims more specifically at students of ELT (English Language Teaching – the process of enabling the learning of English), with or without teaching experience.

The series is intended primarily for college and university students at third or fourth year undergraduate level, graduates (pre-service or in-service) studying TESOL on Masters programs, and possibly some TESOL EdDs or Structured PhDs, all of whom need an introduction to the topics for their taught courses. It is also very suitable for new professionals and people starting out on a PhD, who could use the volumes for self-study. The **readership level** is **introductory** and the tone and approach of the volumes will appeal to both undergraduates and postgraduates.

This series answers a need for volumes with a special focus on **intercultural awareness**. It is aimed at programs in countries where English is not the mother tongue, and in English-speaking countries where the majority of students come from countries where English is not the mother tongue, typical of TESOL programs in the UK and Ireland, Canada and the US, Australia and New Zealand. This means that it takes into account physical and economic conditions in ELT classrooms around the world and a variety of socio-educational backgrounds. Each volume contains a number of tasks which include examples from classrooms around the world, encourage comparisons across cultures, and address issues that apply to each student's home context. Closely related to the intercultural awareness focus is a minor theme that runs throughout the series, and that is language analysis and description, and its applications to ELT. Intercultural awareness is indeed a complex concept and we aim to address it in a number of different ways. Taking examples from different cultural contexts is one way, but the volumes in the series also look at many other educationally relevant cultural dimensions such as sociolinguistic influences, gender issues, various learning traditions (e.g. collectivist vs individualistic), and culturally determined language dimensions (e.g. politeness conventions).

TESOL students need **theory clearly related to practice**. This series is practical and is intended to be used in TESOL lectures and workshops, providing group tasks and independent activities. Students are invited to engage in critical thinking and to consider applications of concepts and issues to their own particular teaching contexts, adapting the tendencies and suggestions in the literature to their own countries' educational requirements. Each volume contains practical tasks to carry out individually, in small groups, or in plenary in the classroom, as well as suggestions for practical tasks for the students to use in their own classrooms. All the concepts and issues encountered here will be translatable into the ELT classroom. It is hoped that this series will contribute to your improvement as a teacher.

The series presents ELT concepts and research issues **simply**. The volumes guide students from the basic concepts, through the issues and complexities, to a level that should make them alert to past and recent teaching and research developments in each field. This series makes the topics accessible to those unaccustomed to reading theoretical literature, and yet takes them to an exam and Masters standard, serving as a gateway into the various fields and an introduction to the more theoretical literature. We also acknowledge that **technology** is a major area within TESOL and this series is aware of the need for technology to feature prominently across its volumes. Issues of technological integration and implementation are addressed in some way in each of the volumes. The series is based on state-of-the-art research. The concepts and issues raised are intended to inspire students to undertake their own research and consider pursuing their interests in a PhD.

Editorial Advisory Board

As well as the two editors, the series has an Editorial Advisory Board, whose members are involved in decisions on commissioning and considering book proposals and reviewing book drafts. We would like to acknowledge and thank members of the Board for all of their work and guidance on the Textbooks in TESOL series:

- **Dr Waad Aljohani**, King Abdulaziz University, Jeddah, Saudi Arabia
- **Dr Averil Coxhead**, Victoria University of Wellington, New Zealand
- **Prof. Do Coyle**, University of Edinburgh, UK
- **Prof. Donald Freeman**, University of Michigan, USA
- **Dr Graham Hall**, Northumbria University, UK
- **Dr Mairin Hennebry-Leung**, University of Tasmania, Australia
- **Prof. Enric Llurda**, University of Lleida, Spain
- **Prof. Mike McCarthy**, University of Nottingham, UK
- **Dr Tom Morton**, Universidad Autónoma de Madrid, Spain
- **Dr Anne O'Keeffe**, Mary Immaculate College, University of Limerick, Ireland
- **Dr Robert Poole**, University of Alabama, USA
- **Prof Jonathon Reinhardt**, University of Arizona, USA
- **Prof. Randi Reppen**, North Arizona University, USA
- **Dr Olcay Sert**, Mälardalen University, Sweden
- **Prof. Ivor Timmis**, Leeds Beckett University, UK

- **Assoc. Prof. Scott Thornbury**, the New School, New York
- **Professor Steve Walsh**, Newcastle University, UK

Edinburgh Textbooks in TESOL

Books in this series include:

Changing Methodologies in TESOL	Jane Spiro
Mixed Methods Research for TESOL	James Dean Brown
Language in Context in TESOL	Joan Cutting
Materials Development for TESOL	Freda Mishan and Ivor Timmis
Practice in TESOL	Fiona Farr
TESOL Teacher Education	Thomas Farrell

LIST OF ACRONYMS

CELTA	Certificate in Teaching English to Speakers of Other Languages
EAL	English as an additional language
EAP	English for academic purposes
EFL	English as a foreign language
ELLs	English language learners
ELT	English language teaching
ESL	English as a second language
ESP	English for specific purposes
IATEFL	International Association of Teachers of English as a Foreign Language
IEP	individualized education program
L1	first language
L2	second language
LTE	language teacher education
MA TESOL	Master's degree in Teaching English to Speakers of Other Languages
NESTs	native English speaker teachers
NNESTs	non-native English speaker teachers
RP	reflective practice
SLA	second language acquisition
TEFL	teaching English as a foreign language
TESL	teaching English as a second language
TESOL	teaching English to speakers of other languages
TPR	total physical response
ZPD	zone of proximal development

INTRODUCTION

I have really been writing this book for a long time; since 1977 to be exact. I had just entered my Higher Diploma in Education program in University College Dublin, Ireland, after having graduated at the same university. I had decided I wanted to become a teacher. In those days, I was required to teach each day (unpaid) for two or three hours in a school as a learner-teacher as part of my teaching practice and then attend lectures and seminars in the university in the late afternoons and evenings. I was teaching a business English class to junior high school students and in my fourth week during one class a student suddenly shouted out: "Teacher you are stupid!" I was astonished, as I had no idea at that point how to respond. Although I was in shock for a few moments, I remember that I said to the boy that he could not and should not say this to me, his teacher, or any teacher, and that he should write a letter of apology to me before I would let him back to my class. I then asked him to leave for the remainder of that lesson. Just before class on the following day he handed me a letter that he said he had written as an apology. In that letter (which I still have today) he wrote the following reason for saying what he had the previous day: "Teacher, I called you stupid because you were stupid because you gave us the same homework the day before and that is why you are stupid."

When I read that note, I realized that he was correct as I had mistakenly given the class the same homework before the previous class. I also realized that even though we may think that our students may not be listening to their teachers, in fact they are. Unfortunately, the student who made the statement was actually deemed a 'problem' student by his regular teachers, in that he was always at the center of any class activity that the teachers had difficulty controlling; however, I had always had a good relationship with him, probably because he reminded me of when I was a student at his age.

I have never forgotten the 'critical incident' with Brian calling me stupid and the weeks after when my supervisor gave me *The Look*, and now, after many years working within the topic of reflective practice, I realize it was my first introduction to Schön's (1983) reflection-in-action (my immediate response to the student's statement) and reflection-on-action (my later responses). Over the years, I have had many more occasions when I have experienced both reflection-in-action moments and reflection-on-action examples in different classrooms, contexts, and countries. However, it was that early classroom example that has stayed with me for many years, as well as the fact that I was not prepared for how to deal with such a critical incident

1

in my teacher education program, which included this experience on teaching practice. In fact, I would now say that the contents of the teacher education program had nothing really to do with my experiences in the classroom that first year of my teaching life, and I survived because of the help of colleagues in the school in which I was placed rather than that of the supervisor, whom I never had any discussions with and only met when she was in my classroom before me for the classroom observations that occurred unannounced that year. (I expect/hope things have changed since then and that pre- and post-observation meetings are the norm with such visits.) I refer to this experience later in the book, but I still remember clearly my first day teaching, and I also remember that I had no idea what I was doing and that I had no resource I could refer to at that time to help me through, except for those wonderful colleagues in that school who saved me.

I discovered reflective practice as a concept in my own teaching years later, and began to arrange my own practice through the lens of reflection to get a better idea of who I am as a teacher and teacher educator and what I was doing and trying to do in the classroom. Thus the preceding forty years (I shudder when I see that number!) have led me to write the current book, with the idea that I can contribute to the education of learner TESOL teachers and better prepare them for the transition from the TESOL teacher education program to the reality of the real classroom where they will spend most of their working lives. I am surprised that I am writing this book, as I thought some other more accomplished scholar would have written this a long time ago. Unfortunately, I still cannot find such a book on TESOL teacher education that encourages reflective practice from the start of the program and includes teaching practice and the early career years.

Hence, I have written this book, *TESOL Teacher Education: A Reflective Approach*, for learner TESOL teachers who are attempting to navigate through their early development, but also for TESOL teacher educators who are trying to guide their teacher learners as they navigate through their learning to teach and want to reflect on their practice. In addition, I hope school administrators, cooperating teachers, and school mentor teachers will also find the contents of this book useful, especially as I promote the idea that all can collaborate for the successful education of future TESOL professionals. The language throughout is straightforward, sometimes general or addressed to teacher educators, but most times addressed to learner TESOL teachers and early career TESOL teachers.

Before I outline the structure of the book, I will point out a few issues I do not cover. This is not because they are not important, but because I have already covered some of them in other venues and want to save the limited space here for what I think is important to cover in this book. The first issue I do not cover in this book concerns learner teachers' language proficiency and their awareness of language development as an essential component of a teacher's subject knowledge. I acknowledge that the proficiency level of a language teacher will in many cases determine the extent to which he or she is able to use many teaching methods appropriately (especially the more communicative methods) and whether the teacher is able to provide a reliable model of target language input for his or her students. I have mentioned before that an important duty of all language teachers, be they so-called non-native speaker teachers or so-called native speaker teachers, is to reflect on their knowledge and usage of English so that they can become more confident in teaching through the medium of English (see Farrell, 2007b: ch. 5 for more on how teachers can reflect on their language proficiency).

Related to the mention above of the dichotomy between non-native English speaker teachers (NNESTs) and native English speaker teachers (NESTs), I have also noted that such a dichotomy is not useful. Many consider language proficiency one of the most noticeable differences between NNESTs and NESTs, but this is a fallacious argument, as language proficiency is just one of many competencies 'qualified' English teachers must acquire. Thus, I have suggested that "it is not who you are in terms of your ethnicity, culture or race as a TESOL teacher, but what you know in terms of your effectiveness as a teacher regardless of your background" (Farrell, 2015c: 80). I have also pointed out that no doubt much of the discrimination and racism within TESOL (Edge, 2011) arises from clients (students and their parents) who think they need a so-called native English speaker to be their teacher, even though some of these native speakers may not be qualified by a recognized certifying granting body. I have pointed out too that when considering terminology these people should be called 'conversation partners', and rather than advertising for 'native speaker teachers' schools should advertise for 'conversation partners' for their students. Thus, I have suggested that it is time to stop this harmful NEST/ NNEST dichotomy and indeed using the nonsensical terms 'NEST' and 'NNEST', and to begin talking about effective teachers regardless of their first language or place of origin. I have suggested that the terms 'NEST' and 'NNEST' in themselves are polarizing and self-defeating and contribute to the perception that there is a division in status and teaching effectiveness between teaching professionals in the ELT field. In addition, I have noted that it is time that we as a profession began to talk about critical competencies of effective teachers and effective teaching regardless of that teacher's background (see Farrell, 2015c for more on this discussion). In other words, it is not who you are in terms of your background that makes you a 'qualified' TESOL teacher, but what you know, and that is what this book is all about: becoming a 'qualified', competent TESOL teacher.

STRUCTURE OF THE BOOK

Each chapter begins with a preamble from real TESOL teachers with real experiences that carry a message from their lived experiences. Learner TESOL teachers and TESOL teacher educators can reflect on and analyze these preambles as they move through the contents of the chapter.

Each chapter also has an abundance of **reflective breaks**, which are addressed mostly to learner TESOL teachers and early career TESOL teachers, but also to all stakeholders who may be interested in the focus of these reflective breaks. Learner TESOL teachers are encouraged to reflect on each of the questions and discuss with peers and their TESOL teacher educators. Teacher educators may encourage their learner TESOL teachers to go through each of these sets of reflective breaks in each chapter, or they may decide not to go through each of these in lockstep and instead choose whichever may be of interest depending on time and contextual relevance. Of course, all readers are invited to include their own reflective breaks that may differ from those in each chapter.

Each chapter has lots of **reading and discussion tasks** dispersed throughout the text that learner TESOL teachers can tackle any time they choose. These readings, for the most part, involve encouraging learner TESOL teachers to read specific research articles (many of which were published recently) related to the topic at hand and to reflect on their contents and what they mean to them as learner TESOL teachers. Some of these readings explore a particular issue in more detail, while others seek to provide a completely different viewpoint than the one discussed in the text leading up to the task. After reflecting on the contents, then the results can be discussed with peers and TESOL teacher educators. Many of these readings (you will note that I have attempted to include each author's first and last name to make them more real) are from the field of TESOL but some are from other fields, such as general education studies. This is both to give readers a broader perspective on the issue at hand and because these readings have a significant message for the learner TESOL teacher and TESOL teacher educator to reflect on. TESOL teacher educators and learner TESOL teachers can decide which of these readings are appropriate for their learning and specific contexts, and as such, not all of these reading and discussion tasks need to be covered in lockstep. In fact, readers may postpone some as they read each chapter, only to return later when time and interest allow such reading.

After this introduction, the first chapter is an orientation that outlines core assumptions of the book. The second chapter, after discussing two inconvenient truths about TESOL teacher education, outlines a 'novice-service' framework that can be adapted to TESOL teacher education. Chapter 3 discusses reflection-as-action and outlines a practical framework for reflecting on practice. This framework has five different stages that learner TESOL teachers can use at any time in their courses, teaching practice, and early career years. Chapter 4 shows how collaboration is important in TESOL teacher education and that collaborative learning can be encouraged through mentoring, 'critical friends groups', team teaching, and peer coaching as well as through the mediational tools of writing, dialogue, action research, and technology. Chapter 5 outlines and discusses teaching practice within teacher education and how learner TESOL teachers learn how to teach through microteaching and field placements. The chapter then discusses the different roles of the TESOL teacher educator/supervisor, cooperating teachers, and learner TESOL teacher. Chapter 6 outlines and discusses a reflective, collaborative approach to teaching evaluation, and suggests that the current deficiencies of the traditional approach to TESOL teaching evaluation can be mitigated if the burden of evaluation is shared by learner TESOL teachers through self-appraisal with the use of reflective teaching portfolios. Chapter 7 outlines and discusses the early career years of teaching and the necessity of support for teachers as they develop their professional identity, and also how early career TESOL teachers can take responsibility for their own development by engaging in teacher research. Chapter 8, "Conclusions," is the final chapter of the book and outlines how learner teachers and novice teachers can use reflective practice to overcome the sometimes debilitating 'imposter syndrome' feeling prevalent when they enter a classroom during teaching practice and/or their first years of teaching. In fact, the chapter notes that they can do this by following the contents of what they have just read and reflected on in this book. In other words, this final chapter is a summary of what was presented in the book.

REFLECTION-FOR-ACTION

This book reflects my experiences working with learner TESOL teachers, TESOL teachers, cooperating teachers, and supervisors over the past forty years across several different locations, including Ireland, Singapore, Canada, South Korea, and the United States, as well as my world travels giving talks and workshop to wonderful TESOL professionals. I am grateful to them all and hope they can see themselves somewhere in the contents of the book.

TESOL TEACHER EDUCATION: GETTING ORIENTED

PREAMBLE

The big day has finally arrived for three newly qualified English as a second language (ESL) teachers. All three are very excited to begin their teaching careers and all have said that they could not wait for their first day as a newly qualified teacher. All three are secure in the feeling that they have just graduated from their second language teacher education programs and, as such, feel that they are ready, or should be ready, to teach. All three novice teachers arrived at the same school and walked in with great anticipation, and then the confusion commenced. After locating the teachers' room, they sought their mentor, or at least the person who told them they were hired, as they had had no communication with the school since they were hired except for an email telling them each to show up at a certain time that morning, but with no other information. All three stood there, as there were no introductions, and the head just told them which classroom to go to. All three ESL teachers immediately felt the sense that the school was a bit chaotic; as one of them said: "you feel thrown in to survive yourself." Another of the three summed up all their realizations of their first week on the job: "We're into the deep water now, and it is kind of sink or swim."

The transition that novice teachers (and novices in many other professions as well) make from training programs to their first year of practice may result in some kind of shock, be it in terms of culture, praxis, or otherwise. As the vignette above suggests, these shocks happened on the very first day of teaching for three ESL teachers in Canada and, in fact, lasted all through their first week on the job. As one of the novice ESL teachers remarked, "It's not welcoming. You don't feel like, 'Hey come on in. Thanks for joining the team. This is what's going on.' You have to find out a lot of things for yourself." She felt that she was "thrown in" and had to figure it all out by herself if she was to survive: "You're just thrown in to survive yourself."

The above initial experiences may have left the three ESL novice teachers reeling in their first week, and even their first semester, but they quickly realized that if they wanted to survive in their new school environment, they would have to come up with some strategies to be able to cope. Fortunately, these three ESL teachers were still in touch with their TESOL teacher educator who acted as their mentor, and thus were able to form a novice teacher reflection group during their first semester with him, where they were able to discuss their various challenges and experiences during that first year (Farrell, 2016a). The teachers reported that they did not have any mentors appointed in their new school, nor did they have any guidance or directions about where they could go or who they could seek out if they had problems; they had to rely on their novice TESOL teacher reflection group discussion along with their TESOL teacher educator/mentor, who facilitated the discussions, for developing survival strategies that first year. Indeed, at the end of the year, they began to move from survival to thriving as early career TESOL teachers, mostly because they got lucky enough to have their TESOL teacher educator not only still in contact with them after their graduation from their TESOL teacher education program, but also willing to act as their mentor-colleague during the first year and into their early career years. But one can ask, what happens to those isolated early career TESOL teachers who do not have anybody to mentor them or offer guidance during their first weeks or first semester? Do their TESOL teacher education programs prepare them well enough for their transition to life in what Donald Schön (1983: 42) has called the "swampy lowlands" of teaching in real classrooms "where situations are confusing 'messes'"?

REFLECTIVE BREAK

- Why do you want to become a teacher of English to speakers of other languages and did you always want to become one?
- Do you agree or disagree with the following statement: "Those that can do, those that can't teach"? Explain your answer.
- Define what the word "teacher" means to you.
- Who is your ideal student?
- What is your ideal classroom set-up?
- Do you think your ideals (above) are realistic in the context of the experience of teaching in real classrooms when you graduate from your TESOL teacher education program?
- What do you want to accomplish in the future as a TESOL teacher?
- What do you want to be known for as a TESOL teacher when you retire (your legacy)?
- What is your opinion of the experiences of the three ESL teachers in their first day, week, and/or semester of teaching?
- Are you surprised to read about their negative experiences?
- Do you think this is an exception to what most ESL teachers will experience when they graduate?
- Do you think this would be similar for you when you begin your teaching career? If yes, why? If no, why not?
- Are you surprised by Donald Schön's (1983: 42) description of classrooms as "swampy lowlands" where teaching "situations are confusing 'messes'"?

INTRODUCTION

It may seem somewhat strange to begin a book on TESOL teacher education with a report on some of the challenges of early career TESOL teachers in their first year as outlined in the preamble above. However, this *fast forward* may be a necessary reality check for learner TESOL teachers about to embark on their journeys to becoming a TESOL teacher, because it offers a glimpse into their future reality. All stakeholders, including learner TESOL teachers, TESOL teacher educators, cooperating teachers, mentor teachers, and any administrators, should be fully oriented to what needs to be accomplished in TESOL teacher education programs. Unfortunately, what has *not* happened is abundantly clear for the early career TESOL teachers in the preamble, as they maintain they were not prepared adequately for their future as TESOL professionals. Rather, their experiences seem to give credence to the old adage that teaching is a "profession that eats its young" (Halford, 1998: 34) because they have not been prepared for the reality of what they will face in a real classroom, and sadly the number of novice teachers who are leaving the profession during the first years in epidemic proportions (OECD, 2018a) bears witness to this fact. Why would they leave if they were prepared adequately for what they will face during their careers?

Indeed, the experiences outlined above by three early career TESOL teachers are not unique to Canada or the school in question. Similar findings have also been reported of the experiences of first year TESOL teacher woes in other contexts (Artigliere and Baecher, 2017; Farrell, 2016a, 2017), with many early career TESOL teachers left to cope on their own without much guidance or support (Higginbotham, 2019). However, and although evidence suggests that this is occurring in the TESOL profession, it is not much talked about by TESOL teacher educators either privately or, especially, in the literature. This is possibly because so many TESOL teacher education programs are so diverse in length (from a weekend course to a Masters degree) and in content that it is difficult to compare them.

For example, many TESOL teacher education programs focus their course content heavily on theory (such as second language acquisition theory or linguistic theory), and fewer focus on how learner teachers can put what they have learned in these programs into practice in real settings (I address the theory/practice gap in more detail in the chapter that follows). In addition, there are not many studies that have been conducted on TESOL teacher education courses'/programs' appropriateness for and impact on what happens in school contexts. Of those few studies that have been conducted, the majority report that novice ESL teachers feel that they were not sufficiently prepared for the demands of these real classrooms in real school settings, because what they learned in their TESOL teacher education program was too theoretical (Macknish, Porter-Szucs, Tomaš, Scholze, Slucter, and Kavetsky, 2017). It seems, though, and as mentioned above, that many TESOL teacher educators are oblivious to the struggles of early career TESOL teachers in their first years. These educators continue to provide foundation/theory courses that are not bad in themselves, as they offer more intellectual reflections for learner TESOL teachers, but we must ask whether these courses are presented at the expense of the learner teachers' more practical needs (Farrell, 2016a). That said, I also note that many times academics' hands are tied by national standards and programs that they have to adhere to when delivering teacher education programs (such as the language benchmarks prominent in many teacher education programs in Canada). What I am really suggesting is that we teacher educators really reflect on the various courses we ask our learner TESOL teachers to study and whether they are fulfilling their needs as future TESOL teachers.

TESOL TEACHER EDUCATION: WHOSE NEEDS?

Unfortunately, for too many years within the TESOL profession those who would push a methods approach have been to the fore, especially at TESOL conferences where they have held center stage in the publishers' hall. TESOL as a profession has allowed this to happen over the years because these same people funded various speakers at conferences and, if truth be told, many of these conferences would not otherwise have been held because of the lack of such funding. A negative byproduct of this methods approach was, and still is, that many learner TESOL teachers want to find 'the method' or want to be told what to do in the classroom, and they take TESOL teacher education programs with the idea that they will be shown methods that can be used to teach reading, writing, speaking, listening, grammar, and/or assessment. Many TESOL teacher education programs and teacher educators have been, and still are, all too willing to give them what they want and transfer this 'knowledge' to their perceived empty vessels, with the idea that once they graduate, they can put these methods into practice during their teaching careers.

In such a knowledge transmission approach, TESOL teacher educators are often considered the experts and gatekeepers of the profession, and learner TESOL teachers as there to absorb their wisdom, without much adherence to Lortie's (1975) consideration of their 'apprenticeship of observation', or their tacit development of knowledge of what it means to be a teacher while they themselves were students. Many such programs offer methodology courses in how to teach the skills of reading, writing, speaking, listening, or grammar without much activation of the learner teachers' prior knowledge of how they learned these (successfully or not) when they were students. (I address how teacher educators can help learner TESOL teachers articulate these prior beliefs in more detail in Chapter 2.) Such a reductionist approach to TESOL teacher education places the power fully in the hands of the 'expert' TESOL teacher educators, and teacher education becomes content coverage at the expense of learner TESOL teacher cultivation.

As a result, it seems that the TESOL profession is now in a bit of a quandary: on the one hand, we have TESOL teacher educators providing the knowledge (both content and pedagogical) they consider important and necessary for learner TESOL teachers to become effective teachers throughout their careers. Yet, on the other, we also have recent evidence from research studies that TESOL teachers are struggling when trying to implement what they have learned in their TESOL teacher education once they begin teaching in their first years (e.g. Farrell, 2016a, 2017; Higginbotham, 2019; Wright, 2010). In addition, we have lots of anecdotal evidence that even experienced TESOL teachers do not believe that TESOL teacher education programs prepare learner TESOL teachers for real classrooms, because they say these programs are still not providing the knowledge necessary to be effective TESOL teachers in real classroom situations, with some telling early career teachers to forget all they have learned in their TESOL teacher education programs as it is of no use (Farrell, 2016a, 2016c; Fradd and Lee, 1997). One of the early studies in the United States to examine ESL teachers' opinions of how their TESOL teacher education programs prepared them for the challenges of their work, and especially about how the program did or did not meet their needs, was conducted by Fradd and Lee (1997). Their results informed them that the program failed to prepare ESL teachers to work with English language learners within special education, and that the teachers needed more extensive field and hands-on teaching experiences, as well as more related to the technology at that time. The main issue here is focus within a TESOL teacher education program: academics tend to focus on the subject matter they think learner TESOL teachers need to know, and not on teaching or how learner TESOL teachers can teach or how they should teach. Indeed, Freeman (2001: 73) has observed that it is "ironic" that TESOL teacher education "has concerned itself little with how individuals actually learn to teach."

In agreement, Faez and Vaelo (2012) maintain that TESOL teacher education programs and courses should be reconsidered and reconfigured in order to work out how the program content could be aligned more closely with the needs of learner TESOL teachers, especially in terms of pedagogical content (how learner TESOL teachers should teach). However, in order to be able to realign a TESOL teacher education program to the needs of novice TESOL teachers, second language teacher educators need to be aware of what those needs really are. In other words, they must be able to identify the various challenges their graduates face every day to see how their TESOL teacher education programs prepare learner TESOL teachers to meet the needs of their students (Gándara, Maxwell-Jolly, and Driscoll, 2005). In fact, Faez and Vaelo (2012) illustrated the importance of soliciting the opinions of TESOL teacher education program graduates when they asked their graduates of these programs to describe the least useful features of their TESOL courses in Canada. These researchers discovered that the graduates stated that most of the courses were heavy on theory but too light on concrete teaching of skills, and although they said the different theories may have been interesting in themselves, they said that they did not find them helpful in the real classroom.

Thus TESOL teacher educators must actively solicit feedback from early career TESOL teachers about the different challenges they are faced with in real classrooms, in an attempt to close the gap between their training and their classroom reality. As Tarone (2007: 3) has succinctly suggested, TESOL teacher educators must

> constantly ask ourselves, as part of our own ongoing needs analysis, "How well prepared are the language teachers we educate? Do they have the skills they need to do accurate analyses of the needs of their students, and then to adapt their teaching to address those needs?"

Although many TESOL teacher educators are probably aware that early career TESOL teachers will face many issues and challenges during their first years, it is interesting to note that many TESOL programs still have only limited information about how their graduates are faring in their induction years, or even what their work lives actually involve (Baecher, 2012). This is probably because not many studies exist about the experiences of early career TESOL teachers in their first years. In addition, some of the shortcomings present in current approaches to TESOL teacher education may be a direct result of the dearth of knowledge about what it means to be a TESOL teacher in a real classroom, as TESOL teacher educators may have had little experience teaching in such real classrooms themselves.

That said, what learner TESOL teachers are being presented with in most TESOL teacher education programs has much merit and, as mentioned above, many of the theories of language learning and teaching may hold important intrinsic interest. However, the 'elephant in the room' that the profession is reluctant to face is that the contents of these programs and courses may not be relevant to the everyday needs of learner TESOL teachers.

REFLECTIVE BREAK

- Whose needs should TESOL teacher education programs serve and why?
- What do you think are your needs as a learner TESOL teacher?

Reading and Discussion Task

Eveli Laats (2020) has suggested that despite their qualifications, novice TESOL teachers have difficulties adjusting and soon leave the profession, and that this is caused by drawbacks in teacher preparation. The researcher surveyed graduate novice English language teachers with the aim of finding out what aspects of their preparation they thought useful, what aspects they did not find useful, and their suggestions for improving teacher education.

- Read and summarize their answers to these questions. What is your opinion of the findings?
- Discuss your findings with a colleague.

[Laats, E. (2020). Novice teachers' satisfaction with teacher preparation and recommendations for improving teacher training. In *Proceedings of the 3rd International Conference on Research in Education, Teaching and Learning*, 1-12. Available from: https://www.dpublication.com/wp-content/uploads/2020/02/33-488.pdf.]

TESOL TEACHER EDUCATION:
BECOMING 'STUDENTS OF TEACHING'

Learner TESOL teachers need to be able to adapt to a variety of different challenges throughout their teaching careers, and preparation for this begins in the TESOL teacher education program. Thus, TESOL teacher educators can help prepare learner TESOL teachers to become 'adaptive professionals' throughout their careers. At present, many TESOL teacher education programs provide theories in general and some courses on methods that TESOL teacher educators presume will be useful when the learner teachers go and teach. However, when they are plunged physically into the real world of classrooms (like the ESL teachers in the preamble above) where the contents of their education program are of no help, they are forced into developing quick fixes through a process of what Dewey (1933: vii) called "blind experimentation" rather than any considered reflection. They just want to survive that particular crisis, and begin to form bad habits that can remain fixed throughout their teaching careers. On the contrary, as Dewey (1920: viii) maintained, teacher education should prepare learner teachers to become "students of teaching," through engaging in reflection and reflective practice so that they can become true adaptive professionals throughout their careers.

This is the main premise of this book: by taking a reflective approach to TESOL teacher education, as learner TESOL teachers, you can become 'students of teaching' not only during your teacher education program and teaching practice but also in your early career years, collaborating with all the important people involved as you develop as teachers: your TESOL teacher educators, cooperating teachers, mentor teachers, and all your school administrators.

I now offer three core assumptions that underlie such development toward you becoming 'students of teaching'.

THREE CORE ASSUMPTIONS

The following three interrelated core assumptions suggest that the knowledge a learner TESOL teacher needs comes from personal investment in learning to teach, as well as from observation and reflection, and is personally owned. Of course this knowledge is passed from second language teacher education preparation programs, but it is the individual learner ESL teacher who personally constructs meaning from his or her own knowledge in order to make personal decisions about practice, based on the particular set of circumstances and unique context. In this way, learner TESOL teachers can become informed decision makers within their own social contexts. Most of the ideas and activities outlined and discussed in this book are based on the following three assumptions:

1. The first assumption is that engaging learner TESOL teachers in reflective practice is a key element in TESOL teacher education, especially as it can act as a bridge between theory and practice for learner TESOL teachers as adaptive professionals, where they can reflect on, evaluate, and adapt their own practice. Reflection in TESOL teacher education is based on the premise that TESOL teachers, through systematic reflections on the nature and meaning of their practice, can learn from their own experiences throughout their education and careers. Thus as Bullough and Gitlin (1991: 52) suggest, "Teacher education programs can start with what teachers know and through the process of text building and reflection on the text enable them to articulate and enhance that

knowledge." Such a reflective approach to TESOL teacher education will help learner TESOL teachers move more smoothly through the phases of adaptation they will experience during their early career years and into their in-service years. As Yost (2006: 61) has noted, "In order for novice teachers to become successful, they require the [reflective] tools necessary for coping with challenges they encounter." Reflection is operationalized by encouraging learner TESOL teachers to reflect on their *philosophy, principles, theory, and practice,* and *beyond practice* (Farrell, 2012b, 2015b, 2019a, 2019b, 2020), because such structured reflective opportunities can enable learner TESOL teachers to grow professionally throughout their careers (Howe, 2006). This assumption permeates most of the contents of this book and is discussed in detail in Chapter 3.

2. The second assumption is that the TESOL teacher preparation/education program is just a beginning and the knowledge provided at this pre-service level about TESOL teaching and learning is in a tentative and incomplete state. Learner TESOL teachers will therefore need regular opportunities to update their professional knowledge immediately after they graduate from the program and especially in their early career years. As Cirocki, Madyarov, and Baecher (2019: 2) point out: "Teacher learning is an ongoing, reflective and constructive process. It begins during university degree programs, or certificate courses, and continues in and outside the classroom throughout teachers' careers." Thus, TESOL teacher education is a process that begins in the TESOL teacher education program that includes practice teaching, and continues through the early career years, when learner TESOL teachers will need continued mentoring and support from their TESOL teacher educator/supervisors, cooperating teachers, and school-appointed mentor teachers. Consequently, this assumption suggests that the old, traditional pre-service TESOL teacher education programs that have an entrance and exit or input–output model, where learner TESOL teachers are dropped on exiting graduation and left, for the most part, to their own devices to survive in their early career teaching years in the real world of classroom teaching, are insufficient. This assumption maintains that TESOL teacher education must also include support for these early career years as well. Thus, TESOL teacher education is conducted through a 'novice-service' (as opposed to pre-service) approach, and the framework is outlined in detail in Chapter 2.

3. The third assumption suggests that, although TESOL teacher learning may begin with a learner TESOL teacher's own personal initiative to enter the teaching profession and thus with seeking to develop a personal sense of one's own practice, TESOL teacher learning is basically a social process, where teachers learn with each other in collaboration and thus become actively involved in furthering each other's learning and development. As Dewey (1933) has noted, reflective practice is a social process and best conducted in the company of others as we attempt to overcome any of our tacitly held biases. Conducting TESOL teacher education with collegial forms of collaboration with other learner TESOL teachers encourages both increased interaction between learner TESOL teachers and peer-based learning, as well as mentoring from TESOL teacher educators, cooperating teachers, and mentor teachers in schools. Such successful collaborative

learning is "grounded in the human moral and social capacity to take the position of the other through numerous forms of reciprocity, mutuality, and give
and take" (Brody and Davidson, 1998: 6). This will be discussed in more detail
in Chapter 4. This core assumption of collaboration in TESOL teacher education
is also extended to how learner TESOL teachers are evaluated. A collaborative approach to teaching evaluation in TESOL teacher education suggests that
learner TESOL teachers will share the evaluation process with TESOL teacher
educator/supervisors and cooperating teachers while on teaching practice (see
Chapter 5) and beyond, thus taking more responsibility for their own assessment, as discussed in detail in Chapter 6.

These three interrelated assumptions offer an alternative to more traditional
approaches to teacher education that have problems with a narrow focus on theory
and less on practice. The chapter that follows outlines and discusses some of the
problems in a traditional approach to TESOL teacher education as 'inconvenient
truths', and offers some alternative ideas about how learner TESOL teachers can be
educated as reflective practitioners.

REFLECTIVE BREAK

- What is your understanding of each of the three core assumptions above?
- How do you think these three assumptions are interrelated?
- What is your opinion of each of the three assumptions above? What do you think
  you may learn from each of them?
- Would you add any more assumptions on how you think learner TESOL teachers
  should be educated?

CONCLUSION

This chapter is designed to get everyone oriented to the content of this book on
TESOL teacher education: a reflective approach that is based on three core assumptions that I believe, when *taken together*, offer an alternative to the narrow, traditional, pre-service, one-stop approach that begins and ends with the TESOL teacher
education program currently popular in many countries worldwide. Hence I call this
reflective approach a *novice-service* approach. The assumptions include the belief that
reflective practice should be and is at the core of educating learner TESOL teachers,
that it begins in a TESOL teacher education program and extends well into the early
career teaching years, and that this process is collaborative in nature throughout
these years, with all stakeholders taking an interest in the successful integration of
novice ESL teachers into the profession.

2

TESOL TEACHER EDUCATION: A NOVICE-SERVICE APPROACH

PREAMBLE

The following short narrative is from the lived experiences of an ESL teacher in the United States with ten years of teaching experience and two TESOL-related qualifications but who *still* does not feel adequately prepared to teach:

I have been in ESL/EFL [English as a second language/English as a foreign language] for over a decade. I did a MA in Linguistics with an emphasis in TESL, since my only qualifications while working overseas were a BA in Linguistics and a 200-hour TESL certificate. All of my teaching experience prior to this past year was done abroad, so I feel quite like I am a new teacher. The systems are completely different now that I am working in higher education.

I am currently working for an IEP [individualized education program] at a private college where my class is comprised of multi-level students, a handful of whom feel they do not belong there. I was hired about a month before starting classes, and was given a sample syllabus and a packet of materials created by another teacher, and told not to use a textbook. I'm fighting every day to keep my head above water.

I also work as an adjunct for a community college. Again, hired weeks before the semester started and only given course objectives and sample syllabi. I scurried to try and pull some ideas together for my two new jobs and talked to as many people as I could to try and figure out why this was so unorganized. I came to the conclusion that this is just the way it is, which you seemed to confirm from what I heard in the podcast episode that you gave some time ago about teacher education.

I feel that my training has failed me for the most part. With TESL being part of the linguistics program (not applied linguistics), the majority of what I studied in my program was research based. Therefore, I've had next to no practical, classroom-ready-type training. I came into this profession out of convenience, but I've stayed because I love helping students succeed. I have no doubt learned a lot over so many years in the classroom, but I was really looking forward to feeling confident about teaching upon finishing my degree.

The reality is quite different. I feel that I lack support and readiness for helping my students. I am planning everything on the fly, staying up until midnight the day before class trying to pull together a coherent lesson. Yet I feel absolutely defeated after every class. I am lost. It's pretty overwhelming.

The above short narrative of a real-life experience from a very qualified TESOL teacher in the United States is a further reality check for all learner TESOL teachers, TESOL teacher educators, cooperating teachers, mentor teachers, school principals, administrators, government officials, and any other stakeholders concerned with the education and development of TESOL teachers. The clear message (in the form of an unsolicited email sent to me recently and used with permission) here is that this TESOL teacher's training has let her down repeatedly and that she has had to scramble to try to discover how to survive not only in her early career years, but also well beyond. The example shows that this ESL teacher's education program (initial and certificates) was mostly of a theoretical nature and had "failed" her when she got to teach in real classrooms. The teacher wondered about how she could handle her reality of teaching and that she is feeling "defeated" although she seemingly (on paper) is well 'qualified' to teach, given her BA and MA in Linguistics as well as a (200-hundred-hour) TESL certificate. It is amazing that this teacher did not join a lot of others and just quit the profession, but by reaching out, she showed that she loves what she does and wants to continue teaching English to speakers of other languages.

REFLECTIVE BREAK

- What balance would you expect between theory and practice in a TESOL teacher education program?
- What is the balance between both in the program you are in at the moment?

INTRODUCTION

'I love teaching, but . . .' is a comment made frequently by many experienced TESOL teachers. This is not necessarily out of abject despair with the profession and their practice, because they are still at it. The 'but' points to some sense that not every-thing is going well, and in fact this is also the case for many people in any profession, because nobody would report that they are completely content with their occupa-tion. However, when this statement is made by early career teachers, defined here as novice teachers from their first to their fifth year of teaching (Gordon, Kane, and Staiger, 2006; Ingersoll and Smith, 2003), the descriptions that follow the conjunc-tion suggest a closer look is warranted. Research in general education (e.g. Olsen and Anderson, 2007) has reported a high frequency of early career teachers making such a statement, and the details given after the conjunction revealed complaints about issues such as having 'plateaued' and 'stagnating' while in these early career years, and an overall feeling of disillusionment with teaching as a career/profession.

This is worrying, as learner teachers entering the teaching profession are said to bring with them enthusiasm, idealism, and recent, new training initiatives from their teacher education programs that can only improve the teaching profession (OECD, 2018a). However, and astonishingly, general education research has revealed that nearly half of all beginning teachers will leave within their first five years (Ingersoll, 2015). Among the various challenges they face in their first years, teachers include that first 'reality/culture shock' (Caspersen and Raaen, 2014) they experience when they transition from their teacher education program to the reality of a real classroom, and also the culture shock of adapting to the context of their new workplace environment. Unfortunately, the research reveals that many early career teachers have to scramble throughout these years in their attempt to survive rather than thrive as teachers.

Within TESOL there have been similar findings on the plight of learner TESOL teachers having serious transition problems from their TESOL teacher education programs, where courses focused more on theory than practice, to the reality of teaching in real classrooms. There, not much was transferable from those courses, and the novice teachers felt abandoned because they were left to cope on their own in a 'sink-or-swim' process (Higginbotham, 2019). Indeed, even for those who do *survive* their first years of teaching, these 'transition traumas' can have lasting and serious repercussions for their future commitment to the TESOL profession, and the built-up feelings of alienation can eventually lead to increased levels of teacher attrition (Lindqvist, Nordänger, and Carlsson, 2014; Fenwick, 2011). When this happens, everyone loses, but most of all the learner TESOL teachers, who could have had an exciting career teaching English to speakers of other languages, and their students, who will miss such wonderful instruction.

Thus it is time for the TESOL profession to address some of the current serious deficiencies in how it is educating learner TESOL teachers, such as the theory/practice divide (or as some others put it: "learn-the-theory-and-then-apply-it model" (Yan and He, 2010: 60)) and the near-complete abandonment of early career TESOL teachers once they graduate from their TESOL teacher education programs. This chapter will focus on these two issues and outline and discuss each as 'inconvenient truths', while also offering ways that both can be rectified in TESOL teacher education programs.

REFLECTIVE BREAK

- What is your understanding of the statement: 'I love teaching, but . . .'?
- Are you surprised to hear that experienced TESOL teachers will have complaints about their teaching experiences?
- Are you surprised to hear that they want to trace these back to feelings of not being adequately trained in their teacher education programs?
- Should learner TESOL teachers expect to be able to learn the theory in the TESOL teacher education program and then apply it all in the real classroom, as Yan and He (2010) mention above?
- Are you expecting to put into practice most if not all of what you learn in your TESOL teacher education when you teach in a real classroom?
- Do you think that some theories you will learn in your TESOL teacher education program will not be transferable to teaching in a real classroom, and that

this is to be expected? If yes, which theories do you think this will or should apply to?
• Do you think that the theory/practice gap and early career TESOL teacher abandonment by the different stakeholders are 'inconvenient truths'? If yes, why? If no, why not?

Reading and Discussion Task

Mairin Hennerby-Leung, Angela Gayton, Xiao Amy Hu, and Xiaohui Chen's (2019) paper on 'Transitioning from Master's studies to the classroom: From theory to practice' outlines the challenges language teachers experience in transitioning between teacher education Master's programs in three locations (Hong Kong, Scotland, and China) and the classroom, particularly regarding the theory–practice nexus, and emphasizes the professional community's key role in providing mentoring and support. Results regardless of location were common and included a sense of isolation, a "sink-or-swim" phenomenon leading to the abandonment of theoretically grounded pedagogical beliefs in exchange for adherence to "safe" practice, confusion regarding the relationship between learning on university programs and the practice of teaching, and weak self-efficacy as transitioning teachers faced internal and external pressures.

• Read this paper and explain your understanding of their points of view.
• Discuss your findings with a colleague.

[Hennerby-Leung, M., Gayton, A., Hu, X., and Chen, X, (2019). Transitioning from Master's studies to the classroom: From theory to practice. *TESOL Quarterly*, *53*, 3, 685-711]

TESOL TEACHER EDUCATION: TWO INCONVENIENT TRUTHS

Yes, these problems (theory/practice divide and early career TESOL teacher abandonment) can be considered as 'inconvenient' truths; 'inconvenient' perhaps because some may not want to acknowledge that such a 'truth' exists, and/or even understand why it exists, since program providers may believe (rightly or wrongly) that they are preparing learner TESOL teachers in the best way that they know how. This may well be true. The fact that many TESOL teacher education programs still put a larger proportion of their focus on theory courses is likely a result of the history and tradition of where such programs have been placed since their inception. Indeed, TESOL language teacher education itself is a very new discipline, and so when it was developed its placement as an academic discipline was not fully considered, with some programs ending up in Faculty of Education departments, some in Linguistics/Applied Linguistics departments, and yet others in English departments. Each of these draws on a completely different knowledge base, and thus the courses that they provide will likely reflect the research interests of each individual faculty.

For example, a TESOL teacher education program that is offered in a department that has a heavy applied linguistics background will probably consider that a necessary knowledge base includes core courses on phonetics, discourse analysis, language description and analysis, sociolinguistics and psycholinguistics, and language teaching methodology. Teaching practice may or may not be an add-on in these departments, as they may not have any faculty sufficiently qualified or interested in supervising, and/or they may not have any resources to place learner TESOL teachers in school or institution settings. However, if the TESOL teacher education program is housed in an education faculty, core courses would be very different and include such foundational courses as general education theory, philosophy of education, sociology of education, curriculum development, materials development, and most likely practice teaching of some kind, as many faculty will have qualifications and interest in supervising learner TESOL teachers teaching in schools.

Although each of the above programs will have different subject matter presented to learner TESOL teachers, with some programs more theoretical than others, they are not all bad, in that they all provide different experiences that may prove helpful for individual teachers. Anyway, as a profession, as Richards (2014) has pointed out, we still do not know what content knowledge is really appropriate in the field of TESOL teacher education. That said, Freeman (2016: 9) has suggested that TESOL as a profession should make more attempts to better link the "so-called parent academic disciplines of language teaching" and "what is done in the classroom."

REFLECTIVE BREAK

- List the courses you are asked to take in your TESOL teacher education program. Which ones are theoretical and which ones are practical?
- What are the advantages and disadvantages of each focus?

INCONVENIENT TRUTH1: THEORY/PRACTICE GAP

You have probably entered your teacher education program in order to take courses that you consider will help you become a teacher of English to speakers of other languages when you enter a real classroom (otherwise why take the program?). In other words, TESOL teacher education programs are in existence to deliver programs and courses that will provide solid knowledge that is considered necessary and relevant to you as a learner TESOL teacher, so that you will be able to function as a TESOL teacher in a real classroom. In addition, you hope that many school administrators (including cooperating teachers and mentor teachers) will hire you because you have graduated from a 'recognized' program (read: a recognized university with an acceptable reputation) as a 'qualified' TESOL teacher. The idea that you and those who hire you have is that you will be able to put into practice what you have learned in these TESOL teacher education programs; after all, the courses you have taken *must be useful* otherwise why would they require you to take them?

At least, this is what is supposed to happen. However, as the preamble in the opening of this chapter from a (well-)'qualified' TESOL teacher has demonstrated (again), this is not always the case. The TESOL profession must sit up and take notice, and reason that something is not working in how it is educating and training learner TESOL teachers. This theory/practice gap was first noticed in the field of TESOL some time ago by Mark Clarke (1994) when he pointed out a dysfunction in the field of TESOL teacher education. Indeed, at that time Clarke (1994: 18) suggested boldly that it is TESOL teachers who should be the agents of change in TESOL teacher education programs, and he said they should do this by "turning the hierarchy on its head – putting teachers on top and arraying others . . . below them." Indeed, as Freeman (2016: 9) has maintained, the function of TESOL teacher education is to act as "a bridge that serves to link what is known in the field with what is done in the classroom, and it does so through the individuals whom we educate as teachers."

Reading and Discussion Task

Megan Peercy (2012) has pointed out that teacher educators have generally considered the 'theory/practice gap' to be constructed uniformly by teachers. However, she said that it is important to examine variations in how pre-service teachers make sense of their teacher education, and to examine their understandings of the theoretical and practical elements of their coursework in relation to the identities they construct for themselves as teachers.

- Read this paper and explain your understanding of its points of view. Do you agree or disagree with them? Are the points valid for TESOL teachers?
- Discuss your findings with a colleague.

[Peercy, M. M. (2012). Problematizing the theory–practice gap: How ESL teachers make sense of their preservice teacher education. *Journal of Theory and Practice in Education*, 8, 1, 20-40]

Although the theory/practice gap still remains a major challenge for TESOL teacher programs today, all is not lost, because regardless of where their programs are academically placed, some scholars within TESOL have begun to take notice. They are heeding Johnson's (2013: 76) sound advice that, yes, it is the responsibility of these programs and teacher educators to present concepts they think are important to teachers, "but to do so in ways that bring these concepts to bear on concrete practical activity, connecting them to everyday concepts and the goal-directed activities of everyday teaching." Indeed, as reported in a recent volume published by TESOL Press, eleven TESOL teacher educators from different parts of the globe 'noticed' that such a theory/practice gap existed in their particular TESOL teacher education programs, and took measures to try to bridge the theory/practice gap (Farrell, 2017).

For example, Farahnaz Faez, Shelley Cooke, Michael Karas, and Mithila Vidwans (2017) explored the effectiveness of online interactive forums through Google Docs, a web-based application for creating and editing documents, to determine whether such forums can facilitate rich discussions to bridge theory/practice gaps in their TESOL teacher education program. They discovered that although an online platform was a useful pedagogical tool, its use did not lead to discussions that were as in-depth as face-to-face communication, and they noted that this limited the opportunity of using it as a sole means of classroom interaction. The authors suggest that online collaborations are best enhanced in combination with face-to-face dialogue. Fiona Farr and Elaine Riordan (2017) also reflected on the usefulness of online modes of learning together with reflective practice strategies as a means of bridging the theory/practice gap in their teacher education courses. Specifically, they examined the usefulness of two Web 2.0 technologies (online blogs and e-portfolios) to encourage pre-service teachers to reflect and to make better connections between theories they are taught in their teacher education courses and how these relate to their practice. These studies lead to posing such interesting questions as: how can TESOL teacher educators exploit technological tools to help close the theory/ practice divide in language teacher education? And how can teacher educators move online discussions beyond descriptions of teaching experiences to actual participant involvement in problem-solving and knowledge-building?

Other TESOL teacher educators in that volume (Farrell, 2017) noticed the need to reconsider the amount of theoretical reading they assign, as well as how theory is delivered. Linda Hanington and Anitha Devi Pillai (2017), for example, realized that their learner TESOL teachers did not notice that the approaches (in this case process writing) their teacher educators were using were the very ones they were hoping the pre-service teachers would use once they began teaching. These authors decided that to make this connection to their learners more explicit, they would have to be clearer in their instruction. In addition, Cynthia Macknish, Ildiko Porter-Szucs, and Zusana Tomaš joined with three recent graduates of their Master's in TESOL program (and now ESL teachers), Andre Scholze, Courtney Slucter, and Adam Kavetsky, in cycles of dialogue and reflection about the usefulness of how theory was delivered in the program and perceived by their learner TESOL teachers. These authors came to realize that they would gain a deeper understanding if theory was taught in more manageable segments. Marcus Artigliere and Laura Baecher (2017) looked at the difficulties that learner TESOL teachers face when they are placed in a co-teaching situation with content-area specialists. These authors realized that part of the theory/ practice gap regarding co-teaching stems from the general way all teacher education programs prepare their learner TESOL teachers for the role of teacher as sole leader of instruction. Yet many learner TESOL teachers in the United States are required to work with content specialists in co-teaching arrangements. These TESOL teacher educators attempted to bridge this gap in their program by providing more co-planning and co-teaching experiences in their courses, as well as a co-taught practicum lesson. These studies also report that explicit modeling of reflective practice is essential to teaching learner TESOL teachers how to make links between theory and practice. (See Chapter 3 for more on how reflective practice can be incorporated into TESOL teacher education programs.)

In addition, TESOL teacher educators Nancy Boblett and Hansun Zhang Waring (2017) noticed that the frameworks and methods in their second language acquisition (SLA) course concerning the literature on corrective feedback were limited for practice TESOL teachers, and so, in order to bridge the gap between the theory of error correction and the practice of implementing it in a classroom, they designed a reflective assignment. They combined a video clip of a real English language class and Brown's (2007) "model for the treatment of classroom speech errors" with the goal of helping their students notice instances of error correction. As a result of seeing corrective feedback on video, the students were able to notice not only the many details involved in implementing a specific type of feedback but also the deeply contextualized nature of corrective feedback. Questions raised from all of these studies include: how can teacher educators make use of reflective practice to link theory to practice? In what ways can teacher educators prepare candidates for the particular teaching contexts they are in? And how can teacher educators incorporate local mandates, program models, instructional approaches, and available curricula into their programs?

Finally, some of the TESOL teacher educators noticed a large gap between the way TESOL methods courses are delivered in traditional campus-based programs, through reading case studies of practice, and observations of TESOL classes with (usually written) reflections. Many campus-based programs ask their candidates to write lesson plans for theoretical classes; this practice, however, led to formulaic understanding of TESOL practice because students lacked classroom experience. The solution was to incorporate service learning (similar to what general education programs have done – see above) into the programs.

Michaela Colombo, Kathleen Brazil, and Lisa White (2017) noted that service learning in a TESOL teacher education program provided a more authentic teaching experience, especially of the political nature of teaching that traditional TESOL methods miss. Therefore, these educators embedded in their TESOL methods course service learning that also provided structure for cycles of action and reflection. Immediately following the service learning experiences, the teacher educator conducted the TESOL methods course at the host school. As a result, these authors noticed that their learner TESOL students were better able to make sense of practice through theory and connect theory to practice. In a similar manner, Zuzana Tomaš, Nathan Moger, Allison Park, and Kimberly Specht (2017) decided to incorporate service learning into their TESOL teacher education program because they also noticed that they needed to provide more authentic teaching experiences for their learner TESOL teachers, as well as become more sensitive to the sociopolitical issues in a particular teaching context. These examples of TESOL teacher educators implementing versions of service learning in their TESOL teacher education programs show how such programs can move from traditional, campus-based, and formulaic presentation of content to providing more authentic teaching experiences for their teacher candidates. The examples raise an important question: should teacher educators consider moving from traditional campus-based delivery of TESOL programs to a more authentic setting?

REFLECTIVE BREAK

- How can teacher education programs exploit technological tools more to help close the theory/practice divide in language teacher education?

- Do you think that online discussions of your teaching experiences are useful for your development as a learner TESOL teacher? If yes, how so? If no, why not?

Reading and Discussion Task

Hao Xu (2017), a TESOL teacher educator in China, noticed that the training of his learner TESOL teachers in classroom observation skills did not necessarily result in their acquisition of teaching knowledge.

He began to think that there seems to be a tendency for TESOL teacher education programs to provide a lot of theoretical information for their learner TESOL teachers that may overwhelm them, because it will be up to individuals to figure out what is most useful for them to learn. He decided to give them 'less rather than more' and developed a short course called 'Focused Observation'.

- Read the chapter and explain your understanding of his 'less rather than more' in the Focused Observation approach.
- Discuss your findings with a colleague.

[Hao, X. (2017). Seeing trees in the forest: Using focused observation in pre-service TESOL teacher education. In T. S. C. Farrell (ed.) *Preservice Teacher Education* (pp. 77-84). Alexandria, VA: TESOL Press]

ENGAGING LEARNER TESOL TEACHERS

One of the striking features of all of the experiences of the TESOL teacher educators in the Farrell (2017) volume (see examples outlined above) is that reflective teacher educators have begun to ask their learner TESOL teachers what *they* think about the contents of their TESOL teacher education courses. In other words, TESOL teacher educators are engaging learner TESOL teachers to articulate their assumptions, beliefs, opinions, and their prior experiences in order to reflect on their continued appropriateness in light of what they are being presented with in their TESOL teacher education program and courses.

TESOL teacher educators can encourage their learner TESOL teachers to articulate their tacitly held prior experiences/beliefs (or move them to a more conscious level), where they can be examined for their appropriateness (rather than being blindly accepted) once the learner TESOL teachers are aware of what they are. Thus by making their prior beliefs more explicit, learner TESOL teachers can raise critically reflective questions so that they can discover whatever dogma, if any, may underlie such beliefs. As Widdowson (2012: 4) points out, "if teachers raise critical questions about theoretical assumptions that underlie the approaches that are proposed, they are in a position to establish their relevance to their own local circumstances and *adapt* rather than just *adopt* them."

Thus, it is vital for TESOL teacher educators to help TESOL learner teachers to articulate their previous experience and beliefs to themselves and others, because of the 'competition' with the received knowledge they are presented with in the

TESOL teacher education program. Lortie (1975) has maintained that these prior beliefs can have more influence on learner teachers' future teaching methods than any information they have received from the various courses they take during the teacher education program. In fact, Richards (1998: 71) has suggested that the influence of these tacitly held prior beliefs can be so strong that they "often serve as a lens" through which learner teachers view and filter the content of the TESOL teacher education program. This is problematic for TESOL teacher educators because any new information taught in TESOL teacher education courses "will have to compete with, replace or otherwise modify the folk theories that already guide" both TESOL teacher educators and learner TESOL teachers (Joram and Gabriele, 1998: 176).

Roberts (1998: 67) cautions, however, that the main problem is not that learner TESOL teachers' prior beliefs are "inherently wrong but [that] they are tacit" and "working from tacit images imprisons the teacher in a single frame of reference, which may be inappropriate" to their future teaching contexts. Thus, and as Roberts (1998: 70) suggests, TESOL teacher education programs should provide interventions "to free [teachers] from tacit images of teaching." One such approach to helping to engage learner TESOL teachers to articulate their tacitly held beliefs is to manipulate existing TESOL teacher education courses. Farrell (2012a) noted that because learner TESOL teachers' tacitly held prior experiences and beliefs are in competition with the received knowledge they are being presented with in their TESOL courses, TESOL teacher educators must endeavor in their existing courses (regardless of the philosophical or theoretical underpinnings of these courses) to help learner teachers make clearer connections to their prior experiences and beliefs.

Farrell (1999) calls his approach to helping his pre-service teachers articulate their prior beliefs and experiences the *reflective assignment* in his teacher education courses. He has his pre-service teachers assess the origins and nature of their beliefs about grammar teaching and learning, and the way these could shape their classroom decision making and teaching. This assignment is in three parts. The first part of the assignment has learner TESOL teachers write about their past experiences of learning English, be it as a first, second, or foreign language. This is followed by having them write a detailed lesson plan on any grammar structure and teach it to some students in a school, or elsewhere. Finally, the learner teachers must reflect on how that lesson went and whether they would change anything as a result of the reflection.

REFLECTIVE BREAK

- Lortie (1975) has noted that learner teachers can be overly influenced by how they were taught when they were in school. He called this the 'apprenticeship of observation', because he noted we spend more than 13,000 hours in our schooling and this has more of an impact than, say, a 200-hour course that you may be taking. Do you think you will be (or are) influenced at the beginning of your teaching career by how you were taught in your schooling? If yes, how much? If no, why not?

Reading and Discussion Task

Thomas Farrell's (1999) reflective assignment, discussed above, recounted how the learner TESOL teacher Ben (a pseudonym) went through the three parts of the assignment to teach a grammar lesson. Ben reported in his own words as follows:

Part I

In my Elementary school, a lot of emphasis was placed on grammar. I still remember how my English teacher used to drill my class in all aspects of grammar. I must admit that her method of teaching (drills) grammar did produce results. On the other hand, her method of instruction also made me feel that grammar is very boring. So I lost any interest in grammar. In fact, I hated it!

Part II

Now I have to "Write A Lesson Plan" . . . But I realize I am conflicted!

My prior experience of grammar was that it was 'boring, yet effective' because we passed required examinations. But I want to make my grammar classes more interesting for my students and myself. Still not sure what way to go? Do I drill (like my teachers) or do I teach inductively (this was emphasized in my course readings)?

Part III

I used an inductive approach because I figured a deductive approach leads to too much passive learning. I don't deny that this is partly due to my past experience as a student – I wanted my students to think for themselves about grammar rather than drilling them. I think the class went well but I was not fully comfortable teaching in this way. I may try drilling next time to see . . .

- Read the paper and answer the following questions:
  - Why do you think Ben was conflicted in part II when writing a lesson plan?
  - Have you even had a similar feeling about how to teach grammar (or any other skill area)?
  - Why would grammar in a drill approach be 'boring yet effective' in terms of examinations?
  - Why would Ben not feel entirely comfortable with his approach to teaching grammar?
  - Have you had any similar experiences to Ben's when approaching any skill area because you may have been influenced in how you learned it in school when you were a student?
- Do this reflective assignment now on any teaching skill in TESOL (listening, speaking, reading, writing, and/or grammar) and compare your results to what you read in Farrell (1999).
- Discuss your findings with a colleague.

[Farrell, T. S. C. (1999). The reflective assignment: Unlocking pre-service English teachers' beliefs on grammar teaching. *RELC Journal*, 30, 2, 1-17]

The above reflective assignment highlights the enormous influence of Lortie's (1975) apprenticeship of observation. Indeed, it is very important that TESOL teacher education programs also provide opportunities for learner TESOL teachers to become more aware of their prior assumptions and beliefs, as the results of Farrell's (1999) case study above have indicated.

Along with reflective assignments, outlined above, another method that can offer windows on that thinking is reflection on case studies. Case studies in TESOL teacher education programs can also allow for a bridging of the gap between theory and practice. Case studies give raw contextualized information (rather than decontextualized theory – see above) on the many different factors that influence instructional decisions from their frames of reference; these studies are particularly helpful for learner TESOL teachers to examine and reflect on because of the insider viewpoint. A case is really a freeze-frame of a classroom situation that allows time for reflection (Schön, 1983), especially delayed reflection, and as Shulman (1992: xiv) has pointed out, it provides learner TESOL teachers with "opportunities to analyze situations and make judgments in the messy world of practice, where principles often appear to conflict with one another and no simple solution is possible." Such case reports outline how real TESOL teachers have dealt with teaching dilemmas and, when deconstructed through a process of questioning and analysis, they can show how learner TESOL teachers' beliefs and knowledge form the basis for how they would act in such situations. For example, learner TESOL teachers can be asked to reflect on what they consider to be dilemmas, and then TESOL teacher educators can examine whether these differ from those identified by the practicing TESOL teacher. TESOL teachers can then begin to explore what kinds of beliefs learner TESOL teachers bring to the dilemmas and where these beliefs originate.

Case materials can be written, and audio/video recorded, in order to provide a detailed means for helping learner TESOL teachers develop a capacity to explore and analyze different unique situations of practice. Early career TESOL teachers can be encouraged to write their case studies as part of their teacher research, and these can be fed back into the TESOL teacher education of other learner TESOL teachers to explore (see Chapter 7 for more on early career teachers). For example, Farrell (2006b, 2007b), again in a Singapore context, used case-based teaching in TESOL teacher education as a means of promoting reflection among learner TESOL teachers. In an investigation of the problematic experience of an early career teacher in his first year of school experience, Farrell (2006b) concluded that an appropriate way of preparing novices for the transition from course to classroom reality is for learner TESOL teachers to work with cases constructed from the narratives of novice TESOL teachers (Farrell, 2007b). He recommends moving away from a concern with language teaching methods in TESOL teacher education courses to the development of the skills of *anticipatory* reflection during the course. This process, he argues, will raise learner TESOL teachers' awareness of what they might experience when they make the transition from the TESOL teacher education program to early career TESOL teacher in the first year of teaching. He proposes linking this learning experience to various reflection tools such as classroom observation, journal writing, and group discussions, developing capacities for reflecting on both teaching and the contexts in which it occurs (see Chapter 3 for more on reflective practice strategies).

REFLECTIVE BREAK

- How is a case study a 'freeze-frame' of a real classroom?
- Do you think that case studies of how early career TESOL teachers have outlined and dealt with various teaching dilemmas can be helpful for learner TESOL teachers to analyze?
- What is your understanding of anticipatory reflection?

Reading and Discussion Task

Daniel Hopper and Bill Snyder (2017) have observed that within English teaching in Japan, a location of tensions stemming from opposing educational and economic interests is the private conversation school (*eikaiwa*) industry. The authors outline a case study exploring how one learner TESOL teacher gained increased awareness of the tensions and issues of identity existing in his work as an *eikaiwa* teacher through both reflective practice and critical interaction with a mentor as part of a community of practice course (Master's degree in Teaching English to Speakers of other Languages (MA TESOL)). The mentoring took place within the context of a pedagogical English grammar course in the MA program, when circumstances allowed the course instructor and learner TESOL teacher to develop a project looking in depth at the teacher's practices for teaching grammar in the *eikaiwa* context

- Read their case study and explain your understanding of their points of view.
- Discuss your findings with a colleague.

[Hopper, D., and Snyder, W. (2017). Becoming a "real" teacher: A case study of professional development in *eikaiwa*. *The European Journal of Applied Linguistics and TEFL*, 6, 2, 183-201]

INCONVENIENT TRUTH 2:
EARLY CAREER TESOL TEACHER ABANDONMENT

The preceding section outlined and discussed the theory/practice divide as an inconvenient truth within TESOL teacher education programs, and concluded that one way to address this gap is to better engage learner TESOL teachers to articulate their prior beliefs through reflective assignments and analysis of case studies. However, there lurks another inconvenient truth within TESOL teacher education, and that pertains to the lack of contact these programs have with their graduating early career TESOL teachers. This section discusses this inconvenient truth. A harsh reality for many newly qualified TESOL teachers is that they may find themselves placed in a context of teaching that may be hostile to their development, and indeed relationships may be already in place in that context that do not foster collegiality (Darling-Hammond, 1997); or as Lortie (1975: 195) put it, a school culture of "live and let live, and help when asked." Indeed, early career TESOL teachers may find themselves in a school that has several different 'teacher cultures' in existence and are then faced with the dilemma of which one to join. Instead of thriving and developing during their first years as early career TESOL teachers, they soon find themselves in survival mode, where many feel isolated and with little or no involvement in important school decision making that impacts their lives as teachers.

Unfortunately, many times what occurs is that on graduation, many early career TESOL teachers have no further contact with their TESOL teacher educators or programs, and although they face the same challenges as their more experienced colleagues from the very first day on the job, they may also have little guidance from the new school/institution. This was the case for the 'qualified' TESOL teacher in the opening preamble of this chapter, as she said that she had no contact with any of the educators or programs she graduated from; she said (and this is worth repeating from above): "I feel that I lack support and readiness for helping my students . . . I am lost. It's pretty overwhelming." Indeed, one could wonder what might have occurred if the TESOL teacher in the preamble could have reached out to her previous TESOL teacher educator(s) in order to seek the advice and support that she so clearly needs to be able to succeed as a TESOL teacher. If we consider TESOL teacher educators as mentors during the teacher education program, then we should also be able to consider these same mentors as acting as 'reflective colleagues' for early career TESOL teachers in their first years as they are socialized into a new community of practice (Lave and Wenger, 1991).

One may wonder what the benefits are of TESOL teacher educators having continued contact with early career TESOL teachers in their first years, once they enter the varied contexts and workplaces where they find teaching employment. A valid question, considering many are very busy with new cohorts of learner teachers entering their programs each year. That said, I believe there are major benefits: TESOL teacher educators would be able to (1) find out more about the lived experiences of their learner TESOL teachers in real teaching contexts, and as a result (2) be able to better mentor them to help mitigate the inevitable 'reality shocks' of teaching in 'real classrooms', and turn survival from a 'sink-or-swim' process into one where early career TESOL teachers thrive and develop throughout their teaching careers (Farrell, 2016a). For example, of the little research that documents the lived experiences of early career TESOL teachers, most reports on their negative experiences or misfortunes, including unreasonable workload demands such as lots of unpaid marking, unpaid increased hours outside of school time on school trips, lack of support from administration, and poor-quality induction programs, as well as large class sizes and unorganized curricula; and all the time, most early career TESOL teachers are left to cope on their own (Johnson, Harrold, Cochran, Brannan, and Bleistein, 2014). For the most part, such 'transition traumas' have been neglected in TESOL teacher education, as many TESOL teacher education programs still have limited contact with and information about how their graduates are faring in their induction years, or even what their work lives involve (Baecher, 2012). As Mattheoudakis (2007: 1273) has correctly observed, "The truth is that we [TESOL] know very little about what actually happens" to TESOL teachers in their first years in teaching.

REFLECTIVE BREAK

- Which (if any) of the following issues do you think you will experience as an early career TESOL teacher?
    - unreasonable workload demands
    - unpaid marking
    - unpaid increased hours outside of school time on trips
    - lack of support from administration
    - poor-quality induction programs
    - large class sizes
    - unorganized curricula
- Do you think incoming learner TESOL teachers should be asked about their expectations when starting a TESOL teacher education program? Why or why not?

Reading and Discussion Task

Randal Johnson, Mycah Harrold, Daisy Cochran, Debi Brannan, and Tasha Bleistein (2014) noted that the first years of work for new teachers can be particularly difficult. The authors explored the perceived levels of loneliness and stress of forty-seven early career TESOL teachers as a vital step toward understanding the factors that influence and improve TESOL professionals' mental health, job satisfaction, and occupational outcomes.

- Read their case study and explain your understanding of their points of view.
- Discuss your findings with a colleague.

[Johnson, K. R., Harrold, L. M., Cochran, D. J., Brannan, D., and Bleistein, T. (2014). An examination of the first years: Novice ESOL teachers' experiences with loneliness and stress. *Pure Insights*, 3, 1–10]

TESOL TEACHER EDUCATION: A NOVICE-SERVICE FRAMEWORK

As mentioned in the previous chapter, a key assumption I take in this book is that TESOL teacher education does not begin and end with graduation from a program for the learner TESOL teacher, and indeed it should also not end then for the TESOL teacher educator; in fact, graduation is just a beginning and TESOL teacher education continues into the early career teaching years. Part of the challenge for TESOL teacher educators as they act as reflective colleagues with their early career TESOL teacher graduates is to be available to provide some kind of support so that the novice teachers can transition smoothly into the school context in which they are placed, and thrive throughout their early career teaching years. One way of maintaining contact

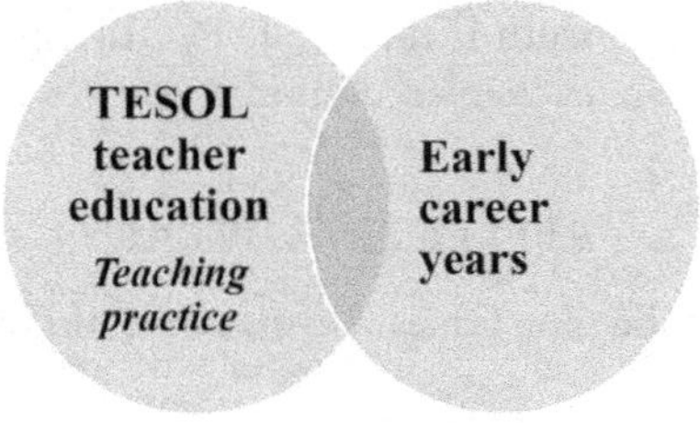

Figure 2.1   TESOL Teacher Education: A Novice-Service Framework

between TESOL teacher educators and programs and learner TESOL teachers, along with partnering schools, is to expand the original pre-service teacher education experience into at least the first five years of the early career (Gordon, Kane, and Staiger, 2006; Ingersoll and Smith, 2003). This period can be called 'novice-service' TESOL teacher education and includes TESOL teacher education or pre-service, teaching practice and evaluation, and the first five early career years of teaching. Figure 2.1 illustrates this basic 'novice-service' TESOL teacher education framework.

A 'novice-service' framework of TESOL teacher education as outlined in Figure 2.1 shows the intersection of the traditional TESOL teacher education period, usually called pre-service (and teaching practice), with the early career teaching years. What can happen, unfortunately, in traditional approaches to teacher education is that some struggling early career TESOL teachers can fall through the period between pre-service education and any in-service development, because many are left without any support during these crucial early years. As Korthagen (2004: 91) has pointed out: "The loss of ideals, and what people experience as a lack of support when it comes to the realization of those ideals, play an important part in cases of burnout and, in some cases, the decision to resign from their position" during these important early career years. Of course, learner TESOL teachers will be prepared for as smooth a transition as possible from the TESOL teacher education programs and teaching practice to their early career teaching experiences, as they are imbued with reflective practices and strategies (the central approach of this book) to be able to face whatever challenges they may meet during their early careers.

This chapter began with a preamble of an experienced TESOL teacher reaching out to this author for help and guidance as she continued her struggles while being a language teacher in several different contexts, and despite her abundant TESOL-related qualifications, including a TESL certificate, an MA in Linguistics, and she later explained to me that she had 'covered' all aspects and theories of second language learning and teaching. She wondered why she had to 'fight every day just to keep [her] head above water' and then, as she mentioned, she realized (from listening to a podcast, https://podcasts.apple.com/us/podcast/19-reflective-practice-thomas-farrell/id933226826?i=1000415356994 & https://mastersoftesol.wordpress.com/2018/07/06/19-reflective-practice-thomas-farrell/?utm_source=feedburner&utm_medium=feed&utm_campaign=Feed%3A+MastersOfTesol+%28Masters+of+TESOL%29, by this author on the deficiencies of TESOL teacher preparation, among other TESOL-related issues) that she was not prepared properly for her role as a

TESOL professional. There is already an abundance of studies that link numerous negative experiences of early career teachers in many different contexts to early career teacher attrition, and these issues include (in no particular order): increased paperwork, lack of resources, feelings of isolation, low salaries, lack of parental support, large classroom sizes, lack of student achievement, lack of administrative support, lack of recognition, student attitudes, increased accountability, job dissatisfaction, burnout, and stress, to mention but a few (Anhorn, 2008; Yost, 2006). As Anhorn (2008: 15) states:

> "Overwhelmed, hectic, isolated, beaten down, unsupported, scared, humiliated, afraid, stressed, and drowning," are not the words a teacher education professor wants to hear from teachers describing their feelings during their first-year of elementary teaching. They are, however, the feelings revealed by a study of first-year elementary teachers.

Many disheartened early career teachers can thus see a link between their teacher preparation programs and how they feel they have been prepared to teach in real classrooms, just as the language teacher teacher in the opening preamble of this chapter noted about her perceptions of the disconnect between how she was prepared and the reality of teaching, which she still cannot get her head around. Many of these teachers generally point to their perceptions of the theory/practice gap in their programs, as outlined earlier in the chapter. The problems with theory and practice in traditional teacher education programs can be traced back to a 'training model' in which as Wideen, Mayer-Smith, and Moon (1998: 167) put it:

> The university provides the theory, methods and skills; the schools provide the setting in which that knowledge is practiced; and the beginning teacher provides the individual effort to apply such knowledge. In this model, propositional knowledge has formed the basis of university input.

A training-model approach involves, according to Richards and Farrell (2005), understanding basic concepts and principles as a prerequisite for applying them to teaching, and the ability to demonstrate principles and practices in the classroom. The main point here is that the biggest input to program content is provided by the university (i.e. the 'experts') through a collection of isolated theoretical courses without many links to actual classroom practices.

However, when learner TESOL teachers enter real classrooms with the idea of putting into practice all they have learned in their TESOL teacher education courses, they soon realize that there may be somewhat of a disconnect or disparity between the content of their courses and the real world of the classroom. The 'shock' of such a transition from the teacher education program to a real classroom is fully realized when learner teachers do not know what to do if/when their students cannot or do not respond to a particular activity. As Hoban (2005: 9) has stated: "what a teacher does in a classroom is influenced by the interaction of many elements such as the curriculum, the context, and how students respond to instruction at one particular time." Thus the impact of such a traditional training approach to educating learner teachers may be limited.

A 'novice-service' approach to teacher education, however, can better prepare learner TESOL teachers for the reality of what they will face in real classrooms, as teacher educators can continue to mentor them, along with school officials, throughout their early career years. This approach also suggests that you, the learner TESOL teacher, fully and enthusiastically collaborate with your TESOL teacher educator/ supervisor, as well as with your cooperating teacher if one has been appointed during teaching practice. In such a manner, TESOL teacher education can take a more realistic and reflective approach to how you as a learner TESOL teacher are prepared for the *real world* of the classroom. The chapter that follows outlines in detail how TESOL teacher educators can provide you with various mediational reflective tools so that you do not just survive in your novice years as a teacher, but really *thrive* in your early years and beyond.

REFLECTIVE BREAK

- Do you think a novice-service framework as outlined above will help you better meet the various adjustment challenges you will inevitably face during your first years teaching in real contexts?

CONCLUSION

Although much has been accomplished in a relatively short period of time in the rather new field of TESOL teacher education, the reality is that we still have some way to go when it comes to preparing learner TESOL teachers for the realities of what they will face in real classrooms and communities during their teaching careers. As this chapter has indicated, there is still a disjuncture between theory provided in TESOL teacher preparation programs and the practices that take place in real classrooms, and this gap needs to be bridged, as I have suggested in this chapter by pointing out two inconvenient truths about TESOL teacher education (the theory/practice gap and early career teacher abandonment). Regarding the second inconvenient truth (lack of contact after graduation), the chapter has suggested that the lack of contact can be bridged by considering the idea of TESOL teacher education extending beyond the pre-service years and into the early career teaching years through a novice-service framework. This would entail greater collaboration between the TESOL teacher educator/program, the school, and the early career TESOL teacher, so that TESOL teacher educators can not only help early career TESOL teachers, but also learn more about their graduates' lived experiences, and such information can be feed back into the TESOL teacher education programs as case studies to be reflected upon.

3

TESOL TEACHER EDUCATION: REFLECTION-AS-ACTION

PREAMBLE

The following narrative account (adapted from Farrell, 2019b) is from an early career TESOL teacher's response to a colleague's observations of some of his lessons.

I am surprised by the sheer volume of questions I ask in a lesson. I know I'm a teacher but four questions a minute seems like a lot. On the other hand in class for 3rd grade I asked under two questions a minute. It feels like a very wide spread. I am interested in how many questions is an appropriate level for students of that age. I also find it shocking how often I allowed less than a second to pass before something was said in the 3rd grade lesson. It is so many times above the other classes that it makes me reconsider what sort of lesson I had. Was it just in my head that students did not understand me? It has the second most questions but dwarfs the 4th grade lesson which has more questions.

I also did not realize how I really lean on "okay." I think it is probably something that I do more with younger students and I can see that happening more, especially after I actually listened to the lesson. I think that it is a good idea to not use that as much, I should be able to use other means for confirmation of understanding with students. Something like TPR [total physical response] or "Simon says" with actions that are involved in the class. This will hopefully help students' comprehension and be a fun activity. These are the most concrete things I have here. I know that I can change these and I look forward to making myself better with this information. I will absolutely try to manage my questions and the time I leave before speaking again better. I don't want to inhibit students by overloading them with language and I need to be more aware of that in the heat of the moment in class.

The above narrative account really demonstrates the power of reflection and the fact that many teachers (understandably) do not know exactly what transpires during an actual classroom lesson. This is not an indictment of the early career TESOL teacher in any way, as many teachers are often unaware of what they do while the teach (reflection-*in*-action) as well as of what has transpired in the whole lesson (reflection-*on*-action). In the example above, the TESOL teacher was unaware of the number and type of questions he asked during his lessons as well as his (over)use of the filler "okay" at stages during lessons.

With regard to teacher use of questions, Farrell (2009: 60) has observed that TESOL teachers are generally "not aware of the number, type, and function of the questions they ask" in their classes because they do not normally consciously reflect on this issue. However, developing awareness of what we actually do when we teach (as opposed to what we *think* we do) is important because, as Knezedivc (2001: 10) has pointed out, it is the beginning of a process of reducing the discrepancy between "what we do and what we think we do." In the preamble above, the TESOL teacher was not aware of his questioning practices or how these practices are informed (or not) by his beliefs, because, as he mentioned to his observer, "I had never reflected on these issues before, hence my surprise at hearing what you told me about my questioning behavior." Thus, as Freeman (2016) and others have advocated, TESOL as a profession should educate learner TESOL teachers to become reflective practitioners throughout their careers, who "look at their work in order to examine the reasons and beliefs underlying their actions and generate alternative actions for the future" (Stanley, 1998: 585).

REFLECTIVE BREAK

- Why would what TESOL teachers think they do be different from what they actually do when they teach?
- Do you think that most TESOL teachers are aware of the number, type, and function of the questions they ask in their lessons? Are you?

INTRODUCTION

A main premise of this book is that a key function and goal of TESOL teacher education programs is that they prepare learner TESOL teachers to be able to successfully meet those challenges and demands of the profession that they will most likely face during their early careers and beyond, so that they will become 'adaptive experts' within the context in which they teach. TESOL teacher education programs can achieve this by educating learner TESOL teachers to become reflective practitioners. Indeed, as Tony Wright (2010: 267) has acknowledged, the goal of TESOL teacher education should be to produce "reflective teachers, in a process which involves socio-cognitive demands to introspect and collaborate with others, and which acknowledges previous learning and life experience as a starting point for new learning." Other TESOL teacher educators have also noted the importance of TESOL teacher education programs encouraging reflective practice for learner TESOL teachers (e.g. Farr and O' Riordan, 2017; Farr, Farrell, and O' Riordan, 2019; Hanington and Pillai, 2017; McCormack, 2017; Mann and Walsh, 2017). Yet one of the persistent issues still unresolved concerning the concept of reflective practice in TESOL (and many other disciplines) is how reflection can be implemented or operationalized by teachers and programs (Freeman, 2016).

Thus although many TESOL teacher educators may agree that some form of reflection is desirable, they still cannot agree on how the concept can be implemented in a TESOL teacher education program. This is mostly because TESOL teachers and teacher educators must choose from a vast array of different approaches with different theoretical backgrounds, usually from within the field of general education rather than the field of TESOL, and this has led to confusion about what approaches are best for TESOL teachers.

Some of the confusion regarding the lack of consensus on the use of reflective practice in teacher education in recent years is due to a lack of understanding of two broad schools of thought on reflective practice: Dewey's (1933) rationalist approach to problem-solving and Schön's (1983) experientialist approach. Schön questioned the belief at that time, prevailing since Dewey's work, that the dominance of 'technical rationality' or knowledge can and should be achieved from scientific approaches to problem-solving. Farrell (2012c) maintains that this is not a dichotomous contrast and any tension between the two approaches can be overcome by considering both together – Dewey's systematic approach and Schön's intuitive approach – because they both lead teachers to use evidence to make informed decisions about their practice.

This chapter is not about *what* reflective practice is conceptually or *why* it should be done (its purpose), as other sources have given these philosophical discussions sufficient coverage already (e.g. Farrell, 2020; Farr, Farrell, and O'Riordan, 2019; Freeman, 2016; Mann and Walsh, 2017; to mention but a few). Moreover, most TESOL teacher educators agree that it is generally a good idea to incorporate reflection into their programs for the development of learner TESOL teachers. Rather, this chapter will focus on specific activities designed to promote evidence-based teacher reflection in TESOL teacher education programs and beyond, as well as examine their products, so that we take learner TESOL teacher needs to the forefront of teacher education. Thus, this chapter is about the *how* of reflective practice in TESOL teacher education: how TESOL teacher educators can implement (or operationalize) reflective practice within their programs and courses through the lens of a holistic reflective practice framework that represents both Dewey's (1933) rationalist and Schön's (1983, 1987) experientialist approaches, but is specifically designed for TESOL teachers. This will be explained in detail below (Farrell, 2015b).

REFLECTIVE BREAK

- What is your understanding of reflective practice?
- Do you think reflection is a solitary act or a collective one undertaken with the guidance of colleagues and mentors?

Reading and Discussion Task

Jason Anderson (2020) summarized key issues in reflective practice.

- Read and summarize his views on reflective teaching.
- Discuss your findings with a colleague.

[Anderson, J. (2020). Key concepts in ELT: Reflection. *ELT Journal*, ccaa039. Available from: https://doi.org/10.1093/elt/ccaa039. https://academic. oup.com/eltj/advance-article/doi/10.1093/elt/ccaa039/5891444]

Thomas Farrell's (2020) book on *Reflective Teaching* discusses the *what* and *why* of reflective practice in the opening chapter.

• Read chapter 1 and summarize his views on reflective teaching.
• Discuss your findings with a colleague.

[Farrell, T. S. C. (2020). *Reflective Teaching*(rev. edn). Alexandria, VA: TESOL Press]

Fiona Farr, Angela Farrell, and Elaine O'Riordan's (2019) book *Social Interaction in Language Teacher Education* has an excellent chapter (chapter 3) devoted to reflective practice (RP) in language teacher education (LTE).

• Read and summarize their overview of RP as a concept and approach in English language teacher education, as well as their critical review of the wide-ranging benefits that can be expected for novice and experienced teachers from engaging in RP, and the various RP modes through which this can be achieved.
• Discuss your findings with a colleague.

[Farr, F., Farrell, A., and O'Riordan, E. (2019). *Social Interaction in Language Teacher Education*. Edinburgh: Edinburgh University Press]

TESOL TEACHER EDUCATION:
MOVING TOWARD REFLECTION-AS-ACTION

Donald Freeman (2016: 208) has pointed out that although reflection offers a way into the less "accessible aspects of teacher's work," the level of accessibility depends on how reflection is implemented in the TESOL teacher education program. As mentioned above, two of the leading scholars on how reflective practice can be implemented in teacher education programs are John Dewey and Donald Schön.

John Dewey (1933) viewed reflection as both a *process* (systematic) and a *product* (problem-solution). For Dewey the process begins with a teacher experiencing a situation in which the teacher finds problems and considers some vague suggestions as possible resolutions of this situation. This reflective process involves the teacher engaging in reflective inquiry that has five steps: 'suggestion' followed by 'intellectualization,' 'hypotheses,' 'reasoning,' and finally 'hypothesis testing.' For Dewey (1933: 116) the above steps (which teachers can experience in different sequences) represent the "indispensable traits of reflective thinking."

The product of reflection is achieving the goal of alleviating the original doubt in reaching a solution. Thus, a Deweyan approach to reflection can be understood as an ends-based model where reflection is initiated by some problem in practice and this problem must be solved in a systematic and rational manner (reflection-*on*-action).

Donald Schön (1983, 1987), having completed his PhD dissertation on Dewey's reflective inquiry, wondered what happens when practitioners are confronted with problems while they are doing something and must react spontaneously. This lead to Schön's (1983: 54) reflection-*in*-action or thinking about "doing something while doing it," as occurs when something unexpected happens while doing and leads to a surprise. For Schön (1983: 276) reflection-*in*-action, or a person's "intuitive knowing," is the core of a practitioner's practice because the spontaneity of the occurrence of any problems means they must be solved on the spot and, as a result, cannot be solved through the rigorous application of scientific approaches. A Schönian approach to reflection thus builds on the Deweyan idea of stepping back from a problem (or reflection-*on*-action) to include reflecting while doing (or reflection-*in*-action). Schön's reflection-*in*-action also eventually leads to retrospective reflection-*on*-action moments as the practitioner considers the meaning in a distancing after the event. Thus, we can say that like Dewey's, Schön's approach to reflection proceeds along a causal chain that is initiated by some problem or moment of uncertainty.

The following example (from Farrell, 2019b) illustrates how such a causal chain can exist for a TESOL teacher teaching a grammar lesson:

- A situation develops which triggers spontaneous, routine responses (such as in knowing-in-action): for example, a student cannot answer an easy grammar question that he or she was able to during the previous class, such as identifying a grammar structure.
- Routine responses by the teacher (i.e. what the teacher has always done) do not produce a routine response and instead produce a surprise for the teacher: the teacher starts to explain how the student had already explained this grammar structure in the previous class and so the teacher wonders why this is the case. The teacher asks the student if anything is the matter and the student says he forgets the answer.
- This surprise response gets the teacher's attention and leads to reflection within an action: the teacher reacts quickly to try to find out why the student suddenly 'forgets' a grammar structure the teacher knows the student has no trouble understanding. The teacher can ask the student directly to explain what is happening.
- Reflection now gives rise to on-the-spot experimentation by the teacher: the student may or may not explain why he or she is crying. The teacher will take some measures (depending on the reaction or non-reaction) to help solve the problem: ignore the situation, empathize with the student, help the student answer the question by modeling answers, and so forth.
- This eventually leads to the teacher bringing the event outside the class for later reflection or reflection-on-action similar to Dewey's, as the practitioner thinks about the events after the event.

According to Schön these sequences of moments are all present and lead to reflection-in-action while the teacher is teaching and eventually reflection-on-action after the lesson. In this case, Schön says that practitioners engage in a process of problem-setting rather than problem-solving.

When we look at both Dewey and Schön together we can see that for both, reflection is concerned with some kind of problem-solving. As Farrell (2012c) has noted, both of these approaches are fine in themselves; however, both approaches also seem to separate the teacher-as-person (see below for an explanation) who is doing the reflection from the problem that is reflected on. It seems that both scholars become somewhat fixated in solving the 'problem' or 'uncertainty' in a manner that separates the person and his or her emotions from the process. One unfortunate result of implementing approaches without examining their underlying principles, as outlined above, is that many teacher education programs have implemented reflective practice in a ritualized, mechanical, and prescriptive problem-solving exercise that provides learner teachers with sets of recipe-following checklists to follow rather than engaging in any deep reflections. Reflective practice, for the most part, has been restricted to a retrospective role, as it focuses mostly on teaching problems in the classroom and separates the teacher-as-person who is doing the reflection from the problem that is reflected on.

This has also been the case in TESOL teacher education programs, where reflective practice has often been limited to such a retrospective approach. Freeman (2016: 217) called this "post-mortem reflection," and it usually consists of asking learner TESOL teachers to answer basic questions about their classroom lessons (such as "what happened?" or "why did it happen?" and "what will you do as a result?"). This sole focus of reflection as an intellectual endeavor of solving classroom problems limits its implementation to 'reflection-as-repair' to fix those problems. Although such retrospective approaches may offer a structured way into reflection, especially for novice teachers, there is a *gap* between the teacher who is doing the reflecting, the problem perceived, and the act of reflection itself. As Akbari (2007: 201) has cautioned, when reflection becomes solely an "intellectual exercise, reduced to a set of techniques, the inner lives of teachers are overlooked," and so reflection is promoted narrowly as an individual, cognitive *tool* that teachers are taught to use to 'improve' their practice rather than themselves as TESOL professionals. This *gap* in the reflective process can be removed if we consider reflection-*as*-action, where the reflective process includes "awareness of the self, the context as well as the problem to be solved" (Bleakley, 1999: 323). Viewing reflection-*as*-action, or the actual implementation of reflection, means that the 'teacher-as-person' is included in a more holistic approach to reflective practice that also includes Dewey and Schön's approaches (Farrell, 2019a).

REFLECTIVE BREAK

- Should teachers just reflect on problems that occur in their teaching or include other teacher activities outside classrooms?
- Should the teacher-as-person be part of the reflective process or should it be just the issue that is being reflected on itself?
- What is the value (if any) of including the teacher-as-person in the reflection process?
- Do you think learner TESOL teachers should become more aware of themselves as human beings as they engage in reflective practice?

FRAMEWORK FOR REFLECTING ON PRACTICE

Farrell (2015b) developed a more holistic approach to reflective practice for TESOL teachers that not only focuses on the intellectual, cognitive, and metacognitive aspects of reflection that many of the other approaches include (and limit themselves to), but also involves reflection on the spiritual, moral, and emotional non-cognitive aspects of reflection. Holistic reflective practice, as Orland-Barak (2005: 27) suggests, provides a "stance towards practice that is both affective and intellectual" and that leads not only to awareness of teaching practices but also to more self-awareness and understanding, and thus equips learner TESOL teachers for personal and professional growth throughout their careers. Holistic reflective practice, as presented in this framework, is grounded in the belief that teachers are whole persons and that teaching and reflection are multi-dimensional because they include the moral, ethical, spiritual, and aesthetic aspects of our practice (Farrell, 2019b).

The framework has five different stages/levels of reflection: *philosophy*, *principles*, *theory*, *practice*, and *beyond practice* (see Figure 3.1). Each of these will be explained in more detail in the chapters that follow.

Figure 3.1 illustrates the framework in the shape of a circle and it can be navigated in three different ways: theory-into-practice, practice-into-theory, or a single-stage application. For learner TESOL teachers, Farrell (2019b) suggests taking a theory-in-practice or deductive approach, because they do not have much classroom practice experience and thus they begin with reflecting on their philosophy. For more experienced TESOL teachers in in-service development, practice-into-theory makes more sense, as they have more classroom teaching experiences that they may want to explore first, and then work their way through other levels of the framework. Some may even just want to focus on one level of interest, and that is fine too. Each of the stages is outlined and discussed with activities that learner TESOL teachers, early career TESOL teachers, and more experienced TESOL teachers are encouraged to practice.

Figure 3.1   Framework for Reflecting on Practice (adapted from Farrell, 2015b)

Reflecting on Philosophy

Unlike any other profession, in teaching the medium is the message and the medium is who and what a person is, and as Goodson (2000: 16) maintains, "In understanding something so intensely personal as teaching it is critical we know about the person the teacher is." The first stage of implementing reflection within the framework examines the 'teacher-as-person' and suggests that professional practice, both inside and outside the classroom, is invariably guided by a teacher's sense of self and identity that originated at birth and has been developing since (Farrell, 2015b). TESOL teacher education should begin with a reflection on who the learner TESOL teacher is, in order to gain more self-knowledge. This can be accomplished by exploring, examining, and reflecting on their life-history backgrounds, or from where they have evolved, and this includes a teacher's heritage, ethnicity, religion, socioeconomic background, and family and personal values. As Parker J. Palmer (1998: 3) has noted, "Good teaching requires self-knowledge. Whatever self-knowledge we attain as teachers will serve our students and our scholarship well." In addition, such a process can help teachers develop and nurture their personal and professional identities, and close any gap between their expected teacher identity and their actual teacher identity.

To access philosophy, teachers reflect on how they got to where they are at present and how their past experiences have influenced the various decisions they have made. One way of exploring a teacher's philosophy is through autobiographical reflections (Farrell, 2015b). Learner TESOL teachers can begin their reflections in such a manner by constructing in-depth autobiographical accounts of the most important events in their lives from birth to present. Parker (1998: 5) urges all teachers regardless of the subject matter they teach to ask the 'who' question: "who is the self that teaches?"

To know one's past is to know oneself, and by reflecting on our autobiographies we can gain an understanding of *who* we are as persons and then as teachers. One method of knowing *who* we are and where we came from is by writing our stories of how have come to be who we are now. As Taggart and Wilson (1998: 164) maintain, teacher autobiographical sketches offer insight "into the past to uncover preconceived theories about teaching and learning." Once these stories have been 'told' in writing they can be analyzed alone or with a peer (a critical friend), so that the peer can give a different insight into the meaning and interpretation of the story than if the story was analyzed alone. Such collaborations with other teachers will be outlined in more detail in the next chapter.

In order to get the story, we must first find a means of capturing details of our journey up to now. One means of capturing this information is by first examining the 'tree of life' that outlines your chronological journey up to the present (Farrell, 2015b) and then using this evidence to write your story. The 'tree of life' (see Figure 3.2) is a visual representation of a teacher's chronological development and represents their personal history, from early experiences growing up to where they find themselves today as either an experienced teacher or a teacher-in-training. We are born within a particular socio-historical moment (e.g. this book was written during the Covid-19 virus that has shut down the world!), and into a family that imparts

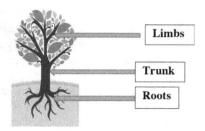

Figure 3.2   The Tree of Life (from Farrell, 2019a)

particular values to us from early on. We are influenced socially, economically, and religiously by the context we are born into, and then we enter a particular education system that also influences the formation and development of our values and beliefs, our roles and relationships, that all define who we have become. The 'tree of life' is divided into *roots*, *trunk*, and *limbs* as follows:

- The *roots* provide the foundations of what has shaped early years, such as family values, heritage, ethnicity, religion, and socioeconomic background.
- The *trunk* captures experiences from early school years all the way to high school years and university years; in other words, educational experiences as a student.
- The *limbs* represent all professional experiences as a teacher.

Reading and Discussion Task

- Fill out 'your tree of life' in the diagram below.

Your Tree of Life

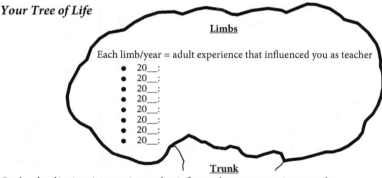

Limbs

Each limb/year = adult experience that influenced you as teacher
- 20__:
- 20__:
- 20__:
- 20__:
- 20__:
- 20__:
- 20__:
- 20__:

Trunk

Grade school/university experiences that influenced your perspective as teacher:
- University:
- High school:
- Elementary school:

Roots

- Family values:
- Heritage:
- Ethnicity, religion:

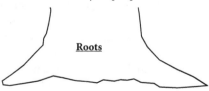

- After filling out 'your tree of life', you can begin to 'see' particular prior experiences and events (both positive and negative) that occurred as being significant for your development as a person and later as a learner TESOL teacher. You can write each part of the tree from the roots to trunk to each important limb.
- After you have written this, look for key events, turning points, early childhood experiences, experiences as a student in elementary school, high school, or university, and significant people who influenced you (positively and negatively) including past teachers, as well as previous language learning experiences, informal and formal.
- Ask yourself how all these histories relate in how you got into language teaching and how your background can shape your teaching assumptions now and in the future.

REFLECTIVE BREAK

- The following is a narrative example of a learner TESOL reflecting on her philosophy as defined in the framework above. As you read her narrative, consider the three parts of her 'tree of life' and how integrated they seem to you. Also comment on how her 'tree of life' can be interpreted. How does this compare to your 'tree of life'?

> As I reflect I see three significant parts from my tree of life that has influenced my career choice as an English teacher. The first part is the root that has shaped my personality and an event that motivated me to learn English. The second part is the trunk which presents my experiences in learning English from elementary school until high school. The last part is from the limb that exposes the benefits that I get from my English skills which made me decide to become an English teacher.
>
> Firstly, the root shows my position as an oldest child has influenced me to be strong-willed and perseverant especially in learning English and continuing my education. Honestly, during my childhood I felt very insecure about my education because in my neighborhood it is not uncommon for women to only graduate from elementary school and then help their parents to sustain family business whilst waiting for a man to marry. However, because my father worked in the capital city of Indonesia, Jakarta, which is more developed than my hometown, he realized how important education is for my future. Then he gave me an English dictionary for children which had colorful pictures on each page to encourage me to perform the best at school. The gift from my father motivated me to learn English.
>
> Secondly, the trunk includes my experiences in learning English which I found challenging. Most of the time, learning English relied too much on memorizing vocabulary and tenses. In my elementary school, I started to learn English in year 5 and only managed to memorize several nouns. Whilst in my junior and senior high school students had to memorize regular and irregular verbs and 16 tenses pattern. I remember that the learning process during my

elementary school was not intimidating because English was not the subject we had to pass in national examination. I could also see that the teacher taught us without burden. Although the lesson seems good to me, the pronunciation of English had challenged me because what I read is different from what I spell. In addition, I felt that most of the time my speaking was interrupted by my fleeting thought about tenses. I could feel that there must be something wrong with my learning but I could not discover why. Although I felt confused and alone, I kept learning English and thought that as long as I used the correct tenses, I would be okay. Luckily, become the oldest child taught me not to give up easily because I had to get something to teach or share with my younger siblings. That time, my goal was to master English.

My motivation to learn English began to spark again during my high school because my English teacher taught me differently. The experiences during high school inspired me to learn English by practicing it. My teacher used various activities so that all students could engage with the lesson. We played drama, fill in the blank of our favorite song's lyric, played games such as "bingo" games, "who am I," and watched movie together. It got me thinking that some of those activities are cognitively challenging so that I could remember some vocabulary more easily than only relying on memorization. As a result, I felt my English proficiency had increased. I could speak in English and had a small talk with my friends and classmates which made me more confident to register myself to an English competition. I registered for English debate competition. Although I could not win the competition, I felt very grateful that I could learn something new to improve my English because the competition gave me a sense like I was in the real conversation, not for learning purpose. This competition motivated me to keep learning English as well as other skills that support it, such as public speaking. At that time, I really believed that someday English would give me a valuable advantage.

Lastly, the limb consists of my work experience which influenced me to choose English teacher as my profession. I worked at a Japanese company in which I had to use English at work. I felt that learning English had helped me to do my job well and got a well-paid job. As a woman who grew up in a society where women can only get elementary education, it was a huge achievement for me. However, the advantages that I got from being able to speak English made me think about my girl-friends in my hometown who are brilliant but could not continue their study. I thought that it was not fair to leave them no choice but to finish their school until elementary school and wait for marry. I considered myself so lucky and the belief that the oldest child must be responsible to the rest of my family made me think to continue my study in English education so that I could teach English to people in my society and I hoped that I would be an inspiration for them that it was not a waste of time and money if women wanted to continue their study in a university. Then I enrolled to a university and chose English language teaching as my major.

In conclusion, my strong interest of English made me determined to learn English although it was challenging. Then I began to feel the benefit during my work which made me want to be an English teacher so that others can get the benefits especially women. There are four lessons that I learnt from those events in my life, firstly in order to keep going you need to keep firing your motivation. Secondly, learning English is not as simple as memorizing words. Cognitively challenging activities which I have mentioned during my high school can help us to practice English without feeling boring. Thirdly, in addition to learning English in the classroom, you must practice your English like in real conversation. Lastly, I hope that by being an English teacher I can help people in my society to get a well-paid job and inspire my students, especially female students to achieve their dreams.

As the story above indicates, learner TESOL teachers can become more self-aware through telling their autobiographical stories, with information garnered from their 'tree of life' that illuminates who they are, how they came to be where they are at present, and why we decided to become a teacher. When learner TESOL teachers reflect about their own lives and how they think their past experiences may have shaped the construction and development of their basic philosophy of practice, they will then be able to critically reflect on their practice, because they will become more mindful and self-aware of their past. Once their story has become explicit as they see it in writing, they can decide whether changes are warranted and a new or different story needs to be developed for their future development. In such a manner, learner TESOL teachers can gain some distance from the self and get more perspective on who they are, what they do, and what they want to do. We will revisit your reflections on philosophy in Chapter 6, as you will use them as part of your teaching evaluation.

Reflecting on Principles

When learner TESOL teachers reflect on their principles they examine their assumptions and beliefs about language teaching and learning. This level of reflection takes the process beyond the previous stage of 'teacher-as-person' and includes the beliefs that learner TESOL teachers possess about the teaching and learning of English to speakers of other languages, because these impact both their perceptions and judgments, and in turn affect their teaching behaviors in the classroom. In this chapter I talk about beliefs mostly because assumptions are a part of beliefs but difficult to articulate, so I subsume assumptions within beliefs because both often remain hidden and need to be articulated. As Kagan (1992: 65) has noted, teacher beliefs are "often unconsciously held assumptions about students, classrooms, and the academic material to be taught."

However, it is not always easy to articulate such beliefs. For example, Farrell and Ives (2015) reported a case study that examined the beliefs of one novice ESL reading (second language (L2)) teacher and compared these to his actual instructional practices while L2 reading, and discovered that although his teaching beliefs mostly converged with his classroom practices, he did not state some of his beliefs that were observed in his practices. This finding suggests that teachers may have difficulty verbalizing the reasons for particular practices because either they are not fully aware of these beliefs or the beliefs were still in formation and thus not fully developed. As Senior (2006: 248) has observed, a teacher's beliefs "are constantly developing and evolving as insights from new teaching situations are fed into their personal frameworks."

REFLECTIVE BREAK

- It is difficult for any teacher, experienced or novice, to talk about their beliefs about teaching and learning a second language. Although the following 'Teacher's Beliefs Inventory' about 'Approaches to ESL Instruction' (adapted from Johnson, 1992) is a bit old, it can help you get started on articulating your beliefs. Read all fifteen statements and then select the five that most closely reflect your beliefs about teaching and learning:

1. Language can be thought of as a set of grammatical structures which are learned consciously and controlled by the language learner.
2. As long as ESL/EFL students understand what they are saying, they are actually learning the language.
3. When ESL/EFL students make oral errors, it helps to correct them and later teach a short lesson explaining why they made that mistake.
4. As long as ESL/EFL students listen to, practice, and remember the language which native speakers use, they are actually learning the language.
5. ESL/EFL students generally need to understand the grammatical rules of English in order to become fluent in the language.
6. When ESL/EFL students make oral errors, it usually helps them to provide them with lots of oral practice with the language patterns which seem to cause them difficulty.
7. Language can be thought of as meaningful communication and is learned subconsciously in non-academic, social situations.
8. If ESL/EFL students understand some of the basic grammatical rules of the language, they can usually create lots of new sentences on their own.
9. Usually it is more important for ESL/EFL students to focus on what they are trying to say and not how to say it.
10. If ESL/EFL students practice the language patterns of native speakers, they can make up new sentences based on those language patterns that they have already practiced.
11. It is important to provide clear, frequent, precise presentations of grammatical structures during English language instruction.
12. Language can be described as a set of behaviors which are mastered through lots of drill and practice with the language patterns of native speakers.
13. When ESL/EFL students make oral errors, it is best to ignore the errors as long as you can understand what they are trying to say.
14. ESL/EFL students usually need to master some of the basic listening and speaking skills before they can begin to read and write.

15. It's not necessary to actually teach ESL/EFL students how to speak English; they usually begin speaking English on their own.
    - Now see which of these (if any) you think you fit into or even agree with the following categories of beliefs:
        - *Skills-based approach*: statements 4, 6, 10, 12, 14. Focus on discrete skills of speaking, listening, reading, and writing.
        - *Rule-based approach*: statements 1, 3, 5, 8, 11. Emphasize the importance of grammatical rules and a conscious understanding of the language system.
        - *Function-based approach*: statements 2, 7, 9, 13, 15. Focus on interactive communication, cooperative learning, and the ability to function in 'real' social situations.
- Reflect and comment on the core beliefs of a group of 167 teachers (from Richards, Gallo, and Renandya, 2001) who reported on the practices they thought facilitated the learning of the language summarized as nine principles:
    - Selectively focus on the form of the language.
    - Selectively focus on vocabulary or meaning.
    - Enable learners to use the language/be appropriate.
    - Address learners' mental processing capabilities.
    - Take account of learners' affective involvement.
    - Directly address learners' needs or interests.
    - Monitor learner progress and provide feedback.
    - Facilitate learner responsibility or autonomy.
    - Manage the lesson and the group.
- Now try to answer the following questions to help you clarify your beliefs about teaching and learning (adapted from Richards and Lockhart, 1994):
    - What are my beliefs about teaching and learning?
    - How do these beliefs influence my teaching?
    - Where do my beliefs come from?
    - What do my learners believe about learning?
    - What do my learners believe about my teaching?
    - How do these beliefs influence their approach to learning?
    - What is my role as a language teacher? (See also the question that follows.)
    - How does this role contribute to my teaching style?
    - What do my learners perceive as my role as teacher?
- In Farrell and Ives's (2015) case study, the teacher indicated that the source of his beliefs related to teaching originated from his past experiences as a learner. He said that he considers it important for students to be active language learners in the classroom. He consistently provided such an environment to allow active learning. He said that this belief derived from his past experiences as a learner. Where do your beliefs come from (source of beliefs)?
    - Your past experience as a student?
    - Your experience of what works or will work best?
    - Established practice in the school you are placed in?
    - Your personality?

- Any research you have read?
- Teaching method(s) you will follow?

One method of helping learner TESOL teachers become more aware of their prior beliefs is to encourage them to examine the metaphors they use to describe teaching and learning. For learner TESOL teachers, the identification and analysis of metaphors they use can be a basis for achieving coherence of thoughts and their future actions when they teach (Bullough, 1990). Furthermore, a close examination of these metaphors may not only provide learner TESOL teachers with some insight into their prior beliefs, but also provide TESOL teacher educators with the same awareness, which in turn can be an important starting point from which to initiate change in such metaphors if they conflict with material presented in their TESOL teacher education courses. As Thornbury (1991: 193) has noted, the beliefs and values embodied in the 'personally significant images' of learner TESOL teachers can also provide "valuable insights for teacher educators." Thus, identification and exploration of teacher metaphors are one means of gaining a window onto the taken-for-granted assumptions and beliefs that learner TESOL teachers possess to make sense of their experiences, or as Block (1992: 51) says, as "explanatory vehicles," and when expressed, can be used for further articulation and reflection.

For example, learner TESOL teachers can be encouraged to explore their use of language to describe students, teaching, and learning subsequent languages such as English. By exploring their use of such language, we can begin to uncover how assumptions may be embedded in learner TESOL teachers' thinking. Farrell (2006a), for example, outlined a case study of how learner TESOL teachers were encouraged to examine their prior beliefs and practices by reflecting on the various metaphors they used during a six-week practice teaching experience in Singapore. The purpose of the study was not only to attempt to understand the nature of the metaphors used by the pre-service teachers, but also to ascertain to what extent these metaphors were maintained or changed as a result of this process of reflection and discussion with the language teacher educator.

Learner TESOL teachers were asked to answer three questions:

- What is the teacher's role in the classroom?
- How should learning take place?
- Complete the statement: "A teacher is_____."

The metaphors were categorized according to Oxford et al.'s (1998) typology covering four perspectives on teaching: (1) social order: for instance, teacher as manufacturer; (2) cultural transmission: for instance, teacher as conduit; (3) learner-centered growth: for instance, teacher as nurturer; and (4) social reform: for instance, teacher as learning partner.

One striking 'social order' metaphor that many of the learner TESOL teachers reported was *the classroom is a battleground* and *the teacher is a general*. One learner TESOL teacher explained the metaphor *classroom as battlefield* as follows: the classroom is "a place of tension" between the teacher and the student "with both waiting to do battle." The learner TESOL teacher continued: "It is a battle between the students and the teacher. In the beginning, both parties do not know a lot about each other. The teacher has to fight to make the students receptive towards him/her." For this learner TESOL teacher the meaning of the word 'battle' included an "internal struggle for both teachers and students" to use appropriate strategies within the classroom. She remarked:

> There is a constant battle of making the right choices. The teacher has to decide
> what materials are suitable for the students. The students, on the other hand,
> have to choose among the choices and come up with a correct answer. In a
> battlefield the General has to decide what strategies to use to defeat the enemies.
> Similarly, the teacher has to think of ways to finish the syllabus in time and also
> to make it interesting and captivating.

When asked to reflect on the use of such a metaphor after actual teaching practice, the learner TESOL teacher said that she found that her actual experiences on teaching practice were different than her initial use and interpretation for the metaphor *the classroom as battlefield*. She said that she realized during practice teaching that her *battlefield* metaphor was not a fact that she observed in the real classroom. Although the formulation of this metaphor was originally based on her prior experiences as a student, she said that she now realized that this was no longer the case. Indeed, after a further period of reflection she used a different metaphor to describe the classroom *as a playground*, and explained it as a place "where I can encourage the pupils to be creative and have fun."

Thus, by a process of being first encouraged to articulate the metaphors she held before, during, and after practice teaching and to reflect on their meaning, she became more aware of the influence of her prior experiences and beliefs (no longer tacitly held) about teaching and learning. Additionally, when challenged about the reality of her present teaching experiences, she acknowledged that some of her previously stated metaphors were no longer appropriate. This important realization resulted in the learner TESOL teacher creating a new reality of her teaching. In fact, and as Roberts (1998: 67) has suggested, the test of the teachers' metaphors is not whether they are 'right or wrong' according to an outsider's perceptions, but "the extent to which they are useful for the teacher."

REFLECTIVE BREAK

- Complete the following sentences:
    - A teacher is_____.
    - A language classroom is a place where_____.
    - Language learning means_____.
- Has your use of metaphors changed between when you first started your TESOL teacher education program and where you are at present?
- If yes, what differences have you noticed?
- What experiences have led to any change you noticed?

- Do you have new metaphors?
- If no changes have occurred in your metaphor usage, what experiences have resulted in this confirmation of your original metaphor usage?
- Revisit the questions above after your TESOL teacher education program has concluded and both before and after practice teaching. Ask yourself whether your metaphors have changed or remained consistent.

Reading and Discussion Task

Farrell (2016b) outlines a case study of the reflections of three experienced ESL teachers in Canada through the use of metaphor analysis. The four categories identified in the Oxford et al. (1998) typology were used to code the metaphors, and 'cultural transmission' metaphors were not found. The following frequency of metaphors was reported by the three teachers (T1, T2, T3) in the other three categories as follows:

	Social order	Learner-centered growth	Social reform	Total
T1	14	15	7	36
T2	11	23	0	34
T3	10	14	0	24
Totals:	35	52	7	94

- Why do you think the three teachers used *learner-centered growth* (52) the most, followed by *social order* (35), then *social reform* (7)?

The teachers used the following metaphors in each category:

Category	T1	T2	T3
Learner-centered growth	Friend Parent Janitor	Facilitator Mother Coach	Nurturer Therapist Coach
Social order	Border guard Guard dog Peacekeeper	King Competitor Police officer Production-line worker	Army general Dictator Judge Micromanaging Boss
Social reform	Learning partner Soldier Archaeologist	N/A	N/A

- What is your understanding of the use of each of these metaphors?
- Do you agree or disagree with them?
- Now read the paper in full and compare your reflections with those the teachers expressed there.

[Farrell, T. S. C. (2016b). The teacher is a facilitator: Reflecting on ESL teacher beliefs through metaphor analysis. *IJLTR,4*, 1), 1-10. Available from: https://files. eric.ed.gov/fulltext/EJ1127419.pdf]

REFLECTIVE BREAK

• Reflect on this example of a learner TESOL teacher's principles by analyzing her use of metaphors. Do you agree with her metaphor and definition of teacher as gardener? What does learner-centered teaching mean to you?

> I believe a teacher is like a gardener, and learners are the seeds that she tends. In order for a plant to grow, the gardener must know its particular characteristics and the kind of conditions in which it will thrive. She must feed it, water it and provide it with the necessary care and attention for it to grow tall and strong. In the same way, a teacher must recognize the characteristics of the students she teaches – their abilities, learning styles, prior knowledge and experiences, and interests – in order to determine their optimal learning conditions. She feeds her students with knowledge; not so much as to overwhelm them, but not so little that they are unmotivated and unchallenged. Then she nurtures them so their knowledge grows, and provides opportunities for them to flourish. I now realize that this metaphor differs from the one I held when I first started this TESOL teacher education program. Then, I believed that teachers were like tour guides, leading students through their learning, explaining the things they encountered and walking a path of ups and downs together with the students. However, through experience, I have realized that leading learners as a group in the same direction does not allow for learner differences. Some may want to stray from the path and explore different things, some may not be able to keep up and others may want to run ahead. From my experience, it is more effective to look at the individual and consider how each student can be nurtured so they can reach their full potential. My style of teaching, therefore, is learner-centered. I teach students new language then give them opportunities to use the language through various tasks and activities. I monitor the students' language and interactions, provide support where necessary and use my observations to help me determine how to further extend their knowledge and skills.

Berliner (1990: 86) has noted that for teachers, "Metaphors are powerful forces, conditioning the way we come to think about ourselves and others." When learner TESOL teachers are encouraged to reveal the metaphors they use, these metaphors can then be challenged as to their relevance given the material they have been presented with in the TESOL teacher education program. Thus, metaphor analysis to reveal a learner TESOL teacher's underlying beliefs is really a two-step process that includes not only articulating, exploring, and reflecting on the metaphors but also challenging them to see whether they need to be adjusted in any way. After being encouraged to articulate her use of language to describe a teacher, the novice ESL teacher in the example above realized that her metaphor usage had changed as a result of reflecting during her TESOL teacher education program. Achieving such awareness is necessary before any change can be considered, and as Thornbury (1996: 284) has noted, without adjustments at the level of awareness of prior beliefs, "the effects of training may only be superficial." When learner TESOL teachers articulate their beliefs through metaphor analysis, they are better able to identify their teaching strengths and areas needed for improvement and gain the overall freedom to be able to continually modify existing beliefs whenever appropriate (Farrell and Bennis, 2013; Farrell and Ives, 2015). We will revisit your reflections on principles in Chapter 6, as you will use them as part of your teaching evaluation.

Reflecting on Theory
When learner TESOL teachers reflect on their theory in stage 3 of the framework, they can become more aware of the different concepts and theoretical principles that underlie their instructional practices. In addition, theory can be reflected on by examining critical incidents that happen in classrooms, either on teaching practice or as written about by practicing TESOL teachers.

In terms of using theory to reflect on future instructional decisions, learner TESOL teachers explore particular skills that are taught (or should be taught) in their day-to-day lessons, and the specific teaching techniques they choose (or may want to choose) to use in their lessons. Thus such teacher planning involves a complex task of thinking about suitable lesson content to teach, suitable methods and activities to use, how to teach all this, and the desired outcomes that the lesson should achieve.

Learner TESOL teachers can consider three different lesson plan designs when considering their plans: *forward, central,* and *backward* designs (see Ashcraft, 2014, for a full discussion). These three designs influence the direction in which the lesson develops, and so teachers should be aware of what each involves. Generally, in *forward planning* the teacher identifies the lesson content first and then decides on the particular teaching methods as well as activities that will be used to teach the content. In *central planning,* the teacher chooses specific teaching methods and activities first and then considers the content and outcomes of the lesson. In *backward planning,* the teacher considers the desired lesson outcomes first, or what students are required to know at the end of the lesson, as well as what type of evidence would be necessary to show that the desired learning has taken place.

Teachers can also engage in collaborative lesson planning. For example, Shi and Yang (2014: 138) examined the reflections of learner TESOL teachers in collective lesson-planning conferences for a writing course, and discovered that

> participants [in collaboration with others] were not only able to develop a shared understanding of lesson planning and by negotiating their own views, make meanings applicable to new circumstances, to enlist the collaboration of others, [and] to make sense of events, but were also able to get a better understanding of the links between their own theories and practices.

REFLECTIVE BREAK

- Reflect on this example of a learner TESOL teacher's lesson planning. Why do you think this teacher took a forward design approach to her lesson planning? What advice would you give to teachers when planning lessons that are curriculum-bound?

As a learner TESOL teacher, my planning followed *forward design* and lesson content was determined by the textbook and planning centered on methods of teaching this content. At the time, this was the only way I knew how to plan. However as I grew in experience, forward planning was increasingly reserved for lessons for cram school students studying for school entrance examinations. In such classes, I had to synchronize lesson content with what the students were studying at school, ensuring they mastered the target language in preparation for their tests. Thus planning for each lesson started by identifying the language the students needed to learn then considering effective ways of presenting it. From this, I determined lesson learning outcomes and assessment methods. I disliked planning in this way as it was textbook- rather than student-centered. However, forward planning helped me cover the content the students needed to learn and ensure their understanding was sufficient to enable application to different exam questions. As a result, all of my students performed well in their English exams.

As I grew more confident and began focusing on students' learning rather than my own teaching, I found myself increasingly employing backward planning; determining first what I wanted students to achieve then planning how this could be accomplished. I found this method useful for all classes as it moved the planning focus from textbook content to the learners' needs while facilitating the forging of connections between new learning and prior knowledge. I determined students' needs by conducting needs analyses, formative assessment, and post-lesson reflections, then found, adapted and presented content to meet these needs.

In classes where I was not curriculum-bound and had more freedom in what I taught, I occasionally used central planning for lessons. These classes were aimed at adult students studying English for overseas travel and communication purposes. As no curriculum existed, I could make lessons activity-based, and consequently encourage the students to freely express themselves, scaffold and support each other while taking more control of their learning. When planning, I looked for activities that would allow students to apply their language knowledge in different contexts and facilitate the sharing of language and strategies. After finding a suitable activity, I would then consider the language I needed to teach and methods of student assessment.

In examining how I plan for teaching, I have seen that my theory of practice centers on adaptation to the needs and situations of my students.

These needs are varied, as is my role as teacher. For students studying for exams, I must ensure a thorough understanding of textbook content and the accurate use and application of target language. Conversely for students studying communicative English, I must identify areas of focus, provide the support they require to meet their goals, and facilitate learner agency. Using combinations of central, forward and backward planning has given me the flexibility to teach according to this theory of practice.

Another means of accessing theory is to explore and examine critical incidents. Indeed, no amount of content study in a TESOL teacher education program can fully prepare learner TESOL teachers for dealing with the full range of issues that language teaching involves (Farrell and Baecher, 2017). For example, oftentimes during a lesson some unplanned incident will occur and is 'too hot' for the teacher to handle as it happens, because it interrupts the taken-for-granted ways of thinking about teaching. This incident becomes 'critical' when subjected to conscious reflection after the class, and by analyzing such incidents teachers can examine the various theories that underpin their perceptions about teaching.

In the field of TESOL, Farrell (2013) has noted the positive effects when teachers analyze critical incidents. As he reported, teachers develop more awareness of how real practices can conflict with expectations and outcomes, and as a result, they can begin to explore assumptions that underlie their practice. Richards and Farrell (2011) have pointed out that some of these issues, incidents, or unforeseen events may arise from working with learners of different cultural, linguistic, and educational backgrounds; some can result from the intrinsic difficulties learning a new language entails; and some may be the result of working with learners who have had difficult life experiences or who have pressing educational and other needs. Thus TESOL teacher education programs should attempt to integrate more of these critical incidents into various courses and materials, so that learner TESOL teachers can get a glimpse of the real-world classroom challenges they will most certainly face when they begin their teaching careers (Farrell, 2015b).

REFLECTIVE BREAK

- Reflect on this example of a learner TESOL teacher's critical incident. Try to tell what happened before the incident, and what happened after the incident. What would you have done?

    This incident happened during the time I taught in a school in [a country in Asia] last year. I was teaching a Grade 11 English class. This incident can be seen as "teaching low" as it made me say to myself, "This is what makes my life as a teacher so difficult." While I was explaining the lesson, a student shouted out, "You are boring."

    I was so shocked at the time that I stared at the boy and asked him to stay after class to have a talk with me. At that moment I thought I would yell at him and ask to see his parents to complain. When I saw him, I asked him why he said such a thing about me in front of everyone. He said I was boring because I talked a lot in every lesson, everyone hated doing boring exercises and they wanted something more interesting to do. He said he liked studying English but he could remember nothing by just doing formal exercises.

I then realized that he was right as my class sequence was always me explaining lessons and students doing exercises. It seemed I followed didactic theory of teaching in which the teacher is regarded as a transmitter of knowledge. I believed such theory would work well as my high school teachers' teaching practice was similar and I was a successful student learning English with them.

I never forgot this event. It let me know the theory I based on was subjective as it came from my own experiences only. That it worked for me in the past does not necessarily mean it may be suitable with different groups of students another time. This incident gave e a chance to reframe my theory of teaching from didactic theory to interactionist theory in which students should interact to gain knowledge. I also realized that students are not often given chances to express and explain what they really think. In fact, those who make such statement about teacher in class like in my incident are often considered to be disrespectful. Besides, the event taught me to be more open to not only students' feedback to improve my own teaching practice but also their mistakes because I make mistakes at times.

Critical incidents also occur outside the classroom (personal critical incidents) and can include an event that resulted in a major change in a teacher's professional life. Indeed, such an event or personal critical incident may have led you to become a learner TESOL teacher. Your 'tree of life' (see 'Reflecting on Philosophy' above) can give you an overall view of what has influenced you to become a TESOL teacher, such as incidents in your youth, school years, and so on that have shaped you and even led you into the field of TESOL. It is important to articulate both personal and professional incidents so that we can be more aware of what is shaping our instructional practices, and that we do not unwittingly teach in reaction to any of these critical incidents. We will revisit your reflections on theory in Chapter 6, as you will use them as part of your teaching evaluation.

Reflecting on Practice
When learner TESOL teachers reflect on philosophy, principles, and theory, they explore the 'hidden' (the invisible) aspects of practice. When they reflect on practice, they explore the more visible and thus observable aspects of practice, namely classroom teaching. This includes not only examination of a teacher's actions but also an examination of student actions and reactions during lessons. Of course, such observable classroom actions on both sides of the desk are directly related to and influenced by our reflections on our theory at the previous level, as well as on our principles and philosophy, and as Widdowson (1984: 87) has observed, "There is no conflict between theory and practice, only between particular theories and particular practices." Thus there is no such thing as teaching actions on their own without also

looking at how these actions are influenced by the 'hidden' aspects of practice, and in turn at how teaching actions can also influence our philosophy, principles, and theory.

Reflections on practice can occur while teaching a lesson (reflection-*in*-action), and/or after a lesson (reflection-*on*-action). When teachers engage in reflection-*in*-action they attempt to monitor and adjust to various circumstances happening during the lesson. When teachers engage in reflection-*on*-action they examine what happened in a lesson after the event. However, reflection-*on*-action can also include some kind of anticipatory reflection, or reflection-*for*-action. Reflection-*for*-action can be a culmination of reflection-*in*-action and reflection-*on*-action as teachers attempt to consider what will come next in light of what went before.

Teachers have several different methods of accessing their reflections on practice. For example, teachers can engage in classroom observations (self-monitoring, peer critical friendships, or group observations), and they can record (audio and/or video) their lessons and later transcribe the recordings for more accurate recounting of what occurred. The main idea here is that learner teachers and novice teachers together with their teacher educators and school mentors have this evidence available for them all to reflect on, and make any informed adjustments to their practice based on this evidence. Some scholars have suggested that language teacher educators can put many of these records of teachers practice together into a collection of written records, to be used in different teacher education contexts as corpus-based evidence that learner teachers can use for reflection during their teaching practice as well as in their early career years (Farr, 2010). As Farr (2010: 623) notes, such "a corpus of classroom language can give a much better insider's perspective, and can complement more traditional LTE (language teacher education) practices of classroom and peer observations, but without the intrusion and time pressure which comes with these." In addition, Farr (2010) notes, language teacher educators can also use such corpus-based approaches as a tool to examine and reflect on their own practices.

Teachers can also consider conducting action research on specific aspects of their practice if they think they need to improve some aspect of their teaching or their students' learning. Because learner TESOL teachers will for the most part not have much teaching experience, they will encounter this experience during their teaching practice or the practicum. Thus I assume that at the time most learner TESOL teachers would be reading this chapter, they might be in the middle of their coursework and thus might not have this teaching practice experience. I will cover the teaching practice in Chapter 8 in more detail, and learner TESOL teachers can then get more ideas that are applicable within stage 4 of the framework above for reflecting on practice.

REFLECTIVE BREAK

- Reflect on this learner TESOL teacher's experience of teaching two lessons. Why do you think she was surprised in the first observed lesson to discover that she may have been favoring one side of the room? What do you think of her questioning behavior in the second observed lesson?

I was observed teaching two classes to 15 and 16 year old high school students. The students have been learning English for more than 10 years, and after 3 years of being placed in the 'Advanced English' class, have chosen to take IB Diploma Program 'Language A: Language and Literature' course which is taught as if English was their first language. After reflecting on my teacher beliefs, I wanted to see if my practice aligned with my beliefs, and if the changes I had tried to make were evident in my practice.

Lesson 1

In my first lesson that I taught I let the students choose their own seating arrangement. The lesson focused on teaching rhetorical devices, analyzing a speech, and identifying the use of different rhetorical devices using examples on the whiteboard. Claudia observed that when I gave instructions, I positioned myself to face the right side of the classroom and that I didn't address the left side of the classroom until later in the lesson when I began asking questions. It was also observed that more students from the right hand side contributed answers than the left hand side, that some students didn't contribute anything and that the interaction was almost 100% teacher–student–teacher, with very little student–student interaction.

This surprised me because I felt that I had been making an effort to address both sides of the classroom evenly, even though I had felt from time to time that it had been difficult to do so partly because the classroom was a rectangle shape, with the whiteboard placed along one of the longer walls. I also found it difficult when the students sat quite spaced out along the length of the back wall. I had been hesitant to tell the students where to sit, or ask them to move closer together, as I prefer that they choose their own seats in order to feel more comfortable in the classroom. After this feedback however I decided to change the seating arrangement for the second lesson to see how this would affect student interaction and participation.

Lesson 2

I taught the concept of ethos, pathos and logos in persuasive speeches for this next lesson. This time I told the students to sit in a circle so that everyone could see each other, and so that I could see each student. I started by giving the students a list of statements about speeches (e.g. a speech is like an essay read aloud), and we had a short discussion activity to see who agreed or disagreed with each statement. The students then read a description from their textbook about pathos, logos and ethos, watched a video of a speech that contained these features, and then finished by writing their own short persuasive speeches. This time when I received feedback it was noted that the amount and type of student interaction had changed. Firstly, with the circle seating arrangement all students had been addressed and each student had contributed an answer during the lesson. The observer also noticed that when I asked the students a question rather than the teacher–student–teacher interaction that had taken place in the previous class, two different types of student interactions were observed: students disagreeing and questioning other students about their response and students agreeing with each other and adding something further to the answer.

The difference in student interaction was very important for me, because the course is about language and literature and requires a lot of classroom participation and discussion. These sorts of discussion activities are incredibly valuable opportunities for the students to develop their critical thinking skills, and oral language in an environment where they receive feedback and guidance from the teacher. Because of this, it is important that all students participate and that they can listen to, disagree with, or extend other ideas. I hadn't previously considered how seating arrangements could affect the type or amount of student interaction. After reflecting on this I decided that in the future I would ask the students to sit closer together as a group, or in a circle seating arrangement.

It was also observed that at times I asked a question and if no-one answered it, I answered it myself. I had waited for the student response, but when there wasn't one I still gave the answer myself instead of asking a specific student or rephrasing the question. I know this is something I struggle with at times, as this year is the first time I have taught this course, and I am still getting to know what the students are capable of, and in which areas of the course they struggle more. I usually try to scaffold the students towards the right answer, but because at times I'm not sure if they are able to get to the right answer themselves, I give them the answer. The observation feedback made me realize that I have been doing this more often than I thought. I hope that with time I can learn more about the students' abilities, have confidence that they will reach the right answer, and focus on scaffolding their learning, rather than giving them the answer myself.

I found the observations and reflections to be a very valuable way of receiving feedback about what I thought I was doing, and what was actually taking place in the classroom. In future observations I hope to be able to further reflect on some of the changes I have made as a result of this first stage of observations, to see if these changes are long-lasting.

When learner TESOL teachers reflect on practice they can become more aware of their daily teaching routines, and how their instructional decisions provide or block opportunities for learning in their lessons, as well as what theory is useful for their practice. For example, Kömür and Çepik (2015) encouraged learner TESOL teachers in Turkey to reflect on practice, and noted their insecurities with classroom management in these lessons and their fear of making mistakes. The authors soon realized the need to use a variety of materials in the classroom to encourage students to participate in the learning process more actively, in order to minimize classroom management problems. As a result of their reflections on their teaching practice, the learner TESOL teachers expressed a concern about the inconsistency between the theory they were provided with in their TESOL teacher education programs and their actual experiences of practice. Thus, they highlighted their need for more

practice in the methodology courses in their teacher education programs and as outlined in the previous chapter. We will revisit your reflections on practice in Chapter
6, as you will use them as part of your teaching evaluation.

Reflecting beyond Practice

Reflecting beyond practice requires learner TESOL teachers to reflect beyond the
technical aspects of practice and look at the sociocultural and moral dimensions of
TESOL. Unfortunately, TESOL as a profession has been slow to reflect at this critical
level over the years and has not openly examined the moral, political, cultural, and
social issues that impact a TESOL teacher's practice both inside and outside the classroom. This dearth of critical reflection could be ascribed to the power that publishers
and governments held over the TESOL profession, especially in the early years, and
it is only since the relatively recent development of TESOL teacher education as a
subfield in its own right that we have begun to highlight the broader sociopolitical
as well as affective/moral issues that impact practice. With such critical reflection on
language education in mind, Julian Edge (2006) put together a collection of articles
from international scholars on critical English language teaching. and he called this
volume *(Re-)Locating TESOL in an Age of Empire.* This excellent collection should
be added to the list of readings on any TESOL teacher education course or in-service
development course.

When learner TESOL teachers reflect beyond practice, they will be able to understand the way particular societal assumptions they may have been following in practice can be socially restrictive and, as a result, develop new ideas that can empower
them to become transformative intellectuals within the TESOL profession and
society in general. Education by its very nature is political and full of ideology, be
it in the classroom, the textbooks and materials, or the administration of a school.
Consequently, reflections beyond practice can assist TESOL teachers in becoming
more aware of the many different agendas and interests that can (and do) shape how
we define TESOL teaching and learning.

Reflection beyond practice is not done in isolation as the fifth stage of the framework, as it involves the teacher-as-person, his or her principles, theories, and practices in combination with each other, and how these are all connected to wider school
and social issues within the community in which they are placed (Farrell, 2018). Such
critical reflection allows learner TESOL teachers to go beyond language instruction
and fulfill educationally oriented promises, such as helping people become critical
thinkers and active citizens (Deng and Yuen, 2011: 450). As Deng and Yuen (2011)
noted, reflection beyond practice on deeper social issues leads to great awareness of
social issues, inequitable relationships and generated roles, thus enhancing learner
TESOL teachers' critical thinking as both teachers and learners.

REFLECTIVE BREAK

- Do you think the TESOL profession should engage in critical reflection?
- Do you think you should look beyond your technical practice and reflect on how
  your practice impacts and/or is impacted by society?

- Do you think that TESOL teachers should be encouraged to take on the role of social agents to promote changes that impact their learners' lives? If yes, why and how? If no, why not?
- Does your status as a TESOL teacher affect your life inside and outside the classroom (positively or negatively)? If so, how do these effects emerge in your teaching practice?
- What links do you perceive between your moral and/or religious beliefs and your practice?
- Do you have any conflicts between your personal morals and anything in your work context: students, colleagues, materials, administrators?

Following on from the answers to the reflective break above, learner TESOL teachers can also reflect beyond practice within the community in which they work, as Crookes (2013) suggested, when they organize, address leadership, fundraise, and engage in action:

- *Organize*: Develop institutional networks, develop connections with parents, and develop networks in the community.
- *Address leadership*: Address leadership but try to see that all are leaders, if provided with the right orientation and skills.
- *Fundraise*: There is a literature on fundraising in education, mainly targeting the post-secondary level, but little guidance for the rest of us.
- *Engage in action*: The old slogan 'direct action gets the goods' is relevant because in many places conventional politicking will not provide what a critical language teacher might need.

Crookes (2013) maintains that learner TESOL teachers can follow the above steps in the community in which they practice in order to solve some injustice they perceive to be present for their students, and/or also TESOL teachers.

REFLECTIVE BREAK

- Reflect on this learner TESOL teacher's reflections beyond practice. What is your understanding of the term 'achievement disease'? Does it apply to your teaching context? How can teachers adhere to the demands of the teaching context that require student success in exams while at the same time keep true to their own teaching and learning beliefs, which may differ? Why do you think the learner teacher in this example engaged in 'self-laceration'? Do you think teachers in general are susceptible to self-laceration? If yes, why? If no, why not?

> Without doubt, as members of society, teachers, including me, cannot be separated from our societal environments, particularly our teaching contexts, where our philosophies, principles, theories of practice and practice are nurtured. Critical reflection can help me as a teacher uncover what societal factors are having an impact on both my professional and personal life,

and offer me more possibilities to critically evaluate my own practice. With reference to my teaching context which is in a [country in Asia] public high school, one of the most influential social factors that I find problematic is "achievement disease" – the hugest burden for teachers of English in [country in Asia] to bear nowadays.

Within [country in Asia] education system, 'achievement disease' can be defined as a phenomenon in which teachers are under pressure to compete with each other for creating more and more good students. The so-called 'good students' are in fact measured by students' test results via which teaching quality is evaluated. In other words, students' academic grades have a significant impact on teachers' competitive scores in the school ranking. As a result, most teachers in my workplace made an attempt to increase such results at all costs. One way of doing this was to "teach to the test" at the expense of students' communicative skills development. As regards communicative teaching, it was considered inessential to ensure high test performance among students, therefore, most English teachers chose to occasionally implement it in their practice when the exams were over.

Superficially, the idea that students were prepared to have higher marks in the school tests seems to satisfy not only the needs of students and their parents but also the requirements of my institution. However, in the long run, such exam-driven instructions cannot effectively contribute to the development of students' communicative competence, which is considered one of the main responsibilities of TESOL teachers. More severely, in order to obtain higher scores in the ranking, some teachers of my department who belonged to the assessment group had a tendency to reveal parts of the school test they compiled by allowing their students to practice the linguistic forms that they knew would be present in the test. To some extent, this can be treated as exam cheating. As a consequence, students whose teachers joined in the school test compilation tended to have higher grades than others, which placed those teachers in higher ranks in the ranking via which the school board made judgment on teaching quality among teachers of English.

The fact that teaching quality is fully reflected through a list was completely inequitable. Actually, within my high school context, 'achievement-disease'-imposed constraints on communicative teaching deviated TESOL teachers from the original goal to facilitate communicative learning, and even had a detrimental effect on their work ethics. As regards learners in my high school, 'achievement disease' was also harmful to them since students' parents usually relied on their grades in discrete point tests to evaluate their English learning progress. While some students managed to communicate well in English, their communicative progress would not be highly appreciated by both their teachers and parents unless they earned high marks in the school examinations. Such an unfair evaluation made most good students lose their interest in learning English, and forced them to focus on studying discrete linguistic forms.

On reflecting upon what happened to my professional life in the past, I found it quite impossible to preserve my communicative teaching without thorough understanding of the strong link between certain social factors, particularly 'achievement disease', and my teaching practice. I myself used to underestimate its impacts on my profession, and ended up forming a bad impression on not only the school board, but also some students' parents. Since I refused to "teach to the test" like other teachers, the majority of my students did not achieve as high scores as their counterparts in other classes. Their results, afterwards, affected my competitive scores, putting me nearly at the bottom of the ranking. Such low rank of mine, however, was inequitably attributed to my inexperience and lack of teaching capability as I was merely a novice teacher during that time. All of these incidents made me start to become doubtful about my teaching capability, and grow a deep sense of despair in terms of my teaching profession.

Had I developed an awareness of how 'achievement disease' manipulated the education system, I would have avoided such self-laceration. Additionally, if I had acknowledged the underlying cause for students' low grades which was the misalignment between their communicative learning objectives and the form-focused assessment outcomes, I could have been more persuasive when explaining to others, including my colleagues, school board, students and their parents, the rationale behind my practice. All of these are parts of critical reflection, one aspect of which refers to 'teaching as a moral activity'. This aspect, indeed, is of great importance to arrest the 'achievement disease' currently dominating most teaching practice in my workplace.

Teaching is heavily influenced by social forces and political trends, as there is the possibility of the presence of different types of discrimination inherent in different educational systems. Encouraging learner TESOL teachers to take a more critical stance to the TESOL profession can, as Abednia (2012: 713) discovered, lead them to became more aware of their old uncritical habits and attitudes and "more conscious of limitations imposed on them by authorities and institutions." In this manner, as a result of critical reflections, the learners Abednia researched also began to rede-fine their own positions, rights, and roles within the profession. As Abednia (2012: 712) observed, many of the teachers experienced a shift from thinking of "ELT as merely aimed at teaching ESL/EFL" to looking beyond the classroom and the impact of teaching on the community. We will revisit your reflections beyond practice in Chapter 6, as you will use them as part of your teacher assessment.

CONCLUSION

Although the concept of reflective practice has been warmly embraced within the field of TESOL, there is still little agreement on how it should be implemented in TESOL teacher education programs. This chapter has outlined and discussed how reflective practice can be implemented through the lens of a holistic framework specifically designed for TESOL teachers (Farrell, 2015a). This framework is different from many other approaches because it not only focuses on the intellectual, cognitive, and metacognitive aspects of practice that many of the other approaches concentrate on, but also explores the spiritual, moral, and emotional non-cognitive aspects of reflection. This acknowledges the inner life of teachers, so that TESOL teachers can become more aware of their philosophy, principles, theories, practices, and how these impact issues inside and beyond practice. Such a holistic approach to reflective practice can produce more integrated learner TESOL teachers who are more self-aware and have the understanding to be able to interpret, shape, and reshape their practice throughout their novice-service years and their entire careers. The information that is produced from reflecting during each stage can be compiled into a teaching portfolio and used for collaborative teaching evaluation purposes, as will be outlined in more detail in Chapter 6.

4

TESOL TEACHER EDUCATION: COLLABORATIVE LEARNING

PREAMBLE

The following is an excerpt from feedback by novice TESOL teachers on a self-initiated novice TESOL teacher reflection group in Canada during the first semester of their first year:

> I liked hearing other ideas. I liked just getting some feedback when I said, 'Oh, this isn't working in my class.' Just to know that sometimes we were going through the same thing like, you know we were frustrated with the administration. We were frustrated with sometimes the students or whatever. So I think that's kind of nice because we created an opportunity to talk about . . . you don't always have that opportunity in your office with a group of teachers. We shared what was happening in our classrooms and professional lives. I don't think we found solutions per se, but I think we provided a forum for each of us as individuals to articulate what was happening and then to share similar experiences in a supportive way. I also found that I created friendships.

> Throughout the group discussions I wasn't concerned by the positives or the negatives or the neutrals. I mean I looked at them and it was interesting and they were not really surprising. So I feel empowered by our group discussion. I truly appreciate the heightened sense of awareness that has been growing within me as time goes on. I find myself stopping to think twice about the choices I make for what I do in the classroom. These two terms of our meeting/sharing/questioning have helped to instill a more consistent habit of reflection for me.

> Now that the group discussions have ended, I must rely on my own decision making and as such I really miss the group discussions. I wondered what the result of this group would be, and genuinely had no idea. Although we are not quite finished, I suspect at this point that the benefits have been to slow down from the hectic pace of teaching and coordinating and to restore a healthy balance to my career and life, to process some of the things that I have learned from both my education and my experience and to look at them more carefully, to develop a closer connection with my two best friends and colleagues and to establish a process or a dialogue that genuinely supports me in my work. I also

feel I have established some degree of control. I went away feeling that we had found some direction and that there were some common interests that we could explore. I hope that I can help to get other people in our department going on Reflective Practice. We all stand to benefit immensely, professionally of course, but also in our relationships with each other.

The three novice TESOL teachers quoted above formed the group as a survival mechanism because they felt they were 'sinking' in their first few weeks. With the aid of a facilitator whom all three knew who managed the process, they were able to survive through the collaborative process of the weekly group discussions and journal writing on their experiences.

The group talked and wrote about many different issues such as classroom management, discipline, and control; how to organize their lessons to motivate reluctant learners; student assessment; and coping with materials they perceived as inappropriate or inadequate. This involved them becoming more aware of their isolation as novice teachers, in that they knew that it was up to them to swim or sink because the school did not provide any particular induction program with mentor teachers to help them in their first year. As Brandt (2005: 21) notes: "Teacher isolation is a salient problem for all teachers, but the lack of collegiate interaction is especially relevant to novice teachers." Therefore, this novice TESOL teacher reflection group acted as a community of practice in which members interacted with each other as a means of "developing particular shared practices, routines, rituals, artifacts, symbols, conventions, stories, and histories" (Wenger, 1998: 6) and allowed them to not only survive, but also thrive during their first year of teaching.

REFLECTIVE BREAK

- Do you consider teacher isolation to be a problem in teaching?
- If yes, why? If no, why not?
- Do you think TESOL teachers should collaborate when reflecting?
- If yes, how should they do this? If no, why not?
- The novice TESOL teachers in the preamble formed a teacher reflection group during their first year. How can a teacher reflection group work for the good of the group while at the same time facilitating individual members' reflections?

INTRODUCTION

The ancient Greek maxim "know thyself" (regardless of who it is attributed to), although very popular, can be considered selfish and even narcissistic because it asks people to individually look inward at themselves. Indeed, reflective practice has also been criticized by some scholars because it can promote such inward examination of individual teachers' teaching (Akbari, 2007). However, although this may seem like a controversial stance, I believe that reflective practice must start with self-reflection in order to 'know-the-self (or 'thyself'), and I agree with Parker Palmer (1998: 3) when he points out that: "The work required to 'know thyself' is neither selfish nor narcissistic. Whatever self-knowledge we attain as teachers will serve our students and our scholarship well. Good teaching requires self-knowledge." Acquiring such self-knowledge through reflective practice, however, does not have to be conducted in isolation from others; as Dewey (1933) has noted, reflection is a social activity and best carried out in interaction with others in a community. Farrell (2015b) has also noted that for TESOL teachers, reflective practice should involve teachers engaging in dialogue with other teachers. Thus, reflection in TESOL teacher education can be seen as a process that is both individual and collaborative, where all learner TESOL teachers can learn through self-dialogue and in dialogue with others, including peers, mentors, supervisors, and students. This chapter outlines and discusses how learner teachers can be encouraged to collaborate throughout their TESOL teacher education program (novice-service) and their careers (in-service).

COLLABORATIVE LEARNING

As outlined in Chapter 1, a core assumption of this book is recognition of the critical role collaborative learning plays in the education and development of TESOL teachers. Such an approach to learning is created in the first instance through the mediation of TESOL teacher educators, who act collaboratively as mentors throughout and beyond the TESOL teacher education program. Within the TESOL teacher education program, *teacher educator-mentors* can help to facilitate such collaborative learning through the development and use of critical friends groups, team teaching, and peer coaching. Such mentorship also continues during the practicum and into the early career years. Teacher educator-mentors can also use such mediational tools as writing, dialogue, and combinations of both with use of technology to help TESOL teacher educators facilitate and encourage the development of a reflective stance in learner TESOL teachers, both during their TESOL teacher education program and into their novice years and in-service years.

MENTORING

TESOL teacher educators play a crucial role when encouraging learner TESOL teachers to develop a reflective stance toward practice. The teacher educators have a critical role in developing the knowledge of learner TESOL teachers through, for example, the careful selection of appropriate readings and providing mentorship in a collaborative process throughout the learner TESOL teachers' development. However, because learner TESOL teachers are in a TESOL teacher education program, they must receive a grade, and as such 'collaborations' are somewhat unequal and therefore 'different'.

Mentoring, defined as a situation in which "a knowledgeable person aids a less knowledgeable person" (Eisenman and Thornton, 1999: 81), is set up as a support system for novice teachers in many educational settings, as they are assigned mentors to assist their socialization into the community of practice of teachers. Such mentoring can take place in the practicum in the form of appointment of a cooperating teacher (for more on this see Chapter 5), and in the early career years (or even in later years), and can help learner TESOL teachers, as Schwille, Dembele, and Schubert (2007: 89) have noted, to "adapt to and learn about their roles as teachers" during these vital first years, because they will need lots of support. Mentors can be very effective in providing such support because of their knowledge and experience gained in their years in the profession.

Within TESOL teacher education programs, the term *teacher educator-mentor* indicates that the teacher educator will ideally act as a mentor for learner TESOL teachers during the program, teaching practice, and in their early careers. Within the TESOL teacher education program, such mentorship entails entering into a collaborative arrangement with learner TESOL teachers in a way that encourages talking with, questioning, and even confronting the learner TESOL teacher to develop a reflective stance toward their practice. This entire book provides various ideas and activities that teacher educator-mentors can use to encourage learner TESOL teachers to achieve such a stance toward practice throughout the program and early career years and into in-service.

Another form of mentorship is provided by schools, where mentors are usually assigned to assist novice teachers with their transition from teacher education programs to teaching in the schools. These *mentor-teachers* have usually been drawn from veteran teachers within a school, who help novice teachers learn the philosophy, cultural values, and established sets of behaviors expected by the schools employing them. Within TESOL, Malderez and Bodoczky (1999: 4) have described five different roles that mentors can play:

1. They can be models who inspire and demonstrate.
2. They can be "acculturators" who show mentees the ropes.
3. They can be sponsors who introduce the mentees to the "right people."
4. They can be supporters who are there to act as safety valves, should mentees need to let off steam.
5. They can be educators who act as sounding boards for the articulation of ideas to help new teachers achieve professional learning objectives.

Malderez and Bodoczky (1999: 4) suggest that most teacher-mentors will be involved "to a greater or lesser degree in all five roles."

Although mentoring is seen as mostly positive, the mere appointment of a mentor to a novice teacher in a school is no guarantee the teacher will be successfully socialized into the school. Mentoring relationships may sometimes be unpredictable. Tomlinson (1995), for example, has suggested that some mentors may feel unclear about their roles and responsibilities. He suggests that as experienced teachers "they may have become so intuitive they find it difficult to articulate what in fact they are doing" (Tomlinson, 1995: 18) and communicate it to other teachers. Thus mentors may be able to talk about their subject content but not about how they applied their knowledge in their classroom teaching.

Thus, mentor-teachers should be informed about the positive benefits of engaging in their own reflective practice so that they can pass their 'insider view' of actions inside and outside the classroom to their less experienced colleagues. Indeed, such reflection can also lead to more professional growth, job satisfaction, and development of leadership skills (Kwan and López-Real, 2010). If the mentor-teacher is not familiar with the concept of reflective practice, the teacher educator-mentor can inform the mentor-teacher about the benefits of reflective practice and the various ways (e.g. via the contents of this book) this has been implemented in the TESOL teacher education programs that the mentee (learner) TESOL teacher is graduating or has graduated from. In such an approach to mentoring, where teacher educator-mentors, teacher-mentors, and learner TESOL teachers engage in reflective dialogue, all can thrive together in a collaborative learning environment that benefits all. Such collaborations can come into play not only throughout the TESOL teacher education program, but also in teaching practice (Chapter 5) and teaching evaluation (Chapter 6). The sections that follow outline how TESOL teacher educator-mentors can help to facilitate collaborative learning throughout the TESOL teacher education programs through the use (either alone or in combination) of critical friends groups, team teaching, and/or peer coaching.

REFLECTIVE BREAK

- Examine the five different roles teacher-mentors can play as outlined by Malderez and Bodoczky (1999) above. Which of these roles will be most important for you as a learner TESOL teacher during your practicum and then in your early career teaching years?
- Can you think of any other roles that it would be suitable for mentors to play?

Reading and Discussion Task

Bede McCormack, Laura Baecher, and Alex Cuenca (2019) noted that despite university supervisors' critical role in the success of learner TESOL teachers, research is limited on how to best prepare supervisors to mentor their supervisees and interact with cooperating teachers and school administrators. The authors explored supervisors' experiences to surface dilemmas of supervisory practice and discovered that they suffer overwhelming workloads, feel marginalized by their institutions, lack ongoing training, and are often unclear as to what their role is.

- Read the article and write a summary.
- Discuss your findings with a colleague.

[McCormack, B., Baecher, L., and Cuenca, A (2019). University-based teacher supervisors: Their voices, their dilemmas. *Journal of Educational Supervision*, 2, 1, 22-37]

CRITICAL FRIENDS GROUPS

The opening preamble above shows how a group of TESOL teachers acted as critical friends while collaborating during discussions in order to improve the quality of their teaching and their students' learning. They did so by questioning and some-times even confronting each other, but in a trusted environment, and as a result, they were able to explore all aspects of their practice both inside and outside the classroom (Farrell, 2001b, 2016a). As Johnson (2009: 101) has noted, critical friends groups all have "common elements: sharing the question or dilemma, inviting questions from the participants, giving and receiving feedback, and promoting self-reflection." These groups meet usually with the help of a facilitator who manages the reflective process.

The opening preamble above identifies comments from the teachers in the critical friends group that indicate that such a collaborative sharing arrangement allowed them to survive some traumatic events of their first week(s) (Farrell, 2016a). The preamble shows how critical friends worked with each other to support each other's professional development need by providing thought-provoking feedback questions that "give voice to a teacher's thinking [as if] looking into a mirror" (Farrell, 2007b: 149). For example, the first day and week were problematic for each of the three novice TESOL teachers in the critical friends group: one teacher noted she "felt com-pletely lost" from the very first day because they did not feel welcomed (no mentor was appointed; see above) and they quickly realized (through group discussions) that they would have to discover everything by themselves if they were to survive their first semester. The teacher continued: "You're just thrown in to survive yourself." In the same group discussion after the first week, another teacher reflected: "The first week felt frenzied because you didn't know if students were coming, or students weren't coming, and lots of that kind of switching around." In fact the teacher said that "The first week is like you're in a swamp." Another group member said: "Yeah, exactly. Like you were on thin ice because you're figuring out what's going on, and then this week is like, okay we're into the deep water now, and it is kind of sink or swim."

More shocks were to occur for all three novice TESOL teachers during their first week(s). One of these shocks occurred for one of the teachers, she said, when the textbook she was told she was going to use in one of her classes was suddenly changed before her first class even though she had already prepared lessons with this book in mind, and moreover, nobody had a copy of this new textbook because it had not arrived at that time. The teacher said that she felt exasperated because when she was informed she was hired and what courses she would be teaching, she was also given a textbook so she could prepare in advance. She remarked: "Then on arrival I was given a different book than what I was told before and they didn't even have it." Then she said that she had had to constantly "nag them" to get a copy of the new book. The teacher continued: "It took me a week of nagging such as asking: 'Where's my book? Where's my book?' Then Friday [end of first week] the book shows up." With that she said that she informed her 'coordinator' that she could only begin preparation of new lesson plans based on this new book from the following week, which situated her, as she noted, "uncomfortably behind in lesson planning." The teacher contin-ued: "I was shocked that they suddenly changed the book and also frustrated because they did not even have it and what was I going to do then with no book?"

Another early shock happened for another member of the group when she realized that she had not received any password to obtain access to necessary software used by the school, and especially for obtaining class lists. The teacher said: "I haven't got on to it [school program] because I have no password yet so I don't know what to do." The teacher remarked that she was then given a hard copy of the class lists, but realized that she would have to input all the names and student numbers into computer files herself. The teacher continued: "I don't understand why the class list with their student numbers cannot be sent to us electronically, so we can add [to them], but it's not. We have to do that [administrative] work ourselves." The teacher then remarked that her attendance sheets were not even correct: "My attendance sheets are a disaster ... all messed up, too because they had students missing. It's ridiculous especially since they use a good computer program anyway."

To compound the shocks outlined above, all three novice TESOL teachers noted that they did not know who they should talk to for guidance. One of the teachers mentioned this when she said that one reason she did not know the other teachers in the school was that a staff meeting planned for the first week was suddenly cancelled without explanation; as she said: "We haven't even had a staff meeting yet [because it was cancelled], so we don't even know all the teachers." To which another teacher responded: "It would be nice to meet – you know: 'Hi. My name is . . . and I teach . . . .'"

The critical friends group of novice TESOL teachers in their first year(s) were able to collaboratively talk through the various shocks and dilemmas they experienced, and to generate their own solutions to many of the problems they encountered during their first week, weeks, semester, and first year (Farrell, 2016a). The group members as critical friends helped each other take risks when trying to solve their issues that they might not have taken had they been left alone with these issues.

Within TESOL teacher education, however, caution should be used by TESOL teacher educators with the makeup of such groups, as some learner TESOL teachers may be culturally sensitive when having to question or offer criticism to other learner TESL teachers for fear of hurting others. For example, Vo and Nguyen (2010) have noted this, reporting that the learner TESOL teachers were initially hesitant to offer any criticism for fear of hurting others, but as the participants gained more trust, they became more comfortable contributing to the group. As Vo and Nguyen (2010: 210) observed, critical friends groups offered novice TESOL teachers "opportunities to learn from colleagues" as they developed a sense of community, and this ultimately led to improvement in their teaching. In a similar conclusion, Lakshmi (2014: 200) also links the collaboration involved in such arrangements with benefits to their overall empowerment as teachers: "teachers realized the need for collaborative work, and sought advice from their senior colleagues to solve their classroom problems and for their self-evaluation." Overall, as Johnson (2009: 101) has noted, "Critical Friends Groups have also been found to strengthen collegial bonds among teachers through close reflection on individual practice and student thinking and learning."

REFLECTIVE BREAK

- What would you have done if you had experienced the shocks outlined by the critical friends group above: (a) feeling unwelcomed – in "a swamp"; (b) the last-minute switch of the textbook; (c) attendance sheet problems?

- Who would you talk to about these issues (assuming you did not have a critical friends group to go to)?
- How would a critical friends group help you get through these 'shocks'?

Reading and Discussion Task

Monica Gonzalez Smith (2019) outlined a case study of how four final-semester learner TESOL teachers engaged in a critical friendship group to reflect on personally recorded videos of instruction delivered to elementary-age ESL students.

- Read her article and give details how her use of *critical friendship* supported these four undergraduate teacher candidates' reflections on ESL teaching and learning.
- Outline and discuss her video-mediated critical friendship framework that ESL teacher educators can use to structure video-mediated dialogue with teacher candidates. I discuss the use of video in more detail in the section on mediational tools below, so also bring your notes about this task to that discussion.
- Discuss your findings with a colleague.

[Smith, M. G. (2019). A video-mediated critical friendship reflection framework for ESL teacher education. *TESL-EJ, 23*, 1. Available from: http://tesl-ej.org/pdf/ej89/a7.pdf]

TEAM TEACHING

Team teaching is another type of critical friendship (see above) arrangement whereby two or more learner TESOL teachers 'team up' and cooperate as equals as they take responsibility for planning, teaching, and evaluating a class (Richards and Farrell, 2005). Team teaching moves reflection beyond the usual practices adopted in many TESOL teacher education programs, especially during the teaching practice components (see also Chapter 5) such as learner TESOL teachers observing lessons before obtaining the responsibility to teach a class alone. Typically in such a collaboration the 'team' share responsibility for planning a class and/or course, then for teaching the class/course, completing follow-up work (i.e. evaluations/assessments), and making various decisions about the class. Teachers usually cooperate as equals, though some elements of coaching (see below for more on peer coaching) may occur (Richards and Farrell, 2005). Such team teaching collaborations better prepare the teachers for the transition from the TESOL teacher education program to teaching in real classrooms. Central to team teaching collaboration is the sharing of experiences and reflective dialoguing (see Mann and Walsh, 2017, and below for more on dialogue as a mediational tool).

From TESOL teacher educators' points of view, one of the main arguments in favor of such collaborative teams in a TESOL teacher education program is that in order to bring about any changes in learner TESOL teachers' beliefs and/or teaching behaviors, they should be given opportunities to engage in dialogue with peers and supervisors about their beliefs and practices (Roberts, 1998), and team teaching offers such a process of collaborative discussions that can bring about any reformulations of beliefs and/or practices. For example, Yang (2013) conducted an ethnographic study of team teaching in a graduate-level internship that included team teaching, and noted that such a team approach can develop skills in cooperative working relationships, interpersonal networks, and intercultural communication. Because the learner teachers got feedback from their co-teachers and supervisors, they could, as Yang (2013) observed, attempt to put TESOL theories learned in teacher education programs into practice, as they gained practical and in-context teaching experience to improve their team teaching in the sessions that followed. The team teaching arrangements allowed the learner teachers to divide up what needed to be done and, as a result, Yang (2013) reported the teachers found it more effective and easier to manage the challenges that many learner teachers initially face.

Richards and Farrell (2005: 162-3) outline some of the following team teaching arrangements that teams can choose from, depending on what best meets their needs:

- *Equal partners*: both teachers see themselves as having equal experience and knowledge, and so all decisions are shared equally for all stages of the lesson: planning, delivery, monitoring, and checking.
- *Leader and participant*: one teacher is given or assumes a leadership role because he or she has more experience with team teaching.
- *Mentor and apprentice*: one teacher is recognized as an expert teacher (and thus take more responsibility) while the other is a novice.
- *Native/Advanced speaker and less proficient speaker*: in some situations (such as in Japan's JET program and Korea's KET program) a native English language speaker or an advanced speaker of English may team teach with a less proficient speaker. In some cases the native/advanced speaker takes responsibility for those aspects of the lesson that are more linguistically demanding, but in many cases the lesson takes place in the less proficient speaker's class, so he or she must take responsibility for setting up the lesson.

From the ESL learner point of view, although this is not widely noted, another positive result of team teaching lessons is the effect on the learners. As Johnston and Madejski (2004: 4) note, when the learners see

> teachers collaborating together, [they] are encouraged to follow suit, to open up and thus to cooperate in building an atmosphere of mutual trust and understanding, which considerably contribute to breaking the isolation of the individual in the classroom – and that means the individual teacher as well as the individual learner.

Gladman's (2014) study of team teaching in a Japanese setting reported that such a collaborative arrangement improved the learners' understanding of their lessons and even encouraged them to ask more questions in class. Indeed, Gladman (2014) suggested that the learners are key participants in any successful team teaching arrangement because the lessons are a co-production of all participants in the room. As Eisen and Tisdell (2000: 1) point out, "team teachers and learners have the capacity to create new knowledge collaboratively."

However, not all team teaching arrangements have reported positive results with learners, Aliakbari and Nejad (2013), for example, reported that learners can sometimes become confused, because team teaching is a novel approach for many given that some cultural expectations of teaching will differ depending on the context. Thus, Aliakbari and Nejad (2013) point out these team teaching arrangements will require consensus, planning, and careful consideration of cultural background, including such variables as the gender composition of the teams.

Within a practicum setting in a TESOL teacher education program, team teaching can appear within any or all of five different models: the *observation model*, the *coaching model*, the *assistant teaching model*, the *equal status model*, and the *team teaching model* (adapted from Cirocki, Madyarov, and Baecher, 2019):

- In the *observation model*, one teacher observes (with a pre-agreed observation protocol) the other teacher teaching, collects information about the lesson, and has no interaction with the students. Both teachers analyze and reflect together after the lesson.
- In the *coaching model*, besides observing as in the previous model, the coach is expected to provide suggestions, assistance, and support in a kind of mentoring capacity.
- In the *assistant teaching model*, one teacher takes the lead, and the other teacher becomes an assistant providing support to learners when necessary during the lesson.
- The *equal status model*, as the name suggests, is a collaborative team teaching arrangement where both teachers have an equal status in all aspects of planning, delivery, and evaluation.
- Finally, in the *team teaching model*, both teachers work collaboratively and share planning, delivery, and evaluation equitably. However, unlike the models above, here both teachers are in front of the class together, taking turns leading a discussion while the other demonstrates something in front of the learners. This model is more elaborate than the other four as it takes more time to set up, because both teachers need to learn more about each other's teaching style.

The above models can be used alone or in different combinations. For example, Gan (2014) reported the positive effects of team teaching arrangements similar to the *observation model* above, for learner teachers, mostly because of the impact of immediate feedback the teachers obtain from their peers and the increase in self-confidence. As Gan (2014: 136) says, "Sharing among the fellow student teachers, most likely developed confidence in 'self as a newcomer' and the timely feedback of peers contributed to valuing of personal experience in capacity to generate knowledge for teaching." Thus, a wide variety of team teaching models (many of which can be combined) are available that promote collaborative learning in TESOL teacher education.

REFLECTIVE BREAK

- Do you think a team teaching arrangement can bring about changes in learner TESOL teachers' beliefs and/or practices? If yes, how? If no, why not?
- Do you think team teaching can have a positive or negative effect on ESL students?
- Why do you think some ESL students in some contexts may be confused with such arrangements?

Reading and Discussion Task

Bill Johnston and Bill Madejski (2004) outline how teachers can '"[run] a team-taught lesson" in four steps: (1) the planning stage; (2) the team teaching lesson; (3) some new ideas; (4) feedback.

- Discuss each of these steps with a colleague with the idea of developing a team teaching lesson.

[Johnston, B., and Madejski B. (2004). A fresh look at team teaching. *The Language Teacher, 29*, 2–7]

Also:
Kathi Bailey, Andy Curtis, and David Nunan (2001: 186) provide a questionnaire about the roles and expectation of team teaching.

- Fill out the questionnaire and discuss your perspectives about the roles and expectation of team teaching with a colleague.

[Bailey, K., Curtis, A., and Nunan, D. (2001). *Pursuing Professional Development: The Self as Source*. Boston, MA: Heinle and Heinle]

PEER COACHING

Peer coaching is another collaborative arrangement between teachers in TESOL teacher education that can promote collaborative learning and reflection. Peer coaching is a "process where teams of teachers regularly observe one another and provide support, companionship, feedback, and assistance" (Valencia and Killion, 1988: 170). However, it is different from the team teaching arrangements discussed above because it is intended to improve specific instructional techniques of one of the peers, usually the observed teacher, in a supportive environment.

The use of peer coaches can enrich teaching practice (see Chapter 5), where, generally speaking, peer coaches observe and record the performance of their peers, provide feedback on the observed teaching practice, help the teacher correct any perceived deficiencies, and thus improve instruction. Although Richards and Farrell (2005) have suggested that feedback in a peer coaching relationship should take the form of "no praise, no blame," there are other ways to provide feedback, such as: (1) mirroring – the coach records data and gives them to the teacher to analyze or make sense of; (2) collaborative coaching – the teacher and coach work together to find ways to improve teaching; and (3) expert coaching – the coach acts as a mentor who gives specific suggestions (Johnson, 2009: 102).

More specifically, there are different types of peer coaching arrangements that TESOL teacher educators can utilize, such as *technical coaching*, where a teacher seeks the assistance of another teacher who is experienced and more knowledgeable in order to learn new teaching methods/techniques (Richards and Farrell, 2005). Another type is *collegial coaching*, where two teacher peers focus on refining their existing teaching practices (Richards and Farrell, 2005). Yet another type is *challenge coaching*, where a problem arises and two teachers work jointly to resolve it (Richards and Farrell, 2005).

Within a US context, these different types of peer coaching arrangements in TESOL teacher education programs were used in combination by Artigliere and Baecher (2017) and DelliCarpini and Alonso (2015). Artigliere and Baecher (2017) is an example of how different combinations of co-teaching arrangements can become complicated for novice ESL teachers when they have to navigate different and sometimes competing models of content-based instruction (CBI), such as: a *push-in* model, where the ESL teacher provides instruction inside the students' content or grade-level classroom; a *pull-out* model, where students receive ESL instruction in small groups in another location; and/or a *team teaching* model, where the ESL and classroom or content teacher jointly provide instruction to English language learners (ELLs). As a result, these teacher educators instituted a policy in their TESOL teacher education courses that the candidates had to deliver at least one co-taught lesson during their practicum (for more on the practicum, see Chapter 5).

DelliCarpini and Alonso (2015) noted that their learner TESOL teachers were struggling with the demands of the academic program in which their ELL students were enrolled, and content teachers had a lack of awareness and understanding of the needs of ELLs in the mainstream classroom. These authors realized that this was an issue related directly to ESL teacher preparation, so they devised what they call "two-way CBI," which extends teacher collaboration and traditional CBI. As a result, they restructured their teacher education program and implemented coursework specifically designed to prepare pre-service teachers to effectively engage in CBI tied to the academic curriculum through ttwo-way CBI and teacher collaboration. Thus, 'teams' (English, Science, Math) developed and worked collaboratively, from discussing relevant issues related to teaching to co-planning and actual co-teaching, as the pre-service teachers learned how to develop both language and content for ELLs in both the ESL and mainstream settings. Two-way CBI promotes collegiality, alleviates the feeling of isolation, and also lowers student–teacher ratios in classrooms so that learner teachers can have more opportunities to develop their reflective skills and teaching repertoires.

Peer coaching is also important as teachers move beyond novice-service teaching experiences into in-service teaching, because they will always need help from a more experienced peer teacher in order to develop new knowledge and skills and a deeper awarness of their own teaching. Thus the more experienced teacher can take on a mentoring role (see above), but both teachers view themselves as peers and equals. For example, Arslan and Ilin (2013) outline the positive effects, in terms of changes to their practices related to classroom management skills, of a peer-coaching activity where teachers were in pairs and observed one another's lessons, exchanged feedback, and repeated the process in a three-week cycle. Indeed, these authors reported that its success lay in that the peers were willing to participate because it was tailored to their particular needs.

Thus peer coaching emphasizes collegiality, as colleagues become empowered to set their own goals by analyzing their practice with each other. Teachers make their own decisions as to what changes, if any, to incorporate into their teaching. In other words, each teacher still has the main responsibility for self-development and does not hand over control to a colleague. Farrell and Jacobs (2020) make the following suggestions as to how teachers can act as coaches to foster language teacher development: informal chats about their teaching in the form of anecdotes about what is happening in their classroom; collaborating to design materials; observing each other's lessons; co-teaching lessons and observing each other's approach and teaching style; and videotaping lessons and watching them together; to name but a few.

REFLECTIVE BREAK

- Which type of peer coaching arrangement would you, as a learner TESOL teacher, be interested in: *technical, collegial,* and/or *challenge* coaching? Why?
- Which kind of feedback would you be most comfortable with from a coach: (1) mirroring; (2) collaborative coaching; or (3) expert coaching? Why?
- What is your understanding of the different models utilized within a US context: *push-in* model, *pull-out* model, and *team teaching* model? Which would you be interested in utilizing and why?

Reading and Discussion Task

Suleyman Goker (2006) studied the impact of peer coaching in a TESOL teacher education program, specifically to test whether student teachers trained using a peer coaching training program after teaching practicum sessions in TEFL would demonstrate greater improvement in instructional skills and self-efficacy than those just receiving traditional supervisor visits.

- Summarize the article's ideas on peer coaching, whether it had an impact, and, if it did, what the impact on the learner TESOL teachers was. Also, how do you think peer coaching can be designed and implemented successfully in TEFL teacher training programs?
- Discuss your findings with a colleague.

[Goker, S. D. (2006). Impact of peer coaching on self-efficacy and instructional skills in TEFL teacher education. *System, 34,* 239–54]

REFLECTION TOOLS

TESOL teacher educators can also use different mediational tools to help support learner TESOL teachers' development of a reflective stance throughout the TESOL teacher education program/courses. Two main reflective tools are the mediation of writing and dialogue, and these can be further combined with the use of various modes of technology to help facilitate and encourage the development of a reflective stance in learner TESOL teachers, not only during their TESOL teacher education program but also into their early career years and in-service years. In addition, action research projects can be introduced into TESOL teacher education programs and courses to encourage learner TESOL teachers to continue their reflective stance in their early career years when they become TESOL 'teachers as researchers' (see also Chapter 7).

Writing

The persistent trend in many TESOL teacher education programs to help facilitate learner TESOL teachers' reflection is mediation by written expression rather than spoken dialogue (see section that follows). This is not surprising, as writing is a valuable reflective tool because it has its own built-in reflective mechanism: teachers must stop to think before they write, and when they have written their thoughts they can further reflect on these written reflections (Farrell, 2013). Thus they can 'see' their thoughts and reflect on these for self-understanding and development (Farrell, 2013). For example, throughout the framework for reflecting on practice presented in Chapter 3, writing will be a significant mode of reflection, especially for 'seeing' their biographical journeys in order to generate greater self-understanding. Such reflective writing can also be expanded as a reflective tool to include written accounts of learner TESOL teachers' thoughts, observations, beliefs, attitudes, and experiences throughout their TESOL teacher education program and into their early career teaching years. TESOL teachers can include a record of incidents, problems, and insights that occurred during their courses, teaching practice, and first year(s) teaching experiences in order to gain new understandings of their own learning and practices.

In TESOL, Hernandez (2015) reported on the benefits of reflective journal writing for both learner TESOL teachers and their TESOL teacher educators when the latter attempted to better integrate theory with practice (see Chapter 2 for more on this). Hernandez (2015) wanted to 'see' how learner TESOL teachers interpreted the use of second language acquisition (SLA) theory in teaching practice, and observed that reflective writing provided valuable information about the impact of the SLA course materials on class activities, and especially how writing helped to raise the learner teachers' awareness of their perceptions of SLA and its impact on their philosophy of teaching. As Hernandez (2015: 147) remarked: "The use of reflective writings allowed documentation of participants' awareness of their role to bring about change in students' lives, thus confirming that personal practical knowledge has a moral and emotional dimension as well."

When learner TESOL teachers write as reflection, they can either write for themselves and keep it private, or they can share their writing with their peers and comment on the contents of each other's writing (dialogical writing). When they write for themselves, they can include their personal thoughts and feelings as well as facts about their practice. They can read these for later reflection with the idea that they can look for patterns over time in the contents of their writing. When they reflect on the patterns they notice in their journal writing, they can become more aware of issues of interest in their practice. For example, Kömür and Çepik (2015) reported that learner TESOL teachers liked writing as reflection because they said they could share their feelings and thoughts comfortably and freely in such a forum.

More often than not, however, learner TESOL teachers write in a TESOL course as a requirement and thus it is graded. However, a perennial problem with the use of writing for reflection in a TESOL teacher education program is that the writing itself can become more important than what the learner TESOL teachers are reflecting on. As Mann and Walsh (2017: 18) point out, when "the focus of attention becomes the actual writing itself" one result can be that the learner TESOL teachers may be faking what they write about because of the demands of the course and the fact that the writing will be graded. One way around this dilemma is to not grade the written reflections of learner TESOL teachers, as Golombek (2015) attempted in her TESOL teacher education course. Although writing weekly journals was a course requirement, Golombek (2015) only responded to the contents of each individual journal without grading them. In this manner she hoped to foster the learner TESOL teachers' reflections as well as learn about what they were thinking and experiencing as they wrote about their expectations of an internship they were about to take up, and about their strengths and concerns as they embarked on their learning-to-teach experience.

Thus, when incorporating writing as reflective practice, TESOL teacher educators are faced with the dilemma of deciding how much of the writing is really critically reflective practice and how much is mere description without much critical reflection. One answer to such a dilemma is for TESOL teacher educators to provide examples of what *they* consider critically reflective writing as they reflect on their *own* practice during the course, and thus their learner TESOL teachers will be able to learn from those reflections as examples of what is expected. For example, during teaching practice (see Chapter 5) Golombek and Doran (2014) encouraged their learner TESOL teachers to write a journal each week as they embarked on their teaching experience. In subsequent journals, the pre-service TESOL teachers wrote descriptions of what they were doing in their classes, and their reactions to their teaching. Golombek and Doran (2014) noted that the dialogic interactions of the journals allowed the teacher educators to not only gain more insight into the reflections of the teachers but also become more self-reflective themselves. As Golombek and Doran (2014: 110) observed, "The iterative nature of writing and responding to reflection journals enables, even compels, teacher educators to engage in their own processes of self-reflection."

There are different modes of writing for reflection, including teacher journals and expanded recently to the use of online writing in blogs, chats, discussion forums, and e-portfolios, to mention a few (for more on these see Farr and O'Riordan, 2017). Now the use of online formats has become popular, especially with learner TESOL teachers because they are easy to use (not requiring an understanding of HTML or web scripting), they are interactive and can be continuously updated (O'Riordan, 2018; Yang, 2009). Indeed, some TESOL teachers report that online writing formats are better than discussions (see below for more on dialogue) because teachers can challenge peers online more easily than when discussing issues face to face (Yang, 2009). Learner TESOL teachers can also use digital formats such as blogging or other online formats to help facilitate their collaborative reflections as they network with other teachers during their early career years and in-service years. Generally, then, when learner TESOL teachers take the time to write about their practice they can express their opinions, hypothesize about their practice, and of course reflect later on what actually happened during their practice, and compare results.

REFLECTIVE BREAK

- Do you like to write?
- Do you think writing can help you to reflect in your TESOL teacher education courses? If yes, what topics would you write about? If no, why not?
- Do you think your written reflections should be graded? If not, why not? If yes, how should they be graded?
- Do you think your TESOL teacher educator should provide examples of his or her written reflections during your courses?

Reading and Discussion Task

Zubeyde Genc (2010) noted the positive effect of regular journal writing for TESOL teachers in becoming more aware of and understanding their beliefs and knowledge about language learning and teaching.

- Read the article and write a summary of how the teachers became more aware of their practice through the mediation of writing.
- Discuss your findings with a colleague.

[Genc, Z. S. (2010). Teacher autonomy through reflective journals among teachers of English as a foreign language in Turkey. *Teacher Development, 14*, 3, 397-409]

Dialogue
The previous section outlined and discussed writing as a main reflective tool for development of learner TESOL teachers. However, written reflection also has a dialogical element when TESOL teacher educators provide some feedback (written, spoken, and/or online interactions). Thus it is rare that writing will be used as a mediational reflective tool without some inclusion of dialogic interaction. If the 'dialogue' is in written feedback, it will have a delay, but if it is spoken, it will be more immediate and itself will require further dialogue (i.e. the natural demand for an answer).

Generally, spoken dialogue in TESOL teacher education programs involves TESOL teacher educators and learner TESOL teachers in face-to-face discussions that are for the most part non-evaluative and supportive. In TESOL teacher education programs, as Mann and Walsh (2017: 8) point out, reflection benefits from such dialogue because it "is a crucial part of the reflection-action-further-action cycle, since it allows for clarification, questioning and ultimately enhanced understanding." Ahmadi, Samad, and Noordin (2013) outlined an example of such face-to-face discussions of the socialization process of their learner TESOL teachers in a graduate TESOL program. In their TESOL teacher education program, the learner TESOL teachers gave oral presentations, engaged in whole-class discussions after oral presentations, did task-based small group discussions, and wrote some reflection papers on the assigned reading materials. Ahmadi, Samad, and Noordin (2013: 1745) reported that reflection during the group discussions "had a very significant influence on the identity construction" of the learner TESOL teachers. As a result of engaging in reflective dialogue throughout the TESOL teacher education program, Ahmadi, Samad, and Noordin (2013: 1765) remarked that the learner TESOL teachers realized that a "TESOL teacher's identity is a continuous process of being informed, formed, and reformed which develops over time mostly through having interactions with other members of their discourse community and also through reflection over teaching practices."

This suggests that engaging in discussions with other peers in a TESOL teacher education program increases the likelihood that learner TESOL teachers will learn something from each other, because each individual will bring a different perspective to the discussions. In such a manner, entering into a discussion with a teacher peer or group of teachers can result in gaining new knowledge, new perspectives, and new understandings that would have been difficult for learner TESOL teachers to acquire by reflecting alone.

In addition, TESOL teacher educators can also enter the discussions to offer support and facilitate learner TESOL teachers to unlock their tacit knowledge and prior beliefs and experiences, and thus find their voice as developing professional TESOL teachers. As Mann and Walsh (2017: 8) point out, learner TESOL teachers can "be 'scaffolded' though their 'Zones of Proximal Development' (ZPD) to a higher plane of understanding through the dialogues they have with other professionals." Mann and Walsh (2017) also maintain that discussions with other teachers can be enhanced if artifacts such as video analysis and other recordings of teaching are included, to promote more systematic dialogue (see below for more on video).

Chick (2015), for example, looked at dialogic interaction during post-teaching practice discussions with a TESOL teacher educator, and examined the ways in which such an approach may help promote the long-term reflective practice involved in developing pedagogic expertise. Chick (2015: 302) reported that dialogic interaction provided "the space for learner teachers to externalize their understandings of the teaching process and thus facilitate mediation by the educator." As a result, Chick (2015) noted that the learner TESOL teachers could learn from each other as they began to uncover their implicit beliefs regarding classroom actions, probe their emerging understandings, and encourage exploration of the teaching and learning process. Chick (2015) concludes that reflective conversations can mediate the development of learner teachers as they learn to teach. In addition, Waring (2013) outlined how TESOL teacher educators can best facilitate and 'scaffold' such discussions for promoting reflection by talking less and being less directive, withholding value judgments or unsolicited feedback, asking mediational questions such as "how do you think the lesson went?" and making open-ended statements about some aspects of teaching.

Dialogue with other teachers will become even more important for learner TESOL teachers when they enter their early career years (see Chapter 7) and beyond, because their reflection will be enhanced when operated through dialogue with a teacher educator-mentor, mentor-teacher, or critical friend, such as within a team teaching or peer coaching arrangement (see above). TESOL teachers can also form their own teacher support groups, development groups, and/or reflection groups, where teachers come together in a mutual-aid-type collaboration in which they explore various issues that directly impact their teaching and/or their practice in general, including their professional identity outside the classroom (Farrell, 2014). These can be informal gatherings and at the same time the teachers can engage in small-scale action research projects (see below for more).

Hung and Yeh (2013), for example, reported positive outcomes for a TESOL teacher reflection group (five TESOL teachers and one group facilitator) for professional development. Hung and Yeh (2013) observed that when the TESOL teachers were encouraged to reflect during nine bi-weekly group meetings in an 18-week period in group interactive discussions, they began to share their practical knowledge as well as co-design several teaching activities and at the same time self-appraise their classroom teaching. Mak and Pun (2015) also reported on a series of planned efforts on cultivating a group of eighteen TESOL teachers in Hong Kong over a period of 10 months. Mak and Pun (2015: 18) noted that the group went through different stages of development, such as "forging a group identity in the midst of tensions arising out of different personalities and/or backgrounds, building common goals, resolving cognitive and psychological dissonances for professional learning and development, as well as assuming communal responsibility for sustainable professional development." These authors also observed that for such teacher groups to survive, it is up to individuals to be committed, honest, self-aware, and sensitive, so that they can "develop their expertise-in-self in the process" (Mak and Pun, 2015: 19).

One final point regarding the reflective approach to TESOL teacher education that the contents of this book and this chapter are built around: it will be important for TESOL teacher educators to allow time in their program and courses to discuss what reflection is and how it is defined in the program. This can be a collaborative discussion between TESOL teacher educators within the faculty and include learner TESOL students, so that they can have a clear conceptualization of what reflective practice entails for that program and all involved. Thus, conceptions of reflective practice can be co-constructed through collegial dialogue. As Dewey (1933) has noted, teacher educators will be better able to model reflection and reflective thought if they so choose once they have conceptualized what reflection is.

REFLECTIVE BREAK

- Do you think spoken dialogue can help you to reflect in your TESOL teacher education courses? If yes, what topics would you speak about? If no, why not?
- Do you think your spoken reflections should be graded? If not, why not? If yes, how should they be graded?
- One study of face-to-face teacher group discussions suggested that even the teachers with many years of teaching experience still needed stimulus and support to promote their continuous learning. Why do you think that such groups will need to be stimulated to reflect on their practice?
- Should learner TESOL teachers be engaged in dialogue with their TESOL teacher educators about what reflective practice is and how to do it?

Reading and Discussion Task

Parviz Ahmadi, Arshad Abd Samad, and Nooreen Noordin (2013) examined how pre-service TESOL teachers' engagement through discourse socialization practices in their graduate TEFL program influenced their professional identity development.

- Read the article and discuss how reflection in group discussions led to a more professional identity over time.
- Discuss your findings with a colleague.

[Ahmadi, P., Samad, A. A., and Noordin, N. (2013). Identity formation of TEFL graduate students through oral discourse socialization. *Theory and Practice in Language Studies*, 3, 10, 1764-9]

Action Research
Another reflective tool that learner TESOL teachers can be exposed to during their TESOL teacher education program and courses is action research. Action research as self-reflection creates a research space for learner TESOL teachers where they can "develop and sustain their own projects without feeling inferior in terms of scale and scope of what they are attempting to achieve" (Mann and Walsh, 2017: 225). Encouraging learner TESOL teachers to engage in action research during TESOL teacher education courses promotes reflective learning and thinking and creativity (Cabaroglu, 2014). In addition, and as Cabaroglu (2014: 84) also noted, by engaging in action research projects throughout their TESOL teacher education program, learner TESOL teachers will improve their "problem-solving skills, and as a result, their teaching [skills]."

Action research involves systematic collection of information or data in a planned manner (some may say planned interventions), followed by some form of analysis of what is revealed by the information or data, then a formal reflection on the implications of these findings for possible further observation and then action (Burns, 2009). The general (cyclical) stages of the action research process are: plan (problem identification); research (literature review); observe (collecting data); reflect (analysis); and act (redefining the problem). This suggests that action research, then, for language teachers serves to address and find solutions to particular problems in a teaching and learning situation, and so is undertaken to bring about change and improvement to a particular teaching practice. Thus, action research entails learner TESOL teachers collecting specific and natural data about an issue or problem of interest or concern, and using the data as a basis for investigating that issue (Richards and Farrell, 2005). Recent initiatives by the British Council have seen a plethora of excellent publications related to TESOL teachers engaging in their own action research, such as *A Handbook for Exploratory Action Research* (Smith and Rebolledo, 2018). This outlines how teachers can engage in exploratory action research and is based on examples from actual experience, including cases from the companion publication *Champion Teachers: Stories of Exploratory Action Research* (Rebolledo, Smith, and Bullock, 2016). The handbook is freely downloadable.

Sowa (2009) encouraged learner TESOL teachers to conduct action research projects together with coursework in order to help them learn more about their English language learners. She observed that the learner TESOL teachers reported that they felt that conducting such research projects had given them "the tools to conduct small research projects in their classrooms and to share their ideas with colleagues" (Sowa, 2009: 1029). Action research projects, as Sowa (2009: 1031) has observed, can help learner TESOL teachers to "start reflecting more critically about their practice particularly with respect to strategies they teach in the classroom to help all students learn." In such a manner, learner TESOL teachers can develop the skills needed to investigate and analyze challenges they may face in their classrooms in the early career years (see also Chapter 7).

Reading and Discussion Task

Timothy Stewart (2001) conducted an action research project on how his Japanese university students used questions in formal debates.

- Read the paper and comment on the way the action research project was set up.
- Discuss your findings with a colleague.

[Stewart, T. (2001).The value of action research in exploring methodology: A case of instruction on questioning in debate. *PAC Journal, 1*, 79-92]

Technology

With advancements in technology, TESOL teacher programs now have many more delivery and collaborative formats at their disposal to encourage learner TESOL teachers to develop a reflective stance. Traditionally, TESOL teacher educators delivered their courses through face-to-face instruction, with classroom presentations and discussions popular along with writing projects for more delayed reflective experiences. Now with these technological advancements, 'discussions' can be promoted beyond the classroom walls, thus providing more opportunities for 'languaging' (or verbalizing thoughts for enhanced learning) and collaborative dialogue (problem-solving dialogue between two or more people) as participants attempt to engage in knowledge-building through online platforms. For example, and as noted in Chapter 2, Faez, Cooke, Karas, and Vidwans (2017) used Google Docs, an online collaborative word processor, as a platform to encourage extra discussions beyond the usual face-to-face mode of the classroom in a TESOL teacher education program. However, when they compared both, they noted that although they all felt that using an online platform for further discussions was a useful pedagogical tool, such a platform did not lead to discussions that were as effective as their face-to-face communications, because the chances for collaborative dialogue to form new knowledge were actually limited. This result indicates that a key consideration in using online interactive forums effectively in TESOL teacher education programs is finding an appropriate balance between these online collaborations and the more traditional face-to-face interactions, in order to provide optimum opportunities for collaborative learning. (See also McCarthy, 2016, for a collection on blended learning and a discussion of attempts to place the use of technology in learning and teaching, and especially of what it means to learn and teach a language.)

That said, there are many advances in communication for TESOL teacher education programs when using virtual environments, where teacher-mentors, TESOL teacher educators, and supervisors can all participate in meaningful exchanges of ideas so that learner TESOL teachers can develop more during and after their formal education. Within TESOL teacher education, for example, Mann (2015) outlined how TESOL teacher educators can use such online collaborations when providing feedback on academic writing tasks and assignments in courses, so that these courses can become more dialogic in nature. Specifically, Mann (2015) detailed how audio feedback through screen capture software (in this case, Jing) can be provided, allowing a supervisor to simultaneously provide a visual focus and auditory commentary, and how this enables more dialogue and reflection by both TESOL teacher educators and learner TESOL teachers. Chik and Breidbach (2011) also noted how such dialogic interaction during post-teaching practice discussions can be beneficial to pre-service second language teacher education. In particular, they used a combination of (wiki) discussion forums, social media, Facebook, and videoconferencing, among other modes of reflection, and observed that the combined online mode helped facilitate the learner teachers' identity development.

It seems that the most popular use of online communications in TESOL teacher education programs and among TESOL teachers includes the use of forums, blogs, and chats to augment the traditional face-to-face discussions in classrooms. In TESOL teacher education, for example, O'Riordan and Murray (2010) maintained that such online communications were different than spoken discourse especially in terms of their interactivity, turn length, and informality. As O'Riordan and Murray (2010: 194) observed, although discussion forums were similar to spoken discourse in terms of interactivity, they "carry a greater resemblance towards the written mode, possibly as a result of the time allowed to ponder over the discourse, thus allowing editing and reformulating of ideas." In a later study, O'Riordan and Murray (2012) noted that blogs and chats were highly interactive, social, and emotional and online discussion forums more cognitive, but reflection is possible within both modes. Overall, O'Riordan and Murray (2010: 194) reported positively about the inter-activity of such online communication because, they said, it had the "potential to aid professional development, by allowing for reflection, support, and collaborative problem-solving."

Another format for learner TESOL teachers to use when interacting with peers in a different program and/or country is by communicating through 'keypals' (similar to penpals but conducted by email). Wach (2015) wondered how learner TESOL teachers would benefit from collaborating online with 'keypals' from another country and what kind of reflections would emerge from their interactions. Wach (2015: 41) reported that the 'keypals' created a "form of support community and the inter-actions were evaluated as both informative and enjoyable and had a positive affective effect on them personally."

Although not new technology, many TESOL teacher education programs world-wide also make use of video as a mediational tool, as it allows both TESOL teacher educators and learner TESOL teachers to 'see' classroom actions, and thus develop their ability to describe and analyze instruction and suggest possible actions. For example, after classroom observations, Eröz-Tuğa (2012) encouraged the learner TESOL teachers to engage in self-evaluation through watching a video of their own teaching together with their TESOL teacher educator. Eröz-Tuğa (2012) observed that such a process helped the learner TESOL teachers become more insightful about their teaching practices. As Eröz-Tuğa (2012: 5) noted, the learner TESOL teachers

> improved self-awareness and displayed a conscious effort in trying to fix the problems the [TESOL teacher educator] warned them about in the first feedback meeting, as well as the ones they noticed themselves. They were able to make comparisons between their first and second videos, pointing to improved aspects of their teaching performance as well as lingering weaknesses.

In an insightful summary of this teacher growth, Eröz-Tuğa (2012: 7) observed:

> In the first feedback session, almost all of the participants were somewhat reluctant about criticizing their own and their partners' performances; they mainly listened to the feedback of the university supervisor and took notes rigorously. Their comments predominantly focused on obvious classroom issues like tone of voice and body language, and they often overlooked critical issues, such as teaching inaccurate forms or time management. However, after the second video viewing, they were so expressive and accurate in their reflections and comments about the videos that the university supervisor did not need to go over all her notes; her points were all already covered by the students or their partner trainees.

Eröz-Tuğa (2012) concluded that the classroom observations (and video of these classes) and feedback sessions had a positive impact on learner TESOL teachers' teaching performance, because they began to depend less on the feedback and more on their own interpretations of watching themselves on video teaching, as they were able to take a more critical perspective. Indeed, Gun (2010) pointed out the true value of the videos in nurturing reflective thinking because the learner TESOL teachers were not only able to identify potential areas of improvement as well as strengths by watching videos of themselves, but also able to transfer their critical reflection into 'on-the-spot' strategies in their classroom. This appears to have greatly helped the learner TESOL teachers to become more autonomous, which is one of the tenets of engaging in reflective practice. As Gun (2010: 7) stated, "watching videos of themselves teach was the most beneficial of all the feedback that came from different sources."

Video can be used in combination with written reflection (rather than memory-based reflection alone) with journals or online writing modes. For example, Ong, Swanto, and Alsaqqaf (2020) used a combination of video and blogs, or vlogs, which were mediated online to encourage learner TESOL teachers in Malaysia to engage in reflective practice. A video blog or vlog is defined by Parks (2010: 219) as "a recorded video of the student speaking while thinking back across their practice, understandings, and sometimes misunderstandings of, and in, their actions in the field." Ong, Swanto, and Alsaqqaf, (2020: 717) reported that although some of the learner TESOL teachers felt a bit awkward and self-conscious sharing videos of themselves with their peers, most had positive responses to the use of vlogs, "where they found the opportunity to reflect deeper by engaging in an effort to reflect critically and having the reflection process captured in vlogs."

TESOL teacher educators and learner teachers play a collaborative role when it comes to the systematic taking up of mediational tools to encourage reflection. TESOL teacher educators can help learner TESOL teachers become more aware of the different types of tools available and how they can impact reflection. However, when planning reflective experiences in a TESOL program, TESOL teacher educators should consider that the use of such tool varies between learner TESOL teachers, with some tools supporting development of one learner TESOL teacher but causing stagnation in the development of another (Farrell, 2001a). Thus, mediational tools should be applied flexibly by TESOL teacher educators, as there is no 'best' tool that will suit all learner TESOL teachers, and as such they should be allowed to choose which works best for them. As the learner TESOL teachers from the preamble in the opening of this chapter noted, their preference was for a combination of different mediational tools to promote their reflections rather than focusing on any one mode of reflection. As it was expressed by one teacher:

I liked the cycle and interplay between the realities of my classroom and workplace, the written journal, the discussion group and then classroom observations. Any of them on their own would have been 'ok' but together they really enriched the experience. It was a full experience. I got to study my classroom and students; reflect upon myself as a teacher (quite specifically and holistically); and feel supported by my colleagues and learn from them.

REFLECTIVE BREAK

- Why do you think that there are conflicting views about which mode of reflection is deeper: face-to-face or online discussions? Which do you prefer and why?
- What is your preference for a mode of reflection: talking, writing, and/or any other?
- Which mode would be easiest for you and why?
- Which mode would be difficult for you and why?
- How do you think online modes of reflective discussions could be different than regular spoken discourse?
- Some researchers say that when blogging, some TESOL teachers do not always dialogue reflectively because they do not challenge each other's opinions or give different ideas or push understandings. Do you agree or disagree?
- Have you ever used or would you ever use vlogs?
- Smith (2019: 6) created a video-mediated critical friendship (VMCF) framework (see also the task in "Critical Friends Groups" above) with the following prompts for her learner TESOL students to use. Do you think this framework would be useful for you when incorporating video as a mediational tool for reflection?

1. Select an ESL instructional goal.
2. Record ESL instruction.
3. Watch the entire video.
4. Select a 5-10-minute video segment that showcases the ESL instructional 'goal in action'.
5. Re-watch the video segment and write down words or phrases that pertain to your ESL instructional goal.
6. Re-watch the selected video segment and analyze the segment with V-Note.
   (a) What patterns do you see?
   (b) How does video evidence show that your ESL instructional goal was met/ not met?
   (c) What ideas or considerations do you have for future ESL instruction?
   (d) What questions or concerns do you still have?

Reading and Discussion Task

Carmen Guerrero-Nieto and Bryan Meadows (2015: 14) encouraged TESOL teachers, both pre-service and in-service, to reflect in online discussions, and were particularly interested in how "graduate TESOL students' dialogues provide them with spaces to activate critical awareness of their global professional identity".

- Read the article and give details how they used a "Schoology Wall" (2015: 15) for posting messages between teachers.
- Discuss your findings with a colleague.

[Guerrero-Nieto, C. H., and Meadows, B. (2015). Global professional identity in deterritorialized spaces: A case study of a critical dialogue between expert and novice nonnative English speaker teachers [Identidad profesional global en espacios desterritorializados: Un estudio de caso de los diálogos críticos entre profesores de inglés no nativos]. *PROFILE: Issues in Teachers' Professional Development, 17*. 2, 13-27]

CONCLUSION

This chapter has outlined and discussed how TESOL teacher education programs can promote collaborative learning during the program, after the program (novice-service), and into in-service experiences. As Roberts (1998: 45) pointed out, TESOL teacher educators can promote teacher learning when they engage learner TESOL teachers in "task focused talk" with peers and others (i.e. TESOL teacher educator-mentors, mentor-teachers, supervisors) that encourages them to take a reflective stance toward issues affecting their practice. Such collaborations are enhanced in TESOL teacher education through the use of critical friends groups, team teaching, and/or peer coaching, and further developed with the use of mediational tools such as writing, dialogue, action research, and combinations of these with online modes of communication. Collaborative learning environments that are encouraged in TESOL teacher education programs are especially valuable for learner TESOL teachers, because such collaborative interaction offers opportunities to clarify their own understandings of what it means to be a TESOL teacher, while at the same time socializing them into communities of practice that support their further development as TESOL professionals. All of these collaborative arrangements can also be utilized during the teaching practice, as outlined in the chapter that follows.

5

TESOL TEACHER EDUCATION: TEACHING PRACTICE

PREAMBLE

The following is a brief account of my own experience while on teaching practice many years ago in Ireland.

She had already arrived and was sitting at the back of the room writing something on a large piece of paper. Oh no! I didn't know she was coming today. Oh my! I should not have gone to that party last night. What is her name anyway? I wonder should I go down and explain why I had just arrived at nine o'clock and not my usual fifteen minutes before.

Oh no! She has stopped writing and is looking up. I guess she expects me to begin. I hope that little Brian is quiet today. Now let me get my notes.

Oh Lord! She is *staring* at me. Ok! Ok! Cool down, 1 had better review yesterday's lesson. Where the hell are my notes? She is still *Looking* at me. Oh boy!

No Brian, don't ask a question. No! [Brian's hand goes up!]

"Yes, Brian?"

"Oh! Mr. Farrell, why are we doing this lesson today, we already finished this last week?"

"Quite right, Brian, thank you for telling me, anyway today we are going to review . . ."

And so went my first experience with *The Look* from my observer. This was, of course, my teaching evaluation from my university practicum days.

This was not the last time I was to get that same *Look*. Oh, no!

When I traveled to South Korea a year later to teach at a prestigious institute at a top-rated university, I got *The Look* again! In fact, it started from the moment when I was interviewed for the job. Yes, that very same "What can you do?" *Look*.

Then after one week teaching, I heard a knock on the door of the classroom I was teaching in. I opened it and in walked the director without any warning. She had *The Look* on her face of, "Let's see what you can do."

"I want to *Look* at you teaching," she said.

"Fine," I said. But it was not really fine.

I coped, somehow, but I still remember that first day in Ireland the observer was sitting in my classroom waiting for me and that first week in Korea experiencing the exact same feeling of an observer/supervisor sitting in the back of the room with a, 'I am the expert, let's see what you can do' type of *Look*. It took me 18 years to write about my first experience of *The Look* but I have never completely recovered from that initial experience. Years later and many workshops and talks in many different countries made me realize that I was not alone when I heard of *so many* similar experiences from highly accomplished TEFL professionals.

Although this is my own experience, I believe much has changed in the past forty years in terms of how classroom observations are carried out, as well as how learner teachers are assigned to teaching practice. At that time, learner teachers out on placement were required to teach (as part of the practicum) in a real school each day fortwo hours and then return to attend lectures (as part of the foundation coursework) in the university in the afternoons and evening, as part of what was called the Higher Diploma in Education that qualifies candidates as recognized by the Ministry of Education in Ireland. For the teaching practice portion, each learner teacher is to be supervised and visited four to six times during the year in the school by a university-based teacher educator-supervisor.

In this author's experience, a university-appointed teacher educator-supervisor arrived unannounced for each of the four observed one-hour lessons during the year. In addition, the supervisor on no occasion either before or after the observed lessons held any discussions with anyone, and so left immediately after. In other words, I had no pre-observation or post-observation lesson discussions, and in fact, never had any discussions with the supervisor from the beginning to the end of teaching practice.

The supervisor was in the room first before I had arrived, and sitting at the back each time for the first 9 a.m. class of the day and left after 45 minutes each time. *The Look* referred to above lasted all four visits and each time I was on the receiving end of it, my anxiety levels in the classroom increased to very high. Thank goodness my students were on their best behavior for each visit; pity the supervisor wasn't: not one time did this observer/supervisor sit down and talk to me about my teaching before or after her observation. Instead, she spent all of these observations writing speedily on paper about what she was 'seeing'; at the end she just said "Thank you" and left the room.

So what does all this mean? I believe that these sessions, still very much prevalent in our profession, are akin to 'drive-by' drop-ins that can turn off a teacher for life if they are judgmental concerning the teacher's teaching skills. Of course if the supervisor does not talk to the teacher, this makes things worse. I got a pass in teaching practice but I never received any report or recommendations, which further traumatized me for future teaching.

Yes, I can never forget *The Look*, but I decided to not ignore it but to educate colleagues about the possible abuses of observing another in class. There is such a power differential that I think it borders on learner teacher abuse if not addressed at the beginning of a learner teacher's life and career. As mentioned above, I fully recognize that those days are probably long gone as there are many positive accounts of teaching practice experiences. particularly when student teachers find it enabling, supportive, and helpful in developing their skills of teaching, as outlined in Farr (2011).

I am personally over this *Look* now, as I have reflected deeply on it and talked to colleagues about their similar early teaching observation experiences, and I have come up with a basic set of questions I now ask any person of authority (e.g. a supervisor or teacher or administrator) who wants to observe my teaching:

1. Why do you want to come to my class? If the answer is to watch me teach, then my answer is no because I am not a model teacher and you are probably going to judge me against some preconceived notion of what constitutes good teaching.
2. What are you going to do in the class? If the answer is just sit at the back, then my answer again is no because I want an observer to help me to observe some aspect of my teaching that I am interested in. So the observer has to be *active*.
3. What are you going to use the observation process for? If the answer is research, then I say hold on; I want to know the exact research project and how I fit into the scheme of things, that is, how *my* class can help in this research. I am not against research and in fact am constantly conducting my own. Rather, I think bad research (not set up with clearly defined objectives) can do more harm than good to the teacher being observed and his or her students who may not like outsiders in the classroom.

I have found that these three questions have helped me to avert *The Look* because when the answers to the questions are to my liking, the observation process can be a wonderful experience. It can be an enlightening exploration of what it is to be a teacher working with other teachers (peer observation), and it can be a learning experience (for focused research). Also, it can be used to evaluate. But evaluators should be able to explain their criteria for evaluation even if these are a preassigned checklist of desirable teaching skills. It would be interesting to see their *look* at that time! That said, if any novice teacher wants to observe me teaching, I do not ask the above questions, but rather I ask them to tell me after the lesson what stood out most for them and why. This, I find, can begin a conversation about teaching, and I let the conversation go wherever the novice teacher wants it to go.

REFLECTIVE BREAK

- What would you do if you experienced *The Look* as in the story above in your teaching practicum?
- Did you have any similar experiences of *The Look* as a learner TESOL teacher?

Reading and Discussion Task

Shosh Leshem and Rivka Bar-Hama (2008) ask how we can evaluate teaching practice experience and the quality of teaching. They conclude that it is important to collaborate with their learner TESOL teachers and provide some space for their voices (unlike what this author experienced in the opening preamble to this chapter).They conclude too that learner TESOL teachers will need explicit criteria for effective teaching in order to identify their strengths and weaknesses and use them as guidelines for improvement.

- Read the paper and outline the authors' explicit criteria for effective teaching. Do you agree or disagree with them?
- Discuss your findings with a colleague.

[Leshem, S., and Bar-Hama, R. (2008). Evaluating teaching practice *ELT Journal*, 62, 257-65]

INTRODUCTION

TESOL teacher education programs usually provide some kind of field experiences in classrooms that attempt to give their learner TESOL teachers some teaching practice, sometimes called the practicum. The main idea of practice teaching in most TESOL teacher education programs is that learner TESOL teachers will have a chance to put some of the material they have learned during academic coursework into action in real classrooms with real students (Farrell, 2007a). (Of course, each course will have different applicability depending on its academic or practical nature, as pointed out in chapter 2 on the theory/practice divide in TESOL teacher education.) Although each context will have different ideas about how the practicum should be placed and implemented in the TESOL program, most would agree that common goals include providing chances for learner TESOL teachers to do the following (Richards and Crookes, 1988):

1. Gain practical classroom teaching experience.
2. Apply theory and teaching ideas from previous coursework.
3. Discover from observing experienced teachers.
4. Enhance lesson-planning skills.
5. Gain skills in selecting, adapting and developing original course materials.

In addition, one of the main functions of the practicum is to help learner TESOL teachers develop an understanding of the different dimensions of effective teaching.

These include, among others, developing discourse skills, developing teacher identity, learning how to apply professional knowledge, understanding the teaching context, and learning how to theorize from practice (Richards and Farrell, 2011). Each is explained briefly here:

- *Discourse Skills*: The practicum can help learner TESOL teachers develop how to use language effectively during classroom lessons, which is a key mark of professional teaching competence. For example, learner TESOL teachers must be able to provide language input at an appropriate level (comprehensible input) for their learners while using appropriate speech that is comprehensible (Richards and Farrell, 2011, call this "teacher talk"), and at the same time providing specific opportunities for interactive and collaborative uses of language among learners. The development of such classroom discourse skills takes time and experience, and novice teachers will need to be aware of how their learners are reacting (or not reacting) to all of what they say while they teach. Discourse skills also involve, as Richards and Farrell (2011) point out, 'talking the talk', or being able to use the professional language associated with language teaching, such as learner-centered instruction, learner autonomy, task-based teaching, and so on. In addition, Farrell (2019) has developed a multidisciplinary approach to corpus linguistics that can be used to illuminate the target models of English that are used by teachers in the EFL classroom context, especially at a time when standard British/American norms are being challenged. That book convincingly argues that suitable target models of English for EFL pedagogy should include more varieties, and especially varieties used by EFL teachers 'at the chalk face'.
- *Teacher Identity*: During the practicum, learner TESOL teachers also begin to construct their professional identity as they become socialized into a community of practice (Farrell, 2001c). Just as they are socialized into 'talking the talk' with discourse skills, so too are they socialized into a professional culture with certain goals, shared values, and standards of conduct, and where learner TESOL teachers must negotiate their involvement. As Burns and Richards (2009) note, learner TESOL teachers' sense of identity (i.e. who they feel they are and who others take them to be) may be shaped by many factors, including their personal biography, gender, culture, age, working conditions, and the school and classroom culture. The practicum will further shape an initial teacher identity assumed (or imagined) during coursework, as learner TESOL teachers get more experience in real classrooms. However, teacher identity is never static; it remains in flux and needs to be negotiated by TESOL teachers throughout the practicum experience and into novice-service years and beyond.
- *Teaching Skills*: The practicum offers learner TESOL teachers some opportunities to develop a repertoire of varied routines and procedures suited to different kinds of learners so that they can become flexible in their teaching. Richards and Farrell (2011) explain this dimension, where learner TESOL teachers develop a repertoire of routines and procedures for such things as opening the lesson, introducing and explaining tasks, setting up learning arrangements (group work, pair work, whole-class learning), checking students' understanding, guiding student

practice, monitoring students' language use, making transitions from one task to another, ending the lesson, and so on. This will involve learner TESOL teachers taking a risk as they try to develop their own routines and generate their own solutions to challenges they face. By trying out new skills, they can gain more experience in reflecting on and analyzing their lessons in terms of appropriate content as well as pacing, and thus develop their pedagogical reasoning skills. Thus, in order to further develop these pedagogical reasoning skills it will be important for learner TESOL teachers to be able to reflect on their teaching while they teach (reflection-in-action), after they teach (reflection-on-action), and before they teach (reflection-for-action) (Farrell, 2015b).

- *Professional Knowledge*: During their TESOL teacher education program, learner TESOL teachers learn various foundational theories and practices that cover different kinds of knowledge, such as disciplinary knowledge (knowledge related to language, linguistics, pedagogy) and pedagogical content knowledge (knowledge related to teaching, such as curriculum planning, teaching the skill areas, assessment). During these courses it is assumed that the disciplinary knowledge, although it is not intended to have practical applications to the classroom, is important for teachers to have when they begin teaching; and that pedagogical content knowledge can help deliver the content from the disciplinary knowledge to their students. However, the successful implementation of this professional knowledge (disciplinary and pedagogical) is not guaranteed in a real classroom during the first year of teaching, because not all teacher education programs emphasize every aspect of this professional knowledge for teachers in training (Richards and Farrell, 2011). In fact there is great discrepancy in what different TESOL teacher education programs provide around the world, with many just promoting disciplinary knowledge over pedagogical content knowledge and thus making the transition for learner TESOL teachers even more challenging (see also Chapter 2). However, as Richards and Farrell (2011: 28) maintain, one would assume that learner TESOL teaches who have a "sound grounding in relevant pedagogical content knowledge [are] better prepared than teachers without such knowledge to understand learners' needs, to diagnose learners' learning problems, to plan suitable instructional goals for lessons, and to select and design learning tasks."

- *Teaching Context*: The practicum can offer learner TESOL teachers experience in many different contexts for their practice teaching, such as private schools or public institutions with mixed-level learners, or institutions offering courses in English for academic purposes (EAP), English for specific purposes (ESP), ESL, or EFL. As they attempt to apply the knowledge they learned in their teacher education programs, learner TESOL teachers will thus quickly realize that each context has something different to offer and presents different challenges to overcome, including discovering what the "hidden curriculum" is in order to be able to function in a particular school context (Richards and Farrell, 2011).

- *Theorize from Practice*: The practicum offers learner TESOL teachers the opportunity to develop a personal system of knowledge, beliefs, and understandings drawn from practical experience of teaching, or their ability to theorize from practice. Richards and Farrell (2011) maintain that this means that learner TESOL teachers reflect on their experiences while teaching their lessons and developing an understanding of the underlying meaning of what they are teaching, in order to better understand the nature of language teaching and learning, which includes observations of how learners learn or fail to learn, and reflections on things that happen during lessons. In such a manner, reflecting on their practice enables learner TESOL teachers to articulate, test, and thus work out theories and concepts that can support and further develop them during their novice-service years and in-service years.

Although learner TESOL teachers enter a TESOL teacher education program in order to learn how to become a TESOL teacher, coursework alone cannot prepare them for real experiences with real students in real classes. Thus, the practicum portion of the TESOL teacher education becomes very important to help them learn the craft of teaching. This includes gaining experiences transforming the various dimensions of effective teaching outlined above into practice with students. Learner TESOL teachers can get this experience in the practicum through microteaching and field placement experiences. These are discussed in the sections that follow.

REFLECTIVE BREAK

- What are your goals during teaching practice?
- What are you looking forward to most during teaching practice?
- What do you expect to learn about teaching during your teaching practice?
- What do you think you can apply from your coursework while on teaching practice?
- How can learner TESOL teachers develop their classroom discourse skills to support classroom language learning?
- How can you develop your teaching identity during your practicum?
- Which teaching skills do you think you need to develop during your teaching practice, and why?
- Who do you think you can go to for help during teaching practice?
- Who would you not go to for help, and why?
- What do you fear most during teaching practice?
- What impact will the context in which you teach have on your experiences during your teaching practice?

Reading and Discussion Task

Bedrettin Yazan (2015) has pointed out that a sociocultural understanding of teacher learning highlights how teacher candidates construct their own learning and adjust or extend their instructional values, priorities, and beliefs within their teaching contexts. He followed five learner TESOL teachers learning to teach English language learners in the teaching practicum and especially how they navigated the school context, established relationships with the teaching community, used the mediating artifacts with the support of mentors and supervisors, found opportunities for constructing a mutually informative and dialogical relationship between theory and practice, and gained closer understanding of ELLs.

- Read the paper and consider your understanding of what issues related to their school context the learner TESOL teachers navigated through and how they did it.
- Discuss your findings with a colleague.

[Yazan, B. (2015). "You learn best when you're in there": ESOL teacher learning in the practicum. *The CATESOL Journal, 27*, 2, 171-99]

LEARNING TO TEACH

Teaching practice, or the practicum, is usually a separate course in most TESOL teacher education programs and, as mentioned above, its main aim is to give learner TESOL teachers some taste of and experience of teaching, with the general idea that what they have learned during coursework can be applied in a classroom. However, and as mentioned in Chapter 2, this application of theory (from TESOL teacher education courses) is not always readily transferable into practice, and thus learner TESOL teachers will need support from their TESOL teacher educators during the period of the practicum to help them make connections between theory and practice. The TESOL teacher educators can design the practicum for such support by providing reflective strategies and activities, including microteaching, classroom observations of other teachers, and classroom teaching during field experiences. In addition, the practicum can make use of the reflective activities outlined in the previous chapter, such as teaching journals, seminar discussions and other dialogue with all stake-holders, team teaching, and peer coaching experiences to encourage learner teacher reflection. This support can be further enhanced when the learner TESOL teachers go out on field placements through a collaborative model in which all stakehold-ers (learner TESOL teachers, TESOL teacher educator-supervisors, school mentors) work in collaboration with each other (as explained in more detail below). The next section outlines and discusses how microteaching can be implemented before learner TESOL teachers go out on their field experiences in a school/institution outside a TESOL teacher education program.

MICROTEACHING

TESOL teacher education programs can provide some teaching experience during the program: learner TESOL teachers can prepare and teach short micro-lessons to peer learner TESOL teachers or volunteer ESL/EFL students in a microteaching class experience. As Richards and Farrell (2011) suggest, such microteaching lessons can be followed up with instant feedback by peers and teacher educators. The duration of such lessons can range from 15 minutes to whole lessons (as in CELTA (Certificate in Teaching English to Speakers of Other Languages) courses) and they can be delivered by one learner TESOL teacher, in teams, or in a peer coaching arrangement (see Chapter 4). During such microteaching, learner TESOL teachers can focus on developing specific skills, such as giving instructions or teaching a particular grammar structure, and then instant feedback can be provided on what was accomplished (Wallace, 1991). Learner TESOL teachers thus benefit from structured teaching in a safe environment where they teach specific strategies and practice teaching skills that prepare them for the practicum (Roberts, 1998).

Richards and Farrell (2011) have suggested that microteaching lessons should follow a basic sequence of plan, teach, and critique. As is common in many TESOL teacher education programs, many learner TESOL teachers will not have much teaching experience, so microteaching lessons offer them opportunities to try out some ideas they may have learned in some of their courses. These type of lessons can be very focused on only one aspect of teaching so that they can attempt to master this, and if they do not, as perhaps the feedback may suggest, they can try again, which would not be an option teaching in a real classroom. Thus, the TESOL teacher educator-supervisor may have to manage the microteaching experiences closely. Wallace (1991) outlined a process that supervisors can consider as follows:

- *Briefing*: The supervisor presents the skill to be practiced and explains how this can be accomplished (e.g. teaching a particular grammar skill). The presentation might be through an oral discussion by the supervisor, or based on readings or checklists, or involve 'modeling' by demonstrating how the skill or technique is used. I would suggest that this stage could be optional for supervisors depending on their confidence in their learner TESOL teachers' abilities to teach.
- *Planning*: The learner TESOL teachers plan their micro-lesson, incorporating the skills they have been assigned to practice or that they have decided they want to try out. This includes preparing a description of the objectives for their lesson.
- *Teaching*: The learner TESOL teachers now teach the micro-lessons either to peers or to real ESL/EFL students, and the TESOL teacher educator-supervisor observes along with peers. The lesson can be audio- and/or videotaped for the feedback/ critique session that immediately follows.
- *Critique*: The lesson is critiqued by all and analyzed in detail through discussion and/or through the use of stimulated recall using a video recording (see also Chapter 4 for more on video). The strengths and weaknesses of the microteaching lesson are noted and, depending on time, the learner TESOL teacher is allowed to reteach.
- *Reteaching*: The learner TESOL teacher reteaches the lesson using the feedback from the previous stage, and the TESOL teacher educator-supervisor provides further feedback.

Although such a skills view to microteaching is artificial and de-contextualized in nature and thus not the same as teaching a real lesson in a real school, less experienced learner TESOL teachers can gain some insight into what they can expect when they enter a classroom, and thus have confidence that they can at least try out ideas and perhaps be their own critiques while teaching. If all learner TESOL teachers practice microteaching, then everyone in the program can gain from observing others teaching and consider what they would do in similar situations, much as if they were watching videos of others teaching.

However, given that a core assumption underlying the contents of this book is that TESOL teacher education should emphasize the development of learner TESOL teachers as reflective practitioners who are adaptive professionals, the above traditional approach may seem very top-down and imposed by the TESOL teacher educator-supervisor. This microteaching approach can be adopted into a more reflective one where, as Richards and Farrell (2011) maintain, the ability to understand and reflect on the cognitive and affective aspects of teaching becomes a central focus.

Such a reflective approach to microteaching will include not only learner TESOL teachers' teaching skills but also many other aspects of practice, such as developing motivation in ESL/EFL classes, using learning strategies effectively, encouraging student participation, and becoming more self-aware of their teaching style. Rather than the TESOL teacher educator-mentor modeling a lesson, he or she can collaborate, provide input into the lesson plan, and suggest procedures and/or activities that can be added. Feedback can consist of the learner TESOL teacher providing an account of his or her experiences of what he or she thought went well, or not well, and why, before the TESOL teacher-supervisor and peers provide their feedback.

In addition, some TESOL teacher education programs may encourage learner TESOL teachers to teach more expanded microteaching lessons when they go out on teaching practice, because the detailed feedback they have already received will give them more confidence to adjust the lesson to fit a whole period of teaching in a real classroom. However, success with this expansion is not guaranteed, as there are many other factors that must also be addressed when learner TESOL teachers go out to real schools, such as the teacher of that class or the cooperating teacher, the students, the curriculum in place, and many more. All of these will be addressed below.

REFLECTIVE BREAK

- Prepare a microteaching lesson (10 to 15 minutes) on any topic (a concept of skill such as reading for gist, writing topic sentences, etc.) teaching English to speakers of other languages.
- Write the main learning objective for your lesson. Start with: "By the end of this 10-to-15-minute lesson, my students will be able to . . .".
- Ask your peers and TESOL teacher educator-supervisor to observe your lesson. Perhaps decide on what particular aspects of your teaching you would like them to look at and/or discuss.
- *After the lesson*: Discuss the following with your peers and supervisor (you go first):
  - What do you think your 'students' learned?
  - How do you know?
  - What did you do well?
  - What did you not do so well?
  - What did you learn about your teaching?

- Is there anything you would change now on reflection after the lesson?
- How well did you in relation to the following aspects?
  - Pacing
  - Explanations
  - Questions: how many, what kind, to whom
  - Feedback to students
  - Creating a positive and supportive atmosphere
- *Re-plan and reteach*: Based on peer feedback and self-evaluation, plan the same lesson and teach it a second time. The goal is to incorporate feedback from the first microteaching session to master the skill being practiced.
- Go through the same cycle of feedback and reflection as above in the first round.

Reading and Discussion Task

Erin Mikulec and Kira Hamann (2020) noted that one of the primary concerns of pre-service secondary teachers is negotiating student behavior and classroom management, and novice teachers cite this as one of the reasons why they leave the profession in the first three years. This is also true for learner TESOL teachers as well as early career TESOL teachers. Consequently, the teacher educators initiated a microteaching project for their learner teachers with a student behavior component. Taking two and a half weeks of the semester, each participant learner teacher completed their project by teaching their lesson to their peers, who were required to "become" high school students when not teaching. In addition to teaching, participants also had to address at least one significant behavior challenge that "arose" during their lesson. The results show that the participants gained a deeper understanding of the complexity of teaching and student behavior and also identified strategies to take with them into their future classrooms.

- Read the paper and consider your understanding of the microteaching project and what the learner teachers gained from it and why.
- Discuss your findings with a colleague.

[Mikulec, E., and Hamann, K. (2020) "My eyes have been opened": Pre-service secondary teachers exploring behavior management through a microteaching project. *Action in Teacher Education*, 42, 2, 102-19]

FIELD PLACEMENTS

As teaching practice is a core component of the practicum in most TESOL teacher education programs, many of these programs will require learner TESOL teachers to teach lessons to ESL/EFL students in a real language classroom. In order for this to happen, TESOL teacher education programs usually have to partner in some manner with either on-campus language schools or off-campus schools, so that learner TESOL teachers can be placed for this experience. There are probably lots of variations in how TESOL teacher education programs implement these field placements and also in how the members of the practicum (TESOL teacher educator-supervisors, cooperating teachers, and school coordinators) carry out their roles in these partnerships. Up to nine different models of various partnerships between teacher education programs and schools have been identified, as follows (I have adjusted some for the purposes of TESOL programs; see Mattsson, Eilertsen, and Rorrison, 2011, for a more detailed discussion of these):

1. *Master–apprentice model*: An expert teacher instructs the learner TESOL teacher in the craft of teaching. This 'craft model', according to Wallace (1991), is akin to '*sitting* with *Nellie*'; that is, the apprentice observes the expert in action and absorbs as much as he or she can of the craft.
2. *Laboratory model*: The TESOL teacher education program has its own school that includes the practicum with whatever system the program decides.
3. *Partnership model*: TESOL teacher education directs the choice of the school placement and, after agreement on expectations, gives the school total control for the teaching practice.
4. *Integrated model*: All stakeholders have equal and shared responsibilities during the program of teaching practice in the school.
5. *Community development model*: Learner TESOL teachers are placed to support an ESL community in need (perhaps recent refugees or immigrants to a country) and to support students in need.
6. *Case-based model*: Learner TESOL teachers not only teach classes but, during their placements, investigate cases of specific students learning under their care and develop a case study of a specific number of students.
7. *Platform model*: Learner TESOL teachers have complete freedom to choose how they want to engage in the practicum.
8. *Community of practice model*: Learner TESOL teachers are socialized as members of a community of practice with the TESOL profession, all with shared goals.
9. *Research and development model*: This scientific approach develops research between TESOL teacher education programs and schools as their main practicum focus.

Although it is difficult to really separate many of the above models, probably the most common approach used by TESOL teacher education programs in many contexts is the *integrated model*, with aspects of other models included as well (Thomas, 2017). In such an integrated model, the learner TESOL teacher is placed in a school and the school arranges for the appointment of a cooperating teacher who will work with him or her throughout the period of the placement; the TESOL teacher educator-supervisor will make periodic visits to observe classes and provide feedback and assessment (as was the case in the preamble to this chapter). In addition, regular dialogue (and journal writing if appropriate) between learner TESOL teachers, their TESOL teacher educator-supervisor, the cooperating teachers, and perhaps other teachers in the placement location will be seen as crucial for the successful experience of the learner TESOL teacher (Cirocki and Farrell, 2017). Such dialogue, according to Edwards-Groves (2014: 163), should be critical in nature, "based on evidence from experiences and actions, accountable for making connections between theory and practice and involve timely responsive feedback and collaborative goal setting." Thus each member of the triad – the TESOL teacher educator-supervisor, the cooperating teacher, and the learner TESOL teacher – has a vital role to play for the success of such integrated field-based experiences.

Another, newer model beginning to make inroads into TESOL teacher education programs in the United States is called 'service learning', where TESOL teacher educators-supervisors help learner TESOL teachers directly make links between theory and practice (see Chapter 2 for more on this), so that they can construct their own understanding of their teaching (Farrell, 2017). For example, immediately following teaching practice in a school, TESOL teacher educators Colombo, Brazil, and White (2017) conducted the TESOL methods course at that school, thus making overt links between the theories presented in coursework and the practice of teaching in a school. In such a manner, learner TESOL teachers are better able to make sense of practice through theory and connect theory to practice, because service-learning occurs in such authentic settings and, in addition, the recursive nature of teachers' theorizing, and an awareness of and sensitivity to the sociopolitical issues, allow the teacher candidates to notice the way the context influences teachers' decision making (Tomaš, Moger, Park, and Specht, 2017). Thus when learner TESOL teachers engage in such service-learning experiences they can not only enhance their teaching skills, but also learn how to reflect critically about less visible aspects of teaching, such as the sociopolitical culture of the context in which they are teaching.

REFLECTIVE BREAK

- Which of the practicum models above would you like to follow for your practicum and why?
- Which of the practicum models above would you not like to follow and why not?

Reading and Discussion Task

Stephen Stoynoff (1999) outlines five principles of an integrated model in the US, one of which is that the delivery emphasizes a team approach that includes mentor teachers (who serve as ESL teachers, models, and coaches); graduate program faculty (who serve as supervising teachers, academic advisors, and graduate course instructors); language institute administrators (who serve as language program managers); and the practicum students (who serve as classroom assistants, observers, and ESL teachers). Each team member is involved in every phase of the year-long experience and participates in a collegial, consultative decision-making process.

- Read the paper and consider your understanding of the team approach in terms of the different roles each member plays. Compare your ideas to what you read below on the roles of three major members of such an integrated

approach: teacher educator-supervisor, cooperating teacher, and learner TESOL teacher.
- Discuss your findings with a colleague.

[Stoynoff, S. (1999). The TESOL practicum: An integrated model in the US. *TESOL Quarterly, 33*, 1, 145-51]

TESOL Teacher Educator-Supervisor

The TESOL teacher educator-supervisor has an important role to play during the practicum in the integrated model, including overall mentoring (see also Chapter 4 for more on mentoring) as well as providing appropriate feedback and assessment throughout each step. Sometimes the triad of TESOL teacher educator-supervisor, cooperating teacher, and learner TESOL teacher all meet together to discuss progress either after classroom observations, or at any time during the period of practice teaching, or at the end of the teaching period. However, in many programs, each member mentioned above has a different level of responsibility. Usually the TESOL teacher educator-supervisor visits the school to observe the learner TESOL teacher teaching specific lessons during the period of the practicum. During these visits the TESOL teacher educator-supervisor provides vital feedback to learner TESOL teachers, although this did not happen in the preamble in the opening of this chapter.

TESOL teacher educator-supervisors can offer such feedback through dialogue, in writing, or through video recall if the observed lesson is recorded (see Chapter 4 for a discussion on all of these modes of reflection). What happens in most visits is that there is a pre-observation meeting with the learner TESOL teacher about what the objectives of the lesson will be, including discussion of the lesson plan and perhaps the materials that accompany the lesson. Then the lesson is observed and possibly videotaped. After the lesson, there is a post-observation discussion (sometimes called a conference) where the TESOL teacher educator-supervisor discusses various aspects of the lesson with the learner TESOL teacher. These post-observation conferences should be a reflective experience for the learner TESOL teacher so that he or she can gain insight into what has occurred during the lessons. The main point is that TESOL teacher educator-supervisors, through dialogue and/or writing, facilitate a reflective process whereby learner TESOL teachers can articulate their thoughts in a supportive environment. Farr (2015), for example, conducts a teaching practice 'input' session, lasting from two to three hours, with her student teachers where they all discuss expectations, look at corpus data from teaching practice feedback sessions, and analyze these so that they can all try to create a more balanced disposition to the imminent teaching practice experience.

Similarly, Waring (2014) suggests that TESOL teacher educator-supervisors should prioritize the learner TESOL teachers' perspectives during teaching practice, so as to invite reflection and thus take a *solution-attentive* approach rather than a *cause-attentive* approach, because the latter can put the learner TESOL teacher on the defensive rather than fostering a real understanding of the issue. Because learner TESOL teachers can use such discussions for defending themselves or displaying their competence as prospective teachers, TESOL teacher educator-supervisors must be aware of any avoidance of making connections between problems observed and their own practice, and thus engaging in lower levels of reflection. As Waring (2014: 117) has noted, it is "difficult to escape the 'testing' aspect of these power-dynamics"; as such, the student "teachers do treat the mentor questions as eliciting reflection, they can approach answering with great caution, orienting to any noticing preceding the question and the question itself as incipient critiques." Thus, TESOL teacher educator-supervisors can provide prompts by asking specific and focused questions in a solution-attentive approach that better scaffolds teacher learning and enables deeper reflections.

REFLECTIVE BREAK

- What role do you expect your TESOL teacher educator-supervisor to play when observing your lessons?
- Should the TESOL teacher educator-supervisor tell you before he or she visits your class or just show up? Explain your answer.
- What kind of feedback do you expect your TESOL teacher educator-supervisor to provide you with?
- Do you want your TESOL teacher educator-supervisor to tell you what he or she thinks you did correctly and incorrectly exactly after your lessons, or would you like to tell that person what you think you did correctly and incorrectly after the lesson first?
- Do you think you would like to experiment with some of your own ideas during teaching practice? If yes, what would you like to try out? If no, why not?
- What do you expect of a pre-observation conference and a post-observation conference?

Reading and Discussion Task

Charles Ochieng' Ong'ondo and Simon Borg (2011), drawing on the perspectives of TESOL teacher educators, cooperating teachers, and learner TESOL teachers, examine the process of supervision by TESOL teacher educators and its influence on learner TESOL teachers during a practicum in Kenya. Results indicate that the supervision was brief and uncoordinated and that the feedback learner TESOL teachers received was mainly evaluative, directive, and focused on general, rather than subject-specific, pedagogy.

- Read their paper and especially look at examples of the supervision, including the sample of the supervisor's written comments in the appendix. Would you teach "plastic lessons" to please your TESOL teacher educator-supervisor?
- Discuss your findings with a colleague.

[Ong'ondo, C. O., and Borg, S. (2011). "We teach plastic lessons to please them": The influence of supervision on the practice of English language student teachers in Kenya. *Language Teaching Research*, 15, 4, 509–28]

Cooperating Teacher

Along with the TESOL teacher educator-supervisor, the cooperating teacher also plays a crucial role in facilitating the practicum experience (Farrell, 2008). Graves (2009) notes the essential role of collaborative relationships between schools and TESOL teacher education programs as well as TESOL teacher educators. These same partnerships, solidified during teaching practice placement, should also be continued as TESOL teachers become socialized into the profession during their early career years (see Chapter 7). Most studies suggest that learner TESOL teachers on teaching practice will need lots of support during their school placement. Farrell (2001c) highlighted the crucial role of the cooperating teacher during this period because he or she spends so much time with these learner TESOL teachers.

If the cooperating teacher has volunteered for this role, then there is every chance that he or she will provide a rich mentoring experience for the learner teacher. If, however, the cooperating teacher was appointed to this role (perhaps because of his or her years of teaching experience), then there is no guarantee that he or she will provide much support beyond what the school requires, especially if this cooperating teacher is controlling, wanting things done his or her way only (Pennington and Urmston, 1998). Unfortunately, there have been instances where some cooperating teachers view the practicum as a break for them, and thus basically abandon learner TESOL teachers to teach on their own without much guidance (Farrell, 2008). Consequently, as Richards and Farrell (2011) point out, the first meeting with the cooperating teacher is very important and learner TESOL teachers should find out what expectations he or she has for them throughout the period he or she is in the school with them (see also Farr, 2015, noted above). Richards and Farrell (2011) point out those discussions should include asking questions that can be considered by *both* the cooperating teacher and learner TESOL teacher, such as the following:

- What are the cooperating teacher's expectations for the practicum?
- What kind of working relationship does the cooperating teacher like to have with learner TESOL teachers?
- How does the cooperating teacher think learner TESOL teachers should prepare for practice teaching?
- What are some things learner TESOL teachers should anticipate while working with the cooperating teacher?
- Will the cooperating teacher allow learner TESOL teachers to observe and teach his or her lessons?
- If yes to both the above, how does the cooperating teacher expect the learner TESOL teachers to teach his or her classes?
- Will the cooperating teacher observe the learner TESOL teachers while they teach these classes?
- Will the cooperating teacher be directive or collaborative in his or her supervision of the learner TESOL teachers during the practicum?

REFLECTIVE BREAK

- What do you think the role of a cooperating teacher in a school should be?
- What would you do if your cooperating teacher was totally controlling of how and what you were teaching in their classroom, as Pennington and Urmston (1998) discovered was the case for learner TESOL teachers in Hong Kong?
- What would you do if your cooperating teacher said to you "Here's the book, go teach the class" and then completely abandoned you for the practicum, as Farrell (2008) reported occurred in a Singapore context?
- What answers would you expect to the questions outlined above by Richards and Farrell (2011)?

Reading and Discussion Task

Caroline Payant and John Murphy (2012) explored cooperating teachers' perceptions of their roles and responsibilities as contributors to the practicum experiences of learner TESOL teachers. The authors discovered a number of issues, such as a perceived lack of communication between cooperating teachers and practicum course instructors, inadequate written descriptions of cooperating teachers' roles and responsibilities, and missed opportunities to develop more fully both the quality of collaborations between cooperating teacher and practicum student and cooperating teachers' recommendations for enhancing the practicum experiences of those involved.

- Read their paper and consider your understanding of these issues and what you would do.
- Discuss your findings with a colleague.

[Payant, C., and Murphy, J. (2012). Cooperating teachers' roles and responsibilities in a MATESOL practicum. *TESL Canada Journal*, *29*, 2, 1-23]

Learner TESOL Teacher

Learner TESOL teachers are not passive participants during teaching practice, waiting to be told what to do at every stage. They can and should take the initiative right from the start of the field experience by finding out where they will be placed – for example, in a campus-based language program, in a local public school, in a community college, or in a private language institute – because each of these contexts will present different notions of the process of learning to teach (Zeichner and Grant, 1981). Thus learner TESOL teachers will realize that there is more to it than just teaching lessons in a classroom, because the classroom is part of a school and thus part of a community of practice that is situated in a community, and/or multiple and overlapping communities, in society (Johnson, 2009). Thus, and as Richards and Farrell (2011) suggest, in order to prepare for a successful practicum, learner TESOL teachers should attempt to discover as much as possible about their placement location, be it a school or institution, and what it actually does. They should also research the kinds of teachers and language students there, and the facilities available there as well.

REFLECTIVE BREAK

- How would you go about researching the site of your placement?
- Richards and Farrell (2011) suggest that learner TESOL teachers should make a preliminary visit to the school of the placement and that this visit should include the following:
    - a short meeting with the school principal;
    - a meeting with the cooperating teacher (and other teachers if possible);
    - observation of some of the classes in the school;
    - familiarization with the layout of the school and its resources;
    - conversations with some of the learners the student teacher will be working with.
- If you could visit your school placement site, would you carry out any of the above suggestions? Why or why not? Can you add more suggestions?
- Richards and Farrell (2011) also suggest that learner TESOL teachers ask specific questions during the preliminary visit, such as:
    - How is the school organized in terms of the administration?
    - Does each department in the school have a Head and are there any level coordinators or skill coordinators?
    - What is the role of the coordinator?
    - Do I attend all staff meetings?
    - Do I have any recess and/or lunch duties?
    - Do I have to go on field trips with the students?
    - What resources would be available to me in terms of computers? Is there a computer room where I can go? Are there any other resources I could use?
    - Who should I go to for photocopying during my teaching practice?
    - Where will I be based during my teaching practice? Will I be in the main teachers' room or is there a separate location for student teachers?
    - How many other student teachers will be placed in the same school with me and will they be located near me during teaching practice?
    - What are the main school rules that I should know about and which ones should I be sure to monitor when I interact with students?
    - What are the school's expectations of student teachers?
    - Is there a dress code for teachers?
    - Are there any rules specific to speaking English in class that I should be aware of?
    - When will my practice teaching take place and how often?
    - Will I be dealing with anyone other than my cooperating teacher?
    - If I have any problems, who should I go to for advice?
    - What discipline procedures should I follow when dealing with students?
    - Who will be giving me overall feedback about my teaching practice performance?

Would you ask these same questions, or would you change any? Explain your answer.

Reading and Discussion Task

Elaine Vaughan (2007) noted that while teacher education programs usually focus on instructing learner teachers about the importance of understanding interaction inside the classroom, or what she calls "frontstage discourse," and this is very important, it is equally significant for learner teachers to be aware of the interaction they are involved with outside the classroom, or "backstage discourse."

- Read her paper and consider your understanding of the importance of becoming more aware of backstage discourse as you learn to teach.
- Discuss your findings with a colleague.

[Vaughan, E. (2007). "I think we should just accept . . . our horrible lowly status": Analysing teacher–teacher talk within the context of community of practice. *Language Awareness, 16*, 3, 173-89]

When entering this new community of practice, learner TESOL teachers will begin to take on new responsibilities associated with their new role as a trainee teacher in a school. Some of these new responsibilities will include fitting in to the new community by, among other things, presenting a professional teacher image that includes following an acceptable dress code and knowing the rules of conduct in the host school (Richards and Farrell, 2011). Learner TESOL teachers will most likely have most interactions with their cooperating teacher (see above for more on this) and therefore attempt to establish good relations with this person, because he or she will help them with all aspects of day-to-day school expectations. In addition, learner TESOL teachers must interact with the TESOL teacher educator-supervisor during his or her visits. Both of these practicum supervisors will engage in classroom observations that may or may not include pre-observation and post-observation conferences (see above for more on these).

During most of the practicum and especially in the integrated practicum model, the cooperating teacher will allow learner TESOL teachers to observe his or her classes before allowing them to teach actual lessons. This observation process may include helping with preparation of teaching materials and activities, to give learner TESOL teachers some experience before they take on teaching a full lesson.

Although some cooperating teachers, as mentioned above, may give learner TESOL teachers full autonomy while teaching lessons, including preparation and delivery, most will attempt to provide mentorship during these teaching experiences. Thus there will be meetings to discuss the lesson and lesson plan before the actual teaching as well as to consider any difficulties that may be anticipated. In addition, the cooperating teacher will inform the learner TESOL teacher how he or she will be evaluated and how and when feedback will be provided. This feedback is usually provided after the lesson, with a review of what went well and any problems or difficulties that were noted.

REFLECTIVE BREAK

• The following is a narrative account of a learner TESOL teacher's experiences during her field placement. What is your opinion of her experiences? What stands out most for you?

I taught first year students EOP (English for Occupational Purposes) courses during my practicum. The two EOP courses I taught were Hotel English and English in Cuisine. These two courses were for the students in two different programs: Hotel English was for the students in Hotel Management, and English in Cuisine was for the Cuisine majors. The courses had no external curriculum, no fixed teaching materials and 100% internal assessment. Instead, the students' needs were at the center of planning.

Before planning, firstly, I thought about what I expected my students to achieve at the end of their learning. So I conducted 'needs analysis' to figure out the goals of teaching. The 'needs analysis' was based on three sources: the existing EOP research in these two domains (usually recommended by the more experienced teachers), the learners and the domain experts (who are experienced professionals in these two domains). For example, one typical 'need' I learned from both the research findings and the domain experts is that these two kinds of job (Hotel Management and Chef) require professionals to have certain level of proficiency in English listening and speaking related to their works. Thus, one of the goals I set up in my teaching plan was to develop the learners' listening and speaking competencies in their working contexts.

After setting up the goals, I began to figure out the specific teaching methodologies and classroom activities to help facilitate the goals as well as the appropriate assessments to measure the students' learning. The interviews with the domain experts made me know the specific activities that the pre-service professionals may use English for. For example, the students in Hotel Management may use English to help their guests check-in and order food. Then, I consulted the relevant theories of second language teaching pedagogies (some were recommended by the more experienced teachers). I found Task-based Teaching might be helpful to achieve the goals. So I designed some oral tasks for each lesson and guided the students to practice and experience the language in the stimulating working contexts.

Reflecting on my plan of teaching in the junior secondary school, in terms of planning of teaching, the situation in the secondary school was very different from the vocational school. Two things made me adjust my way of planning. One thing was the size of the class. There were about 35 students in the class I taught (which was the average size of secondary school classes). However, in the vocational school I worked for, there were about 20 students in each class or even fewer. And another thing was, in secondary schools, the English teaching was highly controlled by the curriculum and syllabus assigned by the Ministry of Education, the high-school entrance examination and the fixed textbooks. The teaching and learning was targeted for a better performance in the exams. The exams (i.e. the final-term exams and the high school entrance exams), however, were mostly designed by the external supervisors who were out of the classroom English teaching for many years. The possibility of implementing 'backward' planning was very little. Instead, I conducted 'forward' planning though it was not the approach I felt comfortable with.

Before planning, firstly, I referred to the curriculum and syllabus to identify what aspects of knowledge and skills the students need to master in each year and after their three years of study. Then, I went over the textbook and had a clear mind of what content I need to cover in teaching in order to match the goals in the curriculum and syllabus. However, I realized that I ignored the learners' English proficiency and needs when setting up the teaching and learning objectives.

Usually, at the beginning and in the middle of each semester, I had discussions with my colleagues regarding the planning of teaching. At the beginning of each semester, our discussion was mainly about planning how much time (or how many lessons) we need to spend in teaching each unit of the textbook (i.e. vocabulary, grammar and language skills related to a topic). While, in the middle of each semester, our discussion focused on analyzing the students' difficulties in achieving the learning objectives so as to adjust some particular exercises to enhance learning.

Finally, I began to match the teaching methods and learning activities with the objectives. The teachers' reference book and the external supervisors' advice were the main evidence. The teaching methods – for example, communicative approach and PPP approach (i.e. Present, Practice and Produce) – and the learning activities (i.e. input and output activities) that helped the learners enhance the required knowledge and skills were also helpful. For example, a listening lesson, the listening materials of a unit were divided into several parts, and then some comprehensive exercises were assigned to check the learners' understandings. There might be some interactions between teacher and students, and students and students.

FEEDBACK DURING FIELD PLACEMENTS

The above account of the experiences of one learner TESOL teacher during her field placement in a school indicates that she had a lot of autonomy and not a lot of supervision as she attempted to design and implement her lessons. There is also no indication that she received much feedback from anyone in the school or from her TESOL teacher education program about her progress during her practicum experience. However, for most learner TESOL teachers a major aspect of field placement is when, where, and how they receive feedback from the various stakeholders, and especially from the TESOL teacher educator-supervisors and cooperating teachers at the institution where they are placed. TESOL teacher education programs may have pre-set and coordinated with the institutions about how their learner TESOL teachers will be evaluated while they are out on teaching practice, and some may provide similar or even the same evaluation forms for the TESOL teacher educator-supervisors and cooperating teachers to fill out. In addition to filling out overall learner TESOL teaching evaluation forms, which are based on observations of teaching in classrooms and probably of adjustment and socialization to the institution's expectations and rules, the TESOL teacher educator-supervisors and cooperating teachers can also provide feedback during the process of teaching practice to learner TESOL teachers/ This can include evaluation during pre- and post-observation conferences with feedback focused on lesson plans, materials, and class observations in terms of strengths and areas necessary for improvement in particular.

Regardless of who provides the feedback during these pre- and post-classroom observations, the manner and style in which the feedback is provided can have different effects on learner TESOL teachers. For example, supervisors who deliver feedback in a directive, authoritative manner will impact learner TESOL teachers more negatively and put them more on the defensive than if the style of delivery is more collaborative and dialogical, with more input from learner TESOL teachers (Wallace, 1991). However, what is most prevalent, according to research, is that supervisors in TESOL settings often struggle to maintain conflicting and paradoxical roles as evaluator and at the same time developer of learner TESOL teachers (Farr, 2011). TESOL teacher educator-supervisors must remain on guard against developing an authoritative position and sounding like 'experts' giving too much direction to learner TESOL teachers (Copland, 2011). This of course is a delicate balance between helping and telling learner TESOL teachers what to do.

I realize that it may be tempting to provide 'expert-like' lectures to learner teachers after teaching practice, and in fact, if truth be told, many learner teachers say this is what they want, or more precisely, "Tell me what to do." I have never told a learner teacher or experienced teacher what to do in my over forty years of practice because I believe that this develops the opposite of reflective practice, in that learner teachers can develop a sense of "learned helplessness" (Abramson, Seligman, and Teasdale, 1978) whereby they will never be able to make informed decisions about their practice. As Fanselow (1988: 115) wonderfully put it: "Helpful prescriptions can stop exploration, since the receiver, as someone in an inferior position being given orders by someone in a superior position, may easily develop the 'ours is not to wonder why' syndrome."

Thus, as Cirocki, Madyarov, and Baecher (2019) maintain, learner TESOL teachers should not be lectured to about their practice, but in fact be given as much time to talk as possible, thus giving them ownership of their own process of learning to teach. These authors suggest that TESOL teacher educator-supervisors and cooperating teachers ask probing questions, so that learner TESOL teachers can reflect on their own processes of learning to teach while also generating their own solutions to whatever issues may have arisen during classroom observations. These authors also advise that learner TESOL teachers be provided with detailed guidelines and rubrics (such as student teaching evaluation form checklists) to follow in the overall assessment process, so that all members can have a shared vision of field placement expectations.

That said, offering feedback to learner TESOL teachers, and carrying out assessment on their progress during the TESOL teacher education program and the practicum in particular, is a complex, challenging, and often daunting task for all those involved. Teacher evaluation and assessment generates a lot of pressure on TESOL teacher educator-supervisors, cooperating teachers, administrators, and especially those who are being assessed: learner TESOL teachers. I address this often neglected area of teacher assessment within the TESOL profession in greater detail in the chapter that follows.

REFLECTIVE BREAK

- What kind of feedback would you expect to receive from your supervisor during field placement?
- Would you expect to be given detailed rubrics (see also the task below) to follow when teaching lessons? If yes, why? If no, why not?
- Do you think that it is possible for you to fail teaching practice?
- Do you know of any learner TESOL teacher who has failed teaching practice? See also the task below about failing the practicum.

Reading and Discussion Task

Thomas Farrell (2007a) has outlined a case study of a learner TESOL teacher who had to repeat her practicum after failing it the first time. One reason she failed her practicum was that she attempted to follow the detailed student evaluation form rubric and ended up teaching the "rubric rather than the students." The case study highlights three main maxims the learner TESOL teacher used after her first classroom observation with a new TESOL teacher educator-supervisor, and how reflecting on these maxims with him contributed to positive changes in her teaching practices to promote more effective learning opportunities for her students, so that she passed her practicum.

- Read the paper and consider your understanding of these problems and what you would do. See also the next chapter on teaching evaluation.
- Discuss your findings with a colleague.

[Farrell, T. S. C. (2007a). Failing the practicum: Narrowing the gap between expectation and reality with reflective practice. *TESOL Quarterly, 41*, 193-201]

The field placement experience for many learner TESOL teachers will no doubt depend on the level of involvement of the cooperating teacher (and the TESOL teacher educator-supervisor) and whether, when, and where team teaching and/ or peer coaching will be considered appropriate in certain cases (see Chapter 4 for more on both). Thus learner TESOL teachers should have a clear understanding not only of their roles and responsibilities while out on field placements, but also of the expectations of those who supervise them while they are on the practicum, such as TESOL teacher educator-supervisors and cooperating teachers.

Since starting this book, the COVID-19 pandemic has engulfed all teacher education production of courses, whether foundation courses and/or teaching practice.

Some 'private' TESOL teacher certificate programs have already begun to set up online practicum experiences, which I believe learner teachers are still trying to adjust to, as are supervisors, who will also evaluate remotely. This is a brave new world we are all entering into with online learning, be it forced on us all or a desired way of learning chosen by some. I am not well versed in how to best conduct all of what I have outlined in this chapter (and all the other chapters in this book), but no doubt readers will be in the thick of it all as they read the book, so any feedback will be welcome. In the meantime, I have found the following commissioned research report valuable reading on this subject: Murray and Christison (2018).

Reading and Discussion Task

John Trent (2010) in a wonderfully titled paper, "My two masters," explored learner TESOL teachers' understandings of the requirements of their teacher education institution and their teaching placement school, their relations with full-time teachers within their placement schools, and their own beliefs about the teaching and learning of the English language in a Hong Kong context. Results indicated that the learner TESOL teachers experienced a dissociation between the demands of their placement schools and those of their teacher education courses.

- Read the paper and consider how supervisors from the teacher education program and cooperating teachers from the teaching placement schools can best provide support for you as learner TESOL teachers during the teaching practicum field placements.
- Discuss your findings with a colleague.

[Trent, J. (2010). "My two masters": Conflict, contestation, and identity construction within a teaching practicum. *Australian Journal of Teacher Education, 35, 7,* 1-14]

CONCLUSION

Teaching practice is regarded as "one of the most important aspects of a teacher education program for learner teachers" (Farrell, 2008: 226). It is vital that at the end of the period of the practicum, as Cirocki, Madyarov, and Baecher (2019: 4) point out, learner TESOL teachers should

(1) be cognisant of their own assumptions and prejudices about human behaviour, (2) understand the students they teach, (3) employ culturally appropriate approaches in classrooms consisting of students from diverse language and culture backgrounds, and (4) show students how to be culturally responsive in the present-day diverse society.

Although TESOL practicum experiences are designed in unique ways in different contexts (for example, see Cirocki, Madyarov, and Baecher, 2019, for an outline of examples of different practicum experiences in thirteen different countries), their common aim is to enable learner TESOL teachers to develop their knowledge of classroom teaching. In order to accomplish this, they require support from various stakeholders, including TESOL teacher educator-supervisors, placement school mentors such as cooperating teachers, and any other parties involved in the process. Part of this process is developing learner TESOL teachers on the road to becoming adaptive practitioners who know what to do when they meet what Dewey (1933) called "forked-road" situations or unpredictable responses from students. Teaching practice can offer learner TESOL teachers experience of facing these situations, rather than turning away, by engaging in reflection throughout the period of the practicum. Such reflective engagement during the practicum can help learner TESOL teachers to move from "students of teaching, to teachers of students" (Cirocki, Madyarov, and Baecher, 2019: 2).

6

TESOL TEACHER EDUCATION: TEACHING EVALUATION

PREAMBLE

The following account of a school placement experience was written by a learner TESOL teacher as part of an MA TESOL program. This program gave all the responsibility for assessment of learner TESOL teachers to the institution and the TESOL teacher educator-supervisors within that institution:

> As a learner TESOL teacher, I have been struggling to fulfill the institution demands where I am placed. They have set certain goals for English teaching in my workplace which is quite optimistic. The reason why they set the high standard is because many of its graduates have some problems especially because their English proficiency is lacking. For example, there is some professional training which is provided by our government that the graduates could not follow because the medium of instruction is English. Also, usually the other requirement is a certain level of English proficiency which is proven by recognized English testing, thus the graduates often miss the training. In addition, the demand of globalization has forced us to be proficient in English as it is one of the most foreign languages spoken in this world. As a result, the second goal of the English program that has been set by the institution is to prepare all graduates to interact and compete, especially in a professional working environment, globally by mastering English.

> Because I need to fulfill the needs of the graduates in improving their English proficiency, honestly, I feel like it is a huge responsibility and a burden. Firstly, the institute has already prepared our teaching materials which consist of twelve topics, from self-introduction to general activities. In addition, most of the students I teach are usually beginner learners of English. I feel overwhelmed by the topics because we only have twenty meetings and each meeting, I have to teach two skills (either listening and speaking or reading and writing). I distinctly remember when I had to teach two classes in order to catch up with the materials so that we had sufficient time to finish the entire target topics. However, the class became overcrowded because there were 70 students in one classroom, and I was having difficulties managing the classroom situation. I could only interact with some of the students who sat in the front row. During the listening section,

113

my audio speaker could not reach all the audiences. I felt that situation was frustrating.

Secondly, the institution also has prepared high stake assessments which usually do not match with the teaching materials or only include certain topics of the teaching contents. There are two high stake assessments held each semester, one is middle term English examination and the other is the English final examination. The good thing about having the high-stake examinations prepared by the institution is I do not have to arrange any test to evaluate my students' study progress. However, I often found that the examinations made by the institution are incongruent with the teaching materials I have given in the classroom. As a learner TESOL teacher, it would be easier for me to focus on the goal of teaching and from that goal we can move backward so that I know how to achieve the goal by creating appropriate content of learning materials.

What has happened is that my classes were visited by an observer from the institution on days of his choosing and he sat at the back of the room and filled out a form as I was teaching. He did not say anything to me before coming and after the class he smiled at me and handed me my 'evaluation' form. This form consisted of a checklist of many different items that were checked off as 'agree' or 'disagree' and an overall comment at the end saying I was doing ok but that I had to make an improvement of some of the items that were checked off as 'disagree'. For example, one of those items was about 'teacher/student rapport' and although I had figured I get on well with my various students and they respect me as their teacher, the supervisor checked it as 'disagree' but he did not write any comment. Another item was 'professionalism' and he checked 'neutral' which is annoying as I think I am very professional.

I feel the evaluation system in the institution and program are so unjust because they evaluate me only if they think I follow what they want me to do as represented only on the checklist and of course that students pass the tests. I was not even asked about what I thought about my teaching or what issues I faced in the classroom. In fact I keep a teaching journal all the time and I can provide strong evidence of my classroom situation and I can give it to the institution to see what I had to face and even to reconsider the teaching contents and curriculum innovations in the institution. I feel the need to change the situation but they only want to evaluate me with what they think is the correct measures based on one long checklist where my supervisor just drops in and makes marks on the sheet and gives it back to me to make 'improvements'. I really don't know what I have learned beyond trying to make sure I do what is on the checklist or otherwise I will get a bad mark in my evaluation. Teaching practice has turned out for me to be an exercise in getting a good mark and not upsetting anyone in the institution so I can just get out and get on with my teaching career. Overall, it was a bad experience for me as I did not learn anything beyond the importance of keeping a low profile and of course the joy of teaching real students. This joy kept me alive and going during these stressful weeks.

As can be inferred from the above account of the learner TESOL teacher while on teaching practice, the institution she was affiliated with used a top-down method of assessment that used a similar checklist for all its TESOL teachers regardless of their level of teaching experience. In this 'one-size-fits-all' approach, teachers were evaluated mostly on the basis of their students' improvement (or not) in their English proficiency levels, and on whether the TESOL teachers followed the rules of the school dutifully.

However, teaching is such a complex activity because it is unpredictable and thus unique to every teacher in terms of how it transpires in lessons, and thus must not be viewed from a 'one-size-fits-all' perspective when it comes to deciding what 'good teaching' or 'bad teaching' is. In addition, teaching and its evaluation are unique to the particular class on that particular day, and so the accuracy of any evaluation will depend on the levels of the TESOL teacher educator-supervisor's skills of being able to notice classroom cues in that moment of teaching and learning (or the ability to notice reflection-in-action, according to Schön, 1983), as well as his or her ability to gather the information after the lesson (or reflection-on-action, according to Dewey, 1933). Thus, TESOL teacher educator-supervisors and school-appointed supervisors themselves should become proficient in noticing classroom cues in the moment of teaching (Schön) and after the lesson (Dewey) for any meaningful learner TESOL teaching evaluation to occur.

This was not the case in the opening preamble above, as it seems the school-appointed supervisor arrived unannounced for each lesson observation 'armed' with an institutional, pre-designed checklist of desired teaching behaviors that he marked off according to his preconceived notions of 'good' or 'bad' teaching. For example, in one instance he checked off that he disagreed that the learner TESOL teacher had 'good' 'teacher/student rapport' without discussing this with the teacher after the observation. What is 'good' or 'bad' 'teacher/student rapport' anyway? For example, if the learner TESOL teacher instituted pair work or group work and the students were loud and active as a result of interacting with each other, in some contexts a TESOL teacher educator-supervisor might consider this to be poor classroom management skills, because the class could seem 'out of control'. The school-appointed supervisor in the preamble above did not talk to the learner TESOL teacher at any time during the evaluation process, with no pre-lesson or post-lesson observation discussions about her ability to reflect on her practice or the importance of engaging in reflective practice during her teaching practice. In fact, the learner TESOL teacher reported that the school-appointed supervisor had no idea of the concept of reflective practice or what its meaning was for TESOL teachers. He was an experienced TESOL teacher who had been in that institution for about twenty-five years.

However, the learner TESOL teacher, although aware of reflective practice tools that would have enabled her to present a more complete picture of who she is as a learner TESOL teacher, was not allowed to give any input into her evaluation and was told to follow the school procedures. She mentioned that one of the criteria on the checklist of teaching evaluation that was used was the ability of all the teachers to follow the school rules. Thus if she wanted to discuss her teaching or the way she was being evaluated or raised any opposition at all, this would have been perceived as being negative and an indication she was not following the rules, which would have adversely impacted her overall evaluation and grade, so she complied with the institution's rules in order to survive her teaching experience. In addition, she reported that she saw no connections between what she had learned in her TESOL teacher education program and what she could use from this while she was on teaching practice, and that she was basically left alone to survive in the institution, as her TESOL teacher educator-supervisor did not take part in her teaching evaluations while she was there.

REFLECTIVE BREAK

- Have you had any experiences like those of the learner TESOL teacher in the preamble above?
- How will you be evaluated during your placement or first year, or how were you evaluated?
- How do you think you should be evaluated?
- Why do you think the institution-appointed observer only used a checklist to evaluate the learner TESOL teacher?
- Do you think checklists are effective for teaching evaluations? If no, why not?
- If yes, what do you think should be on such a checklist?
- In the end in the preamble above the learner TESOL teacher admitted that she just wanted a good mark. How do you feel about that?
- The learner TESOL teacher decided to keep a low profile while on teaching practice. Why do you think she did this and was it effective? Do you intend to keep a low profile while on teaching practice?
- Do you think that the institution-appointed observer should have known something about the concept of reflective practice and how it can be helpful for learner TESOL teachers?

INTRODUCTION

The preamble above is a real story and is more representative than many in the TESOL profession may want to believe or think about when it comes to evaluation of learner TESOL teachers, especially during their teaching practice. I have had similar experiences and such top-down modes of teaching evaluation, defined by Richards, Platt, and Platt (1992: 130) as "the systematic gathering of information for purposes of decision making," can be and unfortunately have been used as a means of enhancing the power differentials between supervisors (be they TESOL teacher educators and/or school-appointed observers) and learner teachers. Indeed, some supervisors who are newly appointed to a teacher educator position may also have limited powers when negotiating what type of teaching assessments are used, especially if the tradition of using top-down modes is long established in that institution. Nevertheless,

I hope to provide some alternative means of gathering information about novice teachers' teaching practices in this chapter, so that both supervisors and learner TESOL teachers can have a developmental as well as an evaluative experience.

The process of teaching evaluation in many TESOL teacher education programs and beyond usually involves TESOL teachers being observed by someone else, normally someone in an administrative and/or supervisory position, who visits the classroom on one or more days to 'evaluate' features of the teacher's teaching. These features or qualities are often predetermined by someone other than the learner TESOL teacher, and even sometimes other than the supervisor (the TESOL teacher educator and/or cooperating teacher), and produced on what is commonly called a teaching evaluation checklist form, as was the case in the opening preamble of this chapter. Of course, this teaching evaluation form can vary from institution to institution, but it invariably includes specific items that are in a checklist mode in which the observer ticks off as 'present' or 'absent', 'agree' or 'disagree', and so on as the lesson proceeds. The observer, who usually sits at the back of the class, gives *The Look* to/at the learner TESOL teacher (see previous chapter), who probably wonders and worries about what the observer is checking off.

Many learner TESOL teachers report that they do not find these evaluations rewarding or stimulating, and some learner TESOL teachers actually resent their supervisors evaluating their teaching just with a checklist of some predetermined categories of what they (or whoever compiled the list) consider to be evidence of 'good teaching'. Some learner TESOL teachers also report becoming somewhat traumatized as a result of these top-down teaching evaluations, and some never recover from them at all and continue to dread being observed throughout their teaching careers. Indeed, if truth be told, some supervisors themselves have indicated that they too feel teaching evaluations, be it on teaching practice or in-service, can be somewhat of a burden for them, because they feel they must complete the form they have been given even if they say they do not agree with all the items on the checklist. Many also realize that such a 'drop-in' mode of teaching evaluation may not be representative of that learner TESOL teacher's overall teaching ability.

Thus, teaching evaluation has become synonymous with a kind of distressing ordeal all TESOL teachers must endure throughout their careers. It is a real burden to them because they do not find the evaluations described above are helpful in any way to improve any aspects of their practice. On the other side of the desk (literally and figuratively), supervisors may also feel that such a checklist approach to teaching evaluation may not be helpful for them when trying to gauge a learner TESOL teacher's performance. However, as outlined in Chapter 2, in a novice-service approach to TESOL teacher education, where TESOL teacher educator-supervisors, learner TESOL teachers, cooperating teachers, and supervisors collaborate and engage in reflective practice through the lens of the framework for reflecting on practice, teaching evaluation can be a more positive experience for all stakeholders involved. This chapter outlines and discusses how such a reflective, collaborative approach can be adopted when evaluating learner TESOL teachers while on teaching practice, where the burden associated with teaching evaluation can be shifted from the supervisor side to be shared by all stakeholders.

Thus, rather than implementing such teaching evaluations from a top-down, authoritarian, controlling perspective, where nobody is satisfied except for those interested in checking off another checklist of their 'doing' the evaluation, learner TESOL teachers can learn from the evaluations and develop their skills as teachers in a non-judgmental setting. The chapter starts by outlining some challenges in many TESOL teaching evaluation approaches that are currently in use, in order to show how these can be changed into more developmental approaches to teaching evaluation not only for TESOL teacher educator-supervisors and learner TESOL teachers, but also for early career TESOL teachers and school supervisors/observers. As noted in Chapter 1, a core assumption of this book is that TESOL teacher education is just the beginning of a learner TESOL teacher's journey, and learning to teach is a career-long journey that requires support all along the continuum from teaching practice, into the early career years, and in the in-service years. While in their TESOL teacher education programs, learner TESOL teachers receive feedback from and are evaluated by their TESOL teacher educators, and this continues during teaching practice and includes school-appointed teacher mentors. This chapter maintains that such feedback should continue to exist from the TESOL teacher educators in the early career years, along with school-appointed mentor teachers in the induction programs, as they all collaborate with the early career teachers in ways that include how they are evaluated. As such, all continue to grow in a collaborative community where feedback and evaluation are shared, with early career teachers taking on more responsibilities for their own self-evaluations and appraisals.

REFLECTIVE BREAK

- What are your expectations of being observed by your supervisor during teaching practice?
- Would you like to share the responsibility between you and your supervisor or should he or she take the full responsibility for evaluating your teaching?

Reading and Discussion Task

Lindsay Wexler (2020) examined how three novice teachers experienced feedback in their learning-to-teach journeys, from their teaching practice experience through their first year teaching. Each learner teacher (called "student teacher" in the article) received feedback on their instruction during student teaching; this came from their mentor teacher (MT), who might also have been a cooperating teacher, from their university supervisor, and from other student teachers. These MTs engaged the student teachers, their mentees, in critical conversations about practice and modeled reflecting on their own teaching. These student teachers reported during student teaching that feedback was an important part of their learning-to-teach experience. The student teachers also wanted to receive feedback during their early career years, and this study reported that while each teacher continued to desire feedback, they had very different experiences seeking, receiving, and using it.

- Read the paper and try to answer its two research questions:
  1. In what ways does the feedback student teachers receive from their mentors influence how they view feedback in the learning-to-teach process?
  2. What experiences do first year teachers have with receiving feedback?
- Discuss your findings with a colleague.

[Wexler, L., J. (2020). How feedback from mentor teachers sustained student teachers through their first year of teaching. *Action in Teacher Education, 42,* 2, 167–85]

TEACHING EVALUATION: CURRENT CHALLENGES

As mentioned above, teaching evaluation is unavoidable for most, if not all, teachers regardless of whether they are just beginning or have been teaching for thirty years. A big part of the traditional evaluation process is lesson observation, where someone other than the students or the teacher teaching the lesson, and usually called a supervisor, evaluates the teacher's teaching and lesson based on some notion of what 'good' teaching is (which also means there is a notion of what 'bad' teaching is; see also Edge and Richards, 1998, on why best practice is not always possible). There are some shortcomings, which I call challenges, in such a traditional approach to evaluation, still common in many TESOL teacher education programs and institutions and schools worldwide, that need to be highlighted so that I can offer a more reflective, collaborative approach that can avoid these challenges.

I now outline six such challenges in teaching evaluation that are representative of more traditional approaches. I fully acknowledge these are general and that not all TESOL teacher education programs conduct their teaching evaluations based on all of these. The six are: *outdated, limited, evaluative criteria; few shared values and assumptions about 'good teaching'; lack of precision in evaluating performance; hierarchical, one-way communication; no differentiation between novice and experienced practitioners;* and *limited administrator expertise* (from Danielson and McGreal, 2000).

OUTDATED, LIMITED, EVALUATIVE CRITERIA

Teaching evaluation has tended to stay very much as it has been for many years since evolving from behavioral psychology research, where evaluation was basically founded on documented observable behaviors such as 'writes objective on board' or 'gives praise to students' and so on (for a complete discussion see Danielson and McGreal, 2000). Supervisors looked for these behaviors and, when they saw them, checked them off their lists; when they did not observer them, their report included the comment that teachers 'should' be performing such a desired teaching behavior. Of course, teachers attempted to memorize such lists because they knew they were going to be evaluated on the behaviors' presence or absence, and so made sure to cover them in as many observed lessons as possible. The result was their supervisor dutifully checked these off when observed, or did not check them off, which usually resulted in negative feedback.

Unfortunately, I was a witness to the harsh reality of this challenge in teaching evaluation during teaching practice (Farrell, 2007a). Although this case study was set as a task in the previous chapter, a few important points are relevant to the current discussion, such as presenting learner TESOL teachers with checklists to follow and their resultant propensity to memorize and 'cover' the checklist items while teaching, rather than teach the lesson objectives and their students. Here is what transpired:

The learner TESOL teacher had failed her practicum and I was asked to act as her *re-practicum* supervisor (.I believe I coined the word "re-practicum," as I had never encountered a learner TESOL teacher anywhere in any context worldwide who had failed the practicum, or what to call repeating the practicum.) As part of this process, I had to review the learner TESOL teacher's initial practicum records, which indicated that she had failed because of "not being well prepared for her classes" and "not [being] focused in her teaching" (Farrell, 2007a: 194-5). I then asked her why she thought she had failed her practicum, and she said it was because she was too nervous when the supervisor and cooperating teachers observed her teaching.

We set up the process for her re-practicum at the same school where she was initially placed for her teaching practice, and we arranged for my first visit to observe her teach a lesson. Problems that emerged immediately during this first observation included her giving me a limited lesson plan ten minutes before the lesson, although she had been asked for it a week in advance; a disastrous beginning to the lesson when she walked in quickly throwing small pieces of rolled-up paper at students in the front of the class, yet nobody knew the class had begun; and an incorrect explanation of grammar rules apparently associated with the throwing of the paper. The lesson could be considered to be fragmented at best.

However, this first lesson offered me a starting point in my attempt to understand this learner TESOL teacher's true reality. Over our discussions I discovered many things about her approach to being observed, and one of them was that she had in fact memorized the entire teaching evaluation form and said that she made sure to 'perform' each item at least once during the lesson. So rather than teaching the students or the material, she said that was always trying to predict what her observers (not just me but all her supervisors and cooperating teachers) wanted to see in her classes, instead of teaching the classes the way she would normally have done. For example, although this learner TESOL teacher said that she did not normally like to conduct pair work activities, she nevertheless attempted this in one class that was observed in her practicum because she heard that there should always be pair work for observed classes, since, as she said, "that was a popular technique" (Farrell, 2007a: 199). When I discovered the teacher was 'trying to give the observers what they want' I told her we would have the next evaluation without any evaluation checklist and so she should teach the way she would normally. It went very well after that.

Thus, TESOL teacher educator-supervisors, cooperating teachers, and learner TESOL teachers need to be very careful when using checklists of any kind to evaluate teaching at any level. The evaluative criteria used should represent the most current research available; and we need to make provisions, as time goes on, to revise those criteria to reflect current findings.

FEW SHARED VALUES AND ASSUMPTIONS ABOUT 'GOOD TEACHING'

As the above challenge suggests, research has moved away from a behaviorist view to teaching toward a more social constructivism view that suggests the process of learning to teach is a dynamic social activity mediated by interaction, language, and the context in which this all takes place (Cirocki, Madyarov, and Baecher, 2019). Indeed, teaching any subject matter becomes a highly personalized affair where no two teachers ever teach in the same way, and learning to teach in a TESOL teacher education program shifts from an "external . . . activity [that is] socially mediated to internal . . . control by individual [teacher] learners, which results in the transformation of both the self and the activity" (Johnson, 2009: 2). As a result, as Cirocki, Madyarov, and Baecher (2019: 2) maintain,

> the socio-cognitive development of student teachers can be regarded as the re-enactment of existing knowledge from other fellow teachers, and as the creation of new knowledge due to the lived experience and varied interactions with other members of the teaching community.

Learner TESOL teachers will develop their own personal view of what constitutes 'good' (or 'bad') teaching, and their priorities in structuring their practice will therefore depend crucially on their own philosophy, principles, and theories about language, learning, and teaching. The concept of 'good' or 'bad' teaching will also be linked to a particular teaching situation. Many new learner TESOL teachers willingly embrace this new approach where learning to teach is a reflective and constructive process beginning in a TESOL teacher education program, continuing through the novice-service years and into in-service. However, and unfortunately, this new view or value is not shared by all administrators in schools or even by some TESOL teacher educators, who remain resistant to relinquishing 'control *over*' for the 'control *with*' that this approach requires. Fortunately or unfortunately, we still do not have a common language to describe what 'good teaching' or 'bad teaching' is, and much of what is said reflects preconceived notions and experiences that are still rooted in behaviorism. Why else do we still have predetermined checklists in a 'one-size-fits-all' approach to defining teaching? On one side of the desk, again, we have learner teachers who are being evaluated on the basis of values and assumptions about 'good teaching' that may not be shared by their evaluators.

LACK OF PRECISION IN EVALUATING PERFORMANCE

As mentioned above, the 'fill-out-the-checklist' approach to teaching evaluation is still very popular in many TESOL teacher education programs worldwide, where learner TESOL teachers are often rated on single dichotomous scales such as 'satisfactory', 'good', or 'needs improvement', or rating scales such as '1 to 4' with '1' bad and '4' good, or 'low', 'medium', and 'high', or 'strongly agree', 'agree', 'disagree' or the like. However, there is little agreement among TESOL teacher educator-supervisors and/or cooperating teachers about what all these really mean; what, for example, constitutes a '3' or 'satisfactory' performance? What do all these mean to individual learner TESOL teachers? The answer is that we do not know, as again these take a 'one-size-fits-all' approach to evaluation. Learner TESOL teachers do not understand the ratings they are given and as a result also do not trust them, and some believe that their supervisors and administrators may give higher ratings to those who 'conform' best to what *they* expect, with little reference to the actual teaching. Indeed, anecdotal evidence suggests that the whole integrity of the evaluation process is often compromised by the perception of favoritism.

Looking at this from the TESOL teacher educator-supervisor's and/or the cooperating teacher's position can also reveal problems, as they too can feel the burden of evaluating by filling out such checklists that lack the precision to interpret their true meaning, as outlined above. Indeed, this can be especially true for many administrators, who may have left teaching a long time ago and have no recent formal training in how to conduct such teaching evaluations other than just to fill out checklists of what they perceive to be 'good' or 'bad' teaching.

HIERARCHICAL, ONE-WAY COMMUNICATION

In many TESOL contexts worldwide, evaluating learner TESOL teachers is still conducted in a traditional manner where TESOL teacher educator-supervisors and cooperating teachers hold all the power and evaluation is considered to be top-down and hierarchical. Typically, the TESOL teacher educator-supervisors and cooperating teachers conduct the observation and evaluation, fill out the checklist, and may take notes and give these in lecture mode as some kind of feedback on the learner TESOL teacher's teaching performance.

Such top-down, one-way communication can generate negative perceptions of TESOL teacher educator-supervisors and cooperating teachers always wanting to, or looking to, find some fault with the learner TESOL teacher's teaching, so that the perception of the evaluation turns out to be as a 'gotcha' experience. Thus, learner TESOL teachers who do the teaching can feel totally left out of the evaluation process because they are not really asked for their opinion (and many feel that they are given their opinion).

NO DIFFERENTIATION BETWEEN NOVICE AND EXPERIENCED PRACTITIONERS

When teaching evaluation involves the use of checklists for all teachers, then there is no consideration of differences in teaching experience. Teaching is probably the only profession that makes the same demands on novices as it does on the more experienced, because from the very moment a novice teacher enters the classroom, he or she is held to the same standards and subjected to the same procedures as his or her more experienced colleagues. Most other professions have an apprenticeship process where novices are officially recognized as being in a learning capacity and thus not held to common standards. This is not, however, reflected in the evaluation process in many institutions, where novice TESOL teachers and experienced TESOL teachers are evaluated using the same checklist/form with the idea that they have the same skills. It is important for TESOL teacher educator-supervisors and cooperating teachers and administrators to remember that novice TESOL teachers have not yet built up a repertoire of skills required to accomplish the same multiple tasks that more experienced teachers have been doing for years.

LIMITED ADMINISTRATOR EXPERTISE

In addition to the above challenges, learner TESOL teaching evaluations are carried out by many TESOL teacher educator-supervisors who themselves have limited expertise in teaching English as a second language in real classrooms, and as a result have limited knowledge about the students in the classroom in which they are evaluating the teacher. Learner TESOL teachers are much more knowledge-able about their students as well as the subject matter they teach than their TESOL teacher educator-supervisors. The exception here is that cooperating teachers are better placed in such a supervisory role; however, there are also problems with such supervision when learner TESOL teachers attempt to implement, for example, more communicative approaches in their lessons, but the cooperating teacher may favor grammar/translation approaches and thus give negative evaluations, because they do not agree with or understand these approaches that the learner TESOL teachers have learned in their TESOL teacher education program.

REFLECTIVE BREAK

- Have you ever experienced any of the six challenges outlined above in terms of how you were evaluated in your teaching at any time so far?
- Define what 'good' and 'bad' teaching mean for you. Give examples of both and say what these examples are based on: fact, research, opinion/feeling?
- What is your opinion of the (real) learner TESOL teaching evaluation form below?

INSTRUCTIONAL SKILLS	NO	YES	EXPERT	COMMENTS
TEACHER TALK MINIMUM Teacher talk is minimized, and students are given ample opportunity to practice.				
CORRECTION AND FEEDBACK Teacher gives immediate feedback on students' questions and errors. Teacher knows what to correct and what to ignore, gives effective encouragement and promotes self-correction.				
EQUAL ATTENTION Teacher gives attention to learners depending on individual need.				
ADEQUATE TIME Teacher allows appropriate amount of time for each activity.				
LEARNER-CENTERED INSTRUCTION Teacher engages students as a) learners and b) designers of their own learning.				

Reading and Discussion Task

Kari Hunt, Rachel Gurvitch, and Jacalyn Lund (2016) ask whether teaching evaluation is "done to you or with you" and point out that the traditional one-size-fits-all approach (or 'generic' evaluation) may not improve teacher effectiveness because it overlooks the actual context in which teaching takes place and disregards the subject matter being taught.

- Read their discussion of 'generic' teaching evaluations and compare it with the challenges noted above.
- Although the suggestions noted in the article are about how physical education teacher education programs can provide observation tools to their teacher candidates to improve teacher effectiveness, reflect on the implications of the contents of the article for TESOL.
- Discuss your findings with a colleague.

[Hunt, K., Gurvitch, R., and Lund, J. L. (2016). Teacher evaluation: Done to you or with you? *JOPERD: The Journal of Physical Education, Recreation & Dance, 87,* 9, 21-7]

"WE TEACH PLASTIC LESSONS TO PLEASE THEM": THE PROBLEM WITH 'CANNED' LESSONS

The result of a more traditional approach to teaching evaluation as discussed in the six challenges outlined above is that it places a wider divide between the supervisors who evaluate and the learner TESOL teachers who are being evaluated. From the learner TESOL teacher perspective, evaluation is 'given', and from the supervisor perspective, evaluation gets 'done'. We are not sure whether there is in fact any or much discussion before such an evaluation or even after, but the learner TESOL teacher is usually provided with some kind of feedback that aims to inform him or her how he or she has performed according to criteria laid out in a teaching evaluation form/checklist. This type of evaluation is sometimes called a 'walk-through' and it usually consists of the supervisor providing a subjective evaluation (be it positive or negative) of the teacher's ability to teach. Because of power differentials in a TESOL teacher education program, learner TESOL teachers do not feel they have the right in many instances either to question what is on the checklist or to seek a definition of what 'good teaching' (or 'bad teaching') really is, not to mention any positive or negative evaluation based solely on a 'one-size-fits-all' checklist for all learner TESOL teachers. In addition, experienced TESOL teachers are only all too aware that such subjective teaching evaluations are not really for developmental purposes, because they rarely produce any meaningful, lasting effects for the teacher to employ in his or her future teaching. Many TESOL teachers, both learners and experienced, therefore become very frustrated with the whole process of being evaluated and many find it a waste of their time, and this can lead to a culture of passivity and self-protection. Learner TESOL teachers try to produce 'canned' lessons (or as Ong'ondo and Borg, 2011, have put it: "We teach plastic lessons to please them") that may attempt to teach all 'behaviors' on the checklist, and/or coach their students before the observations.

Though for the most part well intentioned, these traditional systems are in fact burdensome and not helpful for learner TESOL teachers who are looking to improve their practice. Nor do they assist administrators in making difficult decisions regarding teacher performance. Thus both teachers and their supervisors can feel evaluation is a burden, if truth be told, and in the traditional approach, it ends up as a lose–lose situation for all concerned, most of all for the students who have to put up with stressed teachers and supervisors.

We must ask the question: why do we evaluate? Is it for summative purposes, to make decisions on screening out unsuitable teacher candidates from being certified, and to be able to provide defensible evidence for these reasons? Or is it for formative purposes, to enhance the professional skills of learner TESOL teachers by providing more constructive feedback, where TESOL teacher educator-supervisors and cooperating teachers collaborate with learner TESOL teachers in the collective effort to educate students? We can also ask whether these two are incompatible.

Some educators may think they are so, because the former is supposed to guarantee quality assurance while the latter is all about professional growth. Does accountability for quality assurance always require a strict, hierarchical, top-down approach? Yes, evaluations involve TESOL teacher educators making judgments, but they can also be made more assessable and objective if all stakeholders are involved in the process of making such judgments. TESOL can change the culture surrounding learner TESOL teaching evaluation away from top-down, checklist approaches to one of collegiality and collaboration, where the burden is shifted from being solely on the administrators' side to a sharing approach, and this can be achieved through reflective practice. Indeed, the principal argument of this book is that TESOL teacher education as a whole should be designed around the concept of reflective practice in which TESOL teacher educator-supervisors can mentor, rather than judge, learner TESOL teachers collaboratively on their journey to becoming competent professional TESOL teachers. In such a manner, teaching evaluation would be more of an assessment *for* teacher learning rather than the more traditional assessment *of* teacher learning, as happens currently.

REFLECTIVE BREAK

- Why do you think learner TESOL teachers would teach 'canned' (or plastic) lessons when being observed with a checklist?
- What is the difference between summative and formative teaching evaluations?
- Read Ussher and Earl (2010) and compare your answers above with what the authors say about both modes of assessment.
- Do you think that there is a way to include both types of assessment in learner TESOL teaching evaluations? In other words, how do you think learner TESOL teachers can be evaluated for the dual purposes of accountability and quality (summative) and professional development (formative)?

TEACHING EVALUATION: SHIFTING THE BURDEN

As mentioned above, many teaching evaluations of learner TESOL teachers tend to be top-down and given by an expert TESOL teacher educator-supervisor from a university and/or a cooperating teacher from within a school hierarchy, who evaluate the learner teachers using predetermined checklists or other such 'one-size-fits all' approaches. In addition, in many cases both supervisors and learner TESOL teachers consider this traditional approach not only outdated but burdensome, and as Mercado and Mann (2014) point out, we cannot reduce the complex world of the classroom to causal statements about what we think happens there, and so it is important that the voice of the learner TESOL teacher be included in all evaluations (Farrell, 2007a; Leshem and Bar-Hama, 2008). Such a participatory, collaborative approach to teaching evaluation means that the TESOL teacher educator-supervisor from a university, the cooperating teacher, and learner TESOL teachers share the burden of evaluation, as learner TESOL teachers are given more responsibility to be active in their own reflections, monitoring, and evaluation: a process that is, according to Roberts (1998: 305), "the only possible basis for long-term change."

In other words, we can *shift* the burden of evaluation from lying solely on the shoulders of administrators and supervisors to become more of a sharing process, where each learner TESOL teacher participates actively in the evaluation. So rather than the usual pitting of supervisor against learner TESOL teacher, which can develop into a hostile relationship involving one side exploiting power differentials and an overall lose–lose result, when all stakeholders instead approach teaching evaluation from a collaborative perspective, all sides enter a win–win situation because they all benefit from such a reflective, collaborative approach. Several factors will contribute to the success of promoting such a process to teaching evaluation, including reflection on practice, collaboration, and self-evaluation.

As the central premise of this book suggests, engaging in reflective practice encourages learner TESOL teachers to take more responsibility for making decisions in their practice, and such a reflective approach to teaching evaluation also encourages more ownership of the teacher's self-assessment through reflecting on practice. Some learner TESOL teachers will be able to engage in reflection on practice on their own, but most will find it difficult; however, teaching evaluation that has a foundation of collaboration is better suited to help all stakeholders achieve more positive results. In addition, such a reflective, collaborative approach to teaching evaluation offers a forum where the learner TESOL teachers' voices can be heard as they provide their insiders' view of their practice through the process of self-evaluation. Learner TESOL teachers will have a keen understanding of their own classrooms and students when provided with a safe, respectful, and trusting environment in which to share these self-evaluations, they can grow professionally.

Of course, within the whole process of teaching evaluation, TESOL teacher educator-supervisors will retain most of the responsibility for helping learner TESOL teachers carry out self-evaluation, and as such they play an important role mentoring learner TESOL teachers through this reflective, collaborative process. One of their main challenges will be to provide reflective activities that can promote such self-reflection and that the learner TESOL teachers will recognize and view as valuable to their development. TESOL teacher educator-supervisors can help facilitate the reflections of learner TESOL teachers as they engage in self-evaluation using a number of different mediational reflective tools and procedures. These include dialogue among all stakeholders in critical friends groups, critical incident analysis, team teaching and/or peer coaching arrangements, video-based observations, and writing in a teaching journal for self-reflection and/or in a dialogic journal to share with peers and supervisors (all of these have been outlined and discussed in detail in Chapter 4). Video-based classroom observations are especially appropriate for teaching evaluation for self-reflection and the development of teaching. Indeed, Mercado and Baecher (2014: 75) maintain that self-observation through video analysis can be "a primary catalyst for promoting self-examination, self-assessment, and self-reflection, all of which eventually led to improving instructional effectiveness and student learning."

The above outline of how we can include learner TESOL teachers in the process of evaluating their teaching, through the use of reflecting on 'collaboratively produced artifacts' and/or self-evaluation, does not have to fully replace teacher educators and supervisors having to make decisions about learner TESOL teachers' teaching approaches and methods. I fully recognize that it is a fact of life of most TESOL teacher education programs that decisions must be made and grades given to fulfill institutional and government-mandated standards that must be met for funding and so on, but as mentioned this should be in an 'assessment *for* teacher learning' approach, and can thus better complement such practices and make evaluations of teaching practice easier for those in supervisory positions. In order to make all this work, the novice-service framework to TESOL teacher education becomes even more important. In this framework, learner TESOL teachers, teacher educators, school supervisors, mentors, institutions, and government funding agencies must collaborate with each other so that we provide a meaningful experience for all concerned.

REFLECTIVE BREAK

- Do you think the burden of learner TESOL teaching evaluation should be shifted from the shoulders of supervisors and shared by all?
- Are you willing to take on more responsibility for self-reflection and self-assessment and to communicate this assessment to your supervisors?
- What reflective activities that you have read so far in this book do you think can best promote such self-reflection and self-assessment?
- How do you think you can best report your self-reflection and self-assessment to your supervisors?

TEACHING PORTFOLIOS

The final question asked in the reflective break above is about how to report all the information about learner TESOL teachers' self-reflection and self-assessment to their supervisors. When all of the information outlined above is gathered about teaching, it should be put together to give a full picture of the learner TESOL teacher's journey through the TESOL teacher education program from the start during coursework, through teaching practice and graduation. With a reflective practice approach already adopted in the TESOL teacher education program, learner TESOL teachers will have reflected at various times in the program using the framework for reflecting on practice outlined in Chapter 3, to compile information about their philosophy, principles, theory, practice, and beyond practice. When all of this information is gathered together, it begins to create a picture and story of who the learner TESOL teacher has become as a developing TESOL professional. As mentioned in Chapters 3 and 4, such reflections can be through dialogue and/or writing, with most developed in a combination of these two. For example, starting at stage 1 or philosophy, learner TESOL teachers look at the self and ask questions about their professional identity, where that came from, and where they want to go. Then stage 2 learner TESOL teachers examine their assumptions, beliefs, and conceptions about teaching and learning English as a second or foreign language. For stage 3, they examine their theory of practice, followed by a careful examination of their actual teaching during teaching practice in stage 4.

At stage 4, learner TESOL teachers can really showcase who they are in the classroom and how the previous stages (philosophy, principles, and theory) are represented in their teaching. They can do this by including a statement of philosophy, beliefs, and values regarding language teaching and learning, as well as how they plan lessons. Specifically, it will be important to give a clear picture of how they teach, and therefore a video of a lesson with a lesson plan and student work examples should be included when gathering information about practice, as well as a written description of what the learner TESOL teacher was teaching and after-lesson reflection. Also any feedback, written or otherwise, from a supervisor and/or an administrator should be included, with any classroom observation report from a peer or cooperating teacher.

After reflecting on practice and gathering all the information from these reflections, learner TESOL teachers critically reflect beyond their practice, stage 5, which can include a careful examination of how their teaching and the school they teach in reflect their values. When the information obtained from each of the stages in the framework is compiled by learner TESOL teachers, they can discuss the contents with their supervisors and explain why they choose to include particular items in the collection and what their meaning is for them as learner teachers. Learner TESOL teachers can use the contents to talk about who they are now as TESOL teachers and who they want to become in the future when they begin their teaching careers.

REFLECTIVE BREAK

- The following is an example of the beyond-practice reflections of a learner TESOL teacher (in his own words) as he is about to graduate from an MA TESOL program. What is your understanding of his critical reflections beyond practice? Check your own written reflections beyond practice that you completed in chapter 3 and compare them with the learner TESOL teacher's reflections below. Would you change yours in any way? Why or why not?

I appreciate the critical theory lens which suggests concerning critical reflection that teachers should look at "the influence of the context of knowledge and power in order to be able to understand how social context influences people' s assumptions and how people in turn influence these." This notion really interests me on my thinking regarding to the purpose and end of TESOL professionals based on my philosophy and beliefs. What I have been exploring and constructing is the essence and goals of the personal practices in English language education. I have been trying to build the bridge between my own practice according to my own experience as a private English language tutor teaching English to primary school students, and the possibilities and opportunities of producing social benefits out of TESOL instruction. Brookfield [1995] has mentioned about how critical reflection could benefits teacher in their practice, I have found three points in the list which could be helpful for me to construct my bridge as to the connection with social benefits. Firstly, make informed decisions and actions in teaching. Having examined the consequences (theoretically, practically, socially and morally), teacher can justify to themselves their decision-making; Secondly, because teachers have intensively reflected on philosophy, principles and theory, they developed a rationale for practice; Lastly, they discover a voice, which means that after having critically reflected on practice, teachers can now speak to others about their practice in an organized manner.

After having constructed the foundation of TESOL practices through my critical reflection, I can now build that relationship between the essence of TESOL profession with the social significance according to my own view. One aspect related to the concept of critical reflection is teaching as a moral activity or the teaching of values and morals. This is also the most exciting part for me, because this is how and which I based my critically reflective stance upon. My critical stance towards TESOL profession is that language teachers and tutors should properly convey the teaching of morals and values during their practices rather than trying to avoid them. In this process they put certain significance into the progress of society as being part of social relationship. As Dewey (1933: 58) noted, "every subject, every method of instruction, every incident of school life [is] pregnant with moral possibility." There is no doubt that the teacher, the curricula and the community have important influences on the moral growth of both teachers and students. In order to bridge the gap between teaching language with students in daily practices and create opportunities for the benefits of society, teachers in their TESOL professions have an obligation to influence the morality and value-forming of their students. This also conforms with my belief that teaching is not merely a profession, but more than that, it is a vocation. In the teaching practice, as human being, ESOL teachers 'form' human minds through their reflected practices of language instructions. They do this by choosing the content of lesson, by the way they carry themselves in each class, and by how they interact with and evaluate their students.

While I am talking about moralities, I don't see them as absolute fossilized dogmas whereas teachers should act as centers of activities and students mere receivers. Critical reflection deals with the whole being of the teacher: the contemplative, reflective, cognitive, emotional, ethical, moral and social aspects of both our professional and personal lives. When I am doing reflection beyond practice, I transform reflection from technical to a critical sense in which process I make multiple judgments about "whether professional activity is equitable, just, and respectful of persons or not" (Hatton and Smith, 1995: 35). Through the process of reflection beyond practices and critical reflection, I realized that as TESOL professionals, we are called to enlighten our students with moral perspectives and develop all kinds of creative ideas which could not only reform us as teachers, but also our students, to become transformative intellectuals within their own contexts and carry on the values and moralities of their own society. Brookfield (1995: 126) has reminded teachers that they must be on guard against "dominant or hegemonic assumptions which may influence our practice unwittingly." As we unearth and identify previously unquestioned norms in society and the community within the contexts which they are practiced, we renew and reform every field both in our teaching experience and our lives according to our reflection.

In addition to the information from each stage of the framework for reflecting on practice outlined in Chapter 3, other documents can be added to include a statement of the learner TESOL teacher's development plans and confirm various educational and professional qualifications, such as a résumé, copies of degrees, certificates, honors and awards held, and a list of memberships in TESOL-related professional organizations. For example, learner TESOL teachers can write up a professional development plan that outlines what they intend to achieve professionally in the near future, such as attending certain conferences, seminars, and in-service courses that can upgrade skills, researching certain topics and action research projects that can make one a more effective teacher (see Chapter 7 for more on this), and updating IT-related technical skills online. Learner TESOL teachers can include also descriptions of any leadership positions held, such as head of graduate student committees, curriculum development units, or local TESOL organizations, and any other leadership initiatives.

When all of these reflections are documented, they can be compiled in one place in order to construct a personal teaching portfolio, which can then be used as a basis for discussion with the supervisor and also for the purposes of evaluating the learner TESOL teacher. The creation of a teaching portfolio can provide learner TESOL teachers with a structure and a process for documenting and reflecting on their TESOL teacher education. However, the compilation and development of the portfolio should be mentored by the TESOL teacher educator-supervisor, so that the learner TESOL teacher knows what is important in terms of content for self-evaluation and can generate collaborative discussions that will be used as a basis for evaluation.

In terms of the reality of supervisors having to give evidence of learner teaching as having achieved standards of some kind, mentioned above, it may be necessary to devise some kind of scoring system for such portfolios, and of course this will require careful reflections by teacher educators and supervisors, because some scoring guides can be so detailed that supervisor evaluators can become overwhelmed, while other guides may be so general as to render the scoring process too subjective. The key, then, is to come up with a balanced scoring system. Although the contents of portfolios may vary greatly, each portfolio entry can have a familiar structure that teacher educators can use in collaboration with supervisors and learner teachers, such as the following (adapted from Farrell and Jacobs, 2011):

- *Description*: What is this entry?
- *Reason*: Why did I include this entry?
- *Opinion*: Why do I think this entry is important? What am I proud of in this entry?
- *Reflection*: What did I accomplish with this entry?
- *Supervisor and cooperating teacher comments* (optional): Teacher educators, supervisors, and/or cooperating teachers can add comments after each entry.

Scores can be allotted to each item above in whatever manner all stakeholders agree is appropriate, as each teacher education program decides the relevant scoring weights of each.

Regarding the format of teaching portfolios, each can be paper-based or electronic. Studies of blog-based teaching portfolios have shown positive results in scaffolding reflection, mediating teacher education reform, fostering teacher competencies, and having a positive impact on teacher professional development as well as overall on the institutional environment. Tang (2009) reported that as long as members of online learning communities remain active they can obtain continuous feedback and support from peers and mentors, and discussion and resources can be stored and retrieved at any time, thus providing a powerful tool for the professional development of language teachers. As Farr and O'Riordan (2017: 24) maintain, such blogs and e-portfolios in TESOL teacher education programs are "good mechanisms to promote individual and collaborative reflective practices."

Another type of electronic portfolio, the European Portfolio for Student Teachers of Languages (EPOSTL), was adopted in Europe as a self-assessment tool. The main aim of the EPOSTL is, according to Mirici and Hergüner (2015), to encourage pre-service teachers to reflect on their competences and on the underlying knowledge which feeds these competences. Other aims include the promotion of discussions among pre-service teachers, their peers, and teacher educators and mentors. The idea is that the EPOSTL is an instrument that can help chart the progress of pre-service teachers. Mirici and Hergüner (2015) examined the impact of Turkish pre-service TESOL teachers' use of the EPOSTL as a self-assessment tool, and reported that it not only provided the pre-service TESOL teachers with time and space for reflection on their achievements, but also gave them the opportunity to regularly track their own progress and to determine individual goals for their own learning situations.

It should also be remembered that a teaching portfolio is not a one-time snapshot of where the learner TESOL teacher is at present; rather, it is an evolving collection of carefully selected professional experiences, thoughts, and goals. Thus, teacher portfolios can act as a 'mirror' and a 'map'. The portfolio as a 'mirror' allows teachers to 'see' their development in terms of their principles and practices over time. The portfolio as a 'map' symbolizes creating a plan and setting goals for where teachers want to go in the future. Both of these metaphors are an excellent means for providing structure for teachers who want to engage in self-reflection and self-assessment, and both can act as a catalyst for discussions about assessment with their supervisors.

REFLECTIVE BREAK

- What is your understanding of a teacher portfolio?
- Vanessa Sheu, as part of her MA TESOL program at Columbia University, New York, completed what she called a Teaching E-folio. The contents include a welcome, her philosophy, experience, lesson plans and syllabus, and a teaching video. She has granted permission for you to view these contents at: https://vsheu. weebly.com. Review her portfolio and comment on the contents and what you would include similarly in your portfolio.
- Review the EPOSTL, which is freely available on the internet and includes an introduction, personal statement, self-assessment, and dossier in an 83-page document, and comment on the contents.

- Compile your own teaching portfolio using the information from the activities above.
- Discuss the contents of your teaching portfolio with a colleague and/or with your TESOL teacher educator-supervisor.
  - Do you think your teaching portfolio will give a full picture of who you are as a learner TESOL teacher?
  - How do these contents represent you as a TESOL teacher?

Reading and Discussion Task

Cynthia Houston (2016) has noted that reflective practice is an important skill that teachers must develop to be able to assess the effectiveness of their teaching and modify their instructional behavior. In many education programs reflective narratives, which are often part of teaching portfolios, are intended to assess students' abilities in these areas. Her study explored the portfolio narratives of students in an advanced preparation program to determine the nature and quality of their reflective writing. Results of a content analysis indicate that the level of student reflectivity improved when a reflective writing scaffolding tool was used to assist students with their reflective writing tasks.

- Read the paper and consider what reflective writing scaffolding tools were used and how these can help you write your portfolio narratives.
- Discuss your findings with a colleague.

[Houston, C. R. (2016). Do scaffolding tools improve reflective writing in professional portfolios? A content analysis of reflective writing in an advanced preparation program. *Action in Teacher Education*, *38*, 4, 399–409]

The creation of a teaching portfolio provides learner TESOL teachers with a structured approach to self-evaluation and self-reflection and a basis for collaborative discussions to explain to their supervisors who they are, and how and why they teach the way they do. Such an approach to teaching evaluation in a TESOL teacher education program enhances TESOL teacher educator-supervisor, cooperating teacher, and learner TESOL teacher collaborative discussions in a way that mutually benefits all.

CONCLUSION

The perennial questions that remain in all education, and especially TESOL teacher education, are what is 'good teaching', what is 'bad teaching', and how do or can we measure these? Just as beauty is in the eye of the beholder, so too may definitions of 'good teaching' and 'bad teaching' be in the eye of the beholder within TESOL teacher education programs for learner TESOL teachers, and out in schools and institutions for early career TESOL teachers. What is clear is that if TESOL teacher educator-supervisors and/or school-appointed supervisors approach teaching evaluations with their top-down, personal definition of what 'good/bad teaching' should be, and/or use traditional checklists with predetermined categories in a one-size-fits-all approach, then everybody loses. Learner TESOL teachers and early career TESOL teachers are being judged on ill-defined, unfair, and unrepresentative criteria about their practice, and as a result little of no development takes place. For too long now in the TESOL profession such teaching evaluations have been used and abused in order to exert control over teachers: the whole exercise results in a build-up of resentment over time, and not only do students suffer, but the institution as a whole suffers from unhappy teachers trying to provide 'them' (supervisors) with what they want, or plastic lessons. However, if a more collaborative, reflective approach to teaching evaluation is adopted in TESOL teacher education programs and the early career years, so that learner TESOL teachers and early career TESOL teachers are included in the evaluation process by being allowed to select what best represents their best practices, compiled in their teaching portfolios, then they can be better supported in their professional development journey as TESOL professionals.

7

TESOL TEACHER EDUCATION:
THE EARLY CAREER YEARS

PREAMBLE

The following is a reflection by a novice TESOL teacher wondering about whether she should remain as a teacher after three years in the job.

Should I stay or should I go? I asked myself this question after three years of teaching ESL because I was not satisfied with my experiences up to this. In fact, I had planned to take a break, but a colleague asked me to stay on one more year to see how things would go. I hope they go much better because I am fed up with the school and especially the administration because I feel they do not care much for us ESL teachers and only care about making money for the school itself to make the administrators look good. After three years teaching at that school, I feel the administration do not know us at all and especially our roles as ESL teachers and I really feel underappreciated by them. I have felt constant pressure to pass our students at each level even if some did not deserve it or were ready for the next level and of course we teachers all were indirectly pushed to 'keep the clients happy' – I actually heard this statement. The administration's top priority besides getting new students is to retain the ones that are there now, and it starts to trigger that sense of 'we've got to keep the customers happy. We've got to keep them paying their money and that kind of thing.' We have been made work extra with student retention in mind having to deal with extra-curricular activities and we even bring our students over to our house for dinner and the like even though it is not in our job description nor do they refund any of the extra expenses associated with this although I also like to do this for my students but it would be nice to be appreciated for doing it by the administration. So, I am trying to find a balance between trying to be a 'good teacher' and the many different non-teaching duties that the ESL teachers must do. This all wears you down after a while and now after three years I am in this funk with the whole idea of continuing my career as an ESL teacher.

INTRODUCTION

As mentioned in Chapter 2, most who enter the profession as TESOL teachers really love their job but, at the same time, continue to face dilemmas and obstacles of all kinds during their careers, some of which, if severe enough in the early career years, can lead them to quit teaching altogether. Indeed, the early career TESOL teacher in the opening preamble above shows she is at a really vulnerable point in her early career and is crying out for some help and guidance. Had she not, it is quite possible that she would have already quit the profession. As also mentioned in Chapter 2, the 'but' in the statement 'I love teaching but, . . .' is an indication of the presence of a dilemma being faced and needs to be explored in more detail, especially if such a statement is made by an early career TESOL teacher.

We have also noted that unfortunately teaching as a profession tends to 'eat its young'. As Fantilli and McDougall (2009) have noted, nearly one half of all novice teachers have considered leaving the teaching profession because of the resultant increases in stress levels, anxiety, and overall mental tension, just as the novice TESOL teacher in the opening preamble above is suffering from these. Similar mental stresses have also been reported from novice TESOL teachers, and with a similar problem of many left without any support to help them cope (Higginbotham, 2019).

In addition, some researchers in general education have discovered a noticeable spike in the numbers of early career teachers who leave at the end of their third and fourth years, suggesting that early career teacher attrition may well begin before teachers actually leave the profession (e.g. in the first year) (Clandinin et al., 2015). These first years as a TESOL teacher are crucially important for all stakeholders, as Feiman-Nemser (2001b: 1026) points out, because they "are an intense and formative time in learning to teach, influencing not only whether people remain in teaching but what kind of teacher they become." Learner teachers' experiences in their teaching practice and early career years are influenced by expectations formed during their teacher education programs, and if some of these are unrealistic, they leave early career teachers in a very vulnerable position, as they are unable to cope with the reality of the real teaching world; many suffer this 'praxis shock' (Friedman, 2004).

Consequently, it is imperative for the health of the TESOL profession to continue to support learner TESOL teachers beyond the TESOL teacher education program and well into the early career years, so that they can be helped through any 'transition traumas' they may experience at this crucial time. This support can be provided through a 'novice-service' framework where TESOL teacher educator-supervisors continue to act as mentors, along with cooperating teachers and any school-appointed mentors, for learner TESOL teachers throughout their early career years. This continued involvement, although not practiced at present in many contexts, is vitally important for early career TESOL teachers' development, because the knowledge they have gained during their TESOL teacher education programs can be overshadowed by the new school culture and its demands, if it is allowed to dictate the norms of their pedagogical practices without any reference to the teacher education program. At present, learner TESOL teachers are educated in a 'silo' type of process where they graduate and begin teacher careers completely separate from their initial program and teacher educators, and left to their only means of survival: conforming to the standards of practice that exist within the schools they enter, many of which may differ completely from what they learned in their teacher education program. This chapter outlines and discusses some of the adaptation challenges learner TESOL teachers face during their early career years, and how continued collaboration between TESOL teacher educators, school mentors, and learner TESOL teachers can help reduce the gap between early visions built up during the teacher education program, on the one hand, and the reality of being in a real classroom, on the other.

REFLECTIVE BREAK

- As a result of taking your TESOL teacher education program, including practice teaching, do now you feel prepared for your early career teaching experiences? Why or why not?
- What are you looking forward to most during your early career teaching years?
- What are you not looking forward to most during your early career years?
- What do you think will be your greatest challenges during your early career teaching years?
- How can you overcome such challenges?
- What do you think will be the greatest rewards you will receive?
- Who do you think you can you go to for support or advice during your early career years?

Reading and Discussion Task

Jackie Manuel, Janet Dutton, and Don Carter's (2018) paper "As much as I love being in the classroom . . ." reports on Australian English teachers' work and lives, including their perspectives on workload, motivation, work satisfaction, well-being, and career intentions.

- Read and summarize their findings about the impact of high workloads on the quality of teaching. What would you do if you found yourself in a similar situation when you begin your early career teaching years?
- Discuss your findings with a colleague.

[Manuel, J., Dutton, J., and Carter, D. (2018). "As much as I love being in the classroom . . .": Understanding secondary English teachers' workload. *English in Australia*, *53*, 3, 5-22]

EARLY CAREER YEARS: EXPECTATION VERSUS REALITY

For many early career teachers, the difference between initial expectations of what they perceived the education profession to be, on the one hand, and the realities they then face in a real classroom, on the other, can be so deflating that, after their first year, they begin to realize that teaching is a far more complex career than they had first envisioned (Melnick and Meister, 2008). The first years of teaching can be an anxiety-provoking experience because it involves a balancing act between learning to teach (i.e. furthering what was started during the teacher education program) and, at the same time, attempting to develop an identity within an established culture in a school organization (Calderhead, 1992).

Indeed, several scholars have identified a developing sequence of concerns and adaptation challenges that many early career teachers face during these first years of teaching. Fuller and Brown (1975), for example, describe two general stages of developmental challenges faced by novice teachers. The first stage is characterized by survival and mastery while the second stage presents an either/or dichotomy of development: either settling into a state of resistance to change or staying open to adaptation and change. Vonk (1989) also identified two distinct phases in the professional development of novice teachers: the 'threshold' phase and the 'growing into the profession' phase. The 'threshold' phase is where novice teachers transition from the teacher education program into full-time teaching during their first year. The 'growing into the profession' phase occurs during the following four years, when teachers begin to focus more on their teaching skills and competencies, and culminates with colleagues accepting the novice as a real teacher, usually at the end of the fifth year. Lacey (1977) advocated that novice teachers move through three phases, the 'honeymoon' phase, the 'crisis' phase, and the either/or dichotomy of 'failure' or 'getting by' phase. Although Bullough and Baughman (1993) caution against the notion that teachers move neatly through each stage, what all these stage theorists have in common is their strong recommendation that early career teachers must receive some kind of support, especially in the 'growing into the profession' phase and before they reach the 'failure' phase.

There is general agreement that, for the most part, learner TESOL teachers receive good-quality mentoring throughout the period of their TESOL teacher education program, from TESOL teacher educators and/or cooperating teachers during their teaching practice. As the previous chapter has indicated, learner TESOL teachers receive various forms of important feedback from these mentors during these years; however, when they enter their early career teaching years this support diminishes and even stops, as many become even more isolated behind their closed classroom doors (Farrell, 2016a). This is problematic because early career teachers really yearn for and miss the type of feedback they received within the teacher education program and teaching practice. In fact, they suffer from a complete lack of support in many cases, because they rarely receive the frequent feedback on their instructional practice that they sorely need in order to be able to grow as teachers. Indeed, the level of the support they get or do not get is a really good predictor of whether early career teachers decide to stay or leave the profession. As Korthagen (2004: 91) points out:

> The loss of ideals, and what people experience as a lack of support when it comes to the realization of those ideals, play an important part in cases of burnout and, in some cases, the decision to resign from their position.

When reviewing research about the various reasons that early career teachers have given for resigning and leaving the teaching profession for good, most studies report the top three reasons for leaving as (1) a lack of support, (2) excessive workloads, and (3) feeling unprepared after taking their pre-service teacher education program.

REFLECTIVE BREAK

- Below is the list of reasons the early career teachers cited in the research above gave for leaving the profession. Rank them in order of importance as worries for you teaching in your early career years.

Reasons for leaving the teaching profession	Rank
Lack of support	
Excessive workload	
Feeling unprepared	
Poor climate/physical environment	
Relationship with students and/or students' parents	
Salary	
Personal	
Lack of induction/internships	
Too much personal investment (e.g. time/energy)	
Lack of professional development	
Lack of future prospects	
Lack of collegiality	
Lack of mentorship	
Lack of access to educational materials	
Lack of autonomy	

- Are there any more issues you would like to add to the list above?
- Change each of the above issues into a more positive statement such as "appropriate support," "appropriate workload," "sufficiently prepared," "good work environment or climate," and so on, and then outline how you would turn the negatives into positive experiences for you as a novice TESOL teacher during your early careers.
- Discuss each of these with a colleague and compare your ideas on how you would both achieve each of the above as a positive experience for you during your early career years.

Reading and Discussion Task

Jackie Sydnor (2017) explored the experiences of two first year teachers' tensions involved in becoming a teacher as they transitioned from learner teachers to early career teachers. The study illuminates the multiple discourses such beginning teachers must negotiate as they determine the kind of teacher they will become.

- Read the paper and the author's recommendations of the need for pre-service teachers to create and revise clear visions of becoming a teacher.
- Discuss your findings with a colleague.

[Sydnor, J. (2017). "I didn't realize how hard it would be!" Tensions and transformations in becoming a teacher. *Action in Teacher Education, 39*, 2, 218-36]

EARLY CAREER YEARS: SUPPORT

As stated above, the top reason for early career teachers leaving was experiencing a lack of support in their new position (see also Chapter 2 for Hennerby-Leung, Gayton, Hu, and Chen, 2019, whose research reported that the professional community plays a key role in providing mentoring and support for novice TESOL teachers). That said, not everyone in a school may reach out readily to incoming novice teachers because each school context will have a pecking order, which is not always acknowledged in the learning-to-teach literature (Renard, 2003). In many schools there may be little sympathy among the more experienced teacher colleagues for the plight of early career teachers, because they "often feel that they have paid their dues and that new teachers must do the same. They may view surviving the first few years of teaching as a badge of honor" (Renard, 2003: 63-4). Yet new teachers really want help from within their new context because they feel lost even from their first day. As Johnson (2006: 45) put it, "New teachers yearn for professional colleagues who can help them acclimate to their school's unique culture, help them solve the complicated, daily dilemmas of classroom teaching and guide their ongoing learning."

Novice teachers really want to work in a school where they feel they belong and in a supportive environment. Thus it is the school's role to establish such a supportive environment, especially for incoming novice teachers, where they have emotional support, their professional development is encouraged, and they are encouraged to establish professional relationships with their more experienced colleagues (Farrell, 2003). Such support from the school is vital if the profession wants to avoid early career teacher attrition, and as such, early career teacher support should not be considered a one-off at the start of a learner TESOL teacher's career but rather a sustained program, initiated by the school, in which the novice teacher is placed and where aid is available to the teacher in developing throughout his or her early career years (DeAngelis, Wall, and Che, 2013).

Many schools offer induction programs that, ideally, formally introduce new teachers to the workplace by introducing them to the administration and to both established teachers within the institution and other early career teachers. The purpose of an induction program, according to Schlechty (1990: 37), is "to develop in new members of an occupation those skills, forms of knowledge, attitudes and values that are necessary to effectively carry out their occupational roles." The usual induction program in many schools includes the giving of pamphlets that outline the school rules and regulations, and other school documents that explain the school system, to novice teachers, as well as the appointment of a mentor to guide novice teachers through their first years.

In a review of induction programs for first year teachers, Ingersoll (2012: 50) reports that there is strong evidence demonstrating that early career support, such as induction programs with comprehensive packages that include components such as mentoring, can significantly reduce the likelihood of attrition; however, "only 5% of beginners received such a . . . package." During an interview with Erwing and Smith (2003: 17), a third year kindergarten teacher in Australia who experienced an induction program shared her perceptions of what she had experienced and what she had wished she had experienced, emphasizing the value of both induction programs in particular and early career support in general when she stated that:

> The other staff [was] standoffish because of [her] youth and the fact that [she] was targeted. . . . New teachers need to be inducted into a supportive environment, leadership needs to be shared and modelled and new teachers need to understand how decisions in the school are made.

Although these induction programs can help new teachers to develop a support system and ultimately feel more supported throughout the early stages of their career, research has reported that the quality of these programs varies drastically by region and institution, from being highly involved to completely non-existent (Kardos, Johnson, Peske, Kauffman, and Liu, 2001). When implemented successfully, they can provide early career teachers with confidence by allowing them to familiarize themselves with the school rather than being 'thrown into the job', to learn where and how to access educational materials if they are available, and most importantly to build rapport with the other teachers and establish a support system.

Most induction programs also include a mentorship component where an early career teacher is paired with an established teacher as a support resource (see Chapter 4 for more on mentoring). Such an established teacher mentor can help novice teachers to adapt to the school and also "learn about their roles as teachers" (Schwille, Dembele, and Schubert, 2007: 89).

In addition, the mentor also benefits from helping to socialize the novice teacher into all aspects of the school because the mentor himself or herself must reflect on these aspects before being able to articulate them coherently to the novice teacher (Hobson, Ashby, Malderez, and Tomlinson, 2009). Indeed, in a survey by Manuel and Carter (2016) of early career TESOL teachers who did not experience a mentoring program, "relationships with colleagues" was rated among the top four threats to teacher motivation, with only 58 percent of early career teachers reporting that they felt well supported by their colleagues, and 50 percent stating that their values as a teacher had been challenged either by their peers or by 'the system' at some point. These numbers emphasize the value of implementing induction programs with mentorship components. However, it is important to also consider whether or not receiving support from colleagues is sufficient for early career teachers if they feel unsupported by management and their administration. As Hammond and Cartwright (2003: 54) maintain:

> Those who received support and encouragement are more likely to feel optimistic about the future, and to expect to take on new challenges [while] others may . . . begin to feel dissatisfied with teaching as a career, sometimes because of discontent with senior management.

In terms of substance, Feiman-Nemser (2001a: 18) maintains that early career teachers need to develop an inquiring stance during their first years through the concept of "educative mentoring," where the mentor encourages *reflection* (a core assumption of this book) that supports early career teachers to learn in and from their practice, and to use the knowledge gained from such systematic reflections to guide them forward throughout their teaching careers. Thus, reflection, effective teacher mentoring, and continued 'educative mentoring', as well as the informal social support that teachers provide to one another, such as collaborating with each other on planning or instruction, during these crucial early career years can result in reduced rates of early career teacher attrition (Kelly and Antonio, 2016).

Nonetheless, it should also not be forgotten that teacher retention really begins with and during initial TESOL teacher education programs, in that novice teachers' sense of preparedness to be able to identify and address the various influences, obstacles, and challenges they will face during those early years strongly relates to their successful socialization into the profession (Darling-Hammond, Chung, and Frelow, 2002). In fact, Ingersoll, Merrill, and May (2014) have noted that teachers trained in preparation programs with a focus on applied teaching skills (i.e. practical experience, feedback, and classroom observation) were less likely to leave the profession after their first year of teaching than those who were trained in a more theory-focused program (see also Chapter 2 for more on this). Thus, and as mentioned before, TESOL teacher preparation programs should balance theory with practice while also discussing the multiple dimensions present in the teaching job, so that early career TESOL teachers can make sense of not only the classroom but also the school where they must teach. In other words, early career TESOL teachers need to be able to understand that teaching ESL does not only involve providing classroom lessons, but also that their working conditions are situated and influenced by conditions in the school in which they work. The development of such knowledge, begun in TESOL teacher education programs and continued during teacher induction/mentoring in the schools in which they are placed, can have a positive effect on early career TESOL teachers' retention.

However, early career teachers must also be realistic about what they expect from an induction program and mentorship during their early career years. Gallant and Riley (2017) point out that sometimes there may be somewhat of a disconnect between these expectations and the reality of what they experience, and sometimes this can all be put down to poor communications between the teacher and the mentor. As Gallant and Riley (2017: 901) report, one early career teacher said that the school-appointed mentor abandoned him to teach two different levels on his own, although the mentor was still "officially on the books at the school . . . [as] a mentor." This disconnect suggests a lack of communication among teachers, as well as between teachers and their superiors, of what is expected from all parties (early career teacher, teacher mentor, and administration) in the mentorship and induction programs. The same lack of both collegial and administrative support was outlined in the opening preamble to this chapter. Therefore, any induction program with the inclusion of formal mentorship must be built on a clear understanding on all sides of exactly what processes of the early career teachers' learning it is intended to support and how this will be accomplished (Furlong and Maynard, 1995). Thus, and as pointed out throughout the contents of this book, it is important for TESOL teacher preparation programs and the schools in which early career TESOL teachers work to be aware of the various adaptation challenges that early career ESL teachers are faced with during their first years, so that all stakeholders can reflectively collaborate to ensure they thrive as TESOL teachers throughout their careers.

REFLECTIVE BREAK

- What would you expect to see in an induction program in the school where you are placed during your early career teaching years?
- How do you expect communications to take place between you, your TESOL teacher educator-supervisor/mentor, and the school-appointed mentor during your early career years?
- What do you expect from a school-appointed mentor?
- What do you think your role is as an early career TESOL teacher in order to become a successful teacher in the school in which you are placed?

Reading and Discussion Task

Shirley Andrews, Linda Gilbert, and Ellice Martin (2007) investigated teacher attrition issues and induction/mentoring practices to improve retention rates, especially in the critical first years of teaching. They asked: what types of support do beginning teachers value, and what do they actually receive? What types of support do administrators believe are provided for the beginning teachers in their schools?

- Read the paper and the authors' answers to the questions. What is your understanding of these supports and why would there be discrepancies reported between beginning teachers and the administrators?
- Discuss your findings with a colleague.

[Andrews, S. P., Gilbert, L. S., and Martin, E. P. (2007). The first years of teaching: Disparities in perceptions of support. *Action in Teacher Education, 28,* 4–13]

EARLY CAREER YEARS: IDENTITY DEVELOPMENT

In the above outline of the critical engagement with the context of teaching, one of the important other challenges that early career TESOL teachers will also be reflecting on is their own identities within the formal and informal spaces of school, and across personal and professional contexts, in the early career teaching years (Pennington and Richards, 2016; OECD, 2018a, 2018b). As Burns and Richards (2009: 5) have noted, identity "reflects how individuals see themselves and how they enact their roles within different settings." This includes all the functional roles a teacher plays while performing his or her duties, what he or she feels and believes about teaching and being a teacher, and how these are shaped by a teacher's evolving (and ever changing) *philosophy, principles, theory, practice,* and *beyond practice* (for more on these see Chapter 3).

Professional role identity includes the concept of 'self' as an essential consideration of a teacher's self-image, but many teachers' conceptualizations of their self-image and the various roles they play are usually held at the tacit level of awareness. Indeed, Ji Hong (2010) explored the different perceptions of pre-service and beginning teachers' professional identity in relation to their decisions to leave the profession. The findings of this study showed that pre-service teachers tended to have naive and idealistic perceptions of teaching, and dropout teachers showed most emotional burnout. As such, reflection and reflective practice are a key component associated with unlocking this tacit understanding of the self so that teachers can become more aware of who they are professionally; as Beijaard, Meijer, and Verloop (2004: 114) have pointed out, "it is impossible to speak about the 'self' when there is no reflection." It is important for early career TESOL teachers to be able to bring these professional role identities to the level of awareness so that they can reflect on their usefulness.

Professional role identity formation usually begins in pre-service teacher education programs; however, evidence suggests that in many such pre-service TESOL teacher education programs, as Franzak (2002: 259) has noted, this formation is "best seen as a by-product of teacher education programs rather than a targeted outcome, at least from the student teacher's perspective." Then when TESOL teachers begin their careers in a real school setting, issues related to role identity resurface, but this time its development entails, as Achugar (2009: 65) has observed, "positioning oneself in relation to others by differentiating, affiliating, challenging, or accepting certain ways of constructing knowledge, being, and doing in the world." In fact, Miller (2009: 174) has pointed out that within TESOL there seems to be a "serious hiatus between language teacher education courses and the lived experiences of teachers." Consequently, Miller maintains that there needs to be a shift in language education to "critical sociocultural reflection, which takes account of identity and related issues of individuals in specific contexts, and of the role of discourse in shaping experience" (Miller, 2009: 178). For example, learner TESOL teachers while still on pre-service TESOL courses can be asked to reflect in an anticipatory manner on three umbrella identity clusters and what they mean for them (see reflective break below). They can also be asked to consider other roles that they may have to take on in the future once they have graduated, and how their identity will change from pre-service teacher to early career TESOL teacher.

Early career TESOL teachers will for sure form and develop their professional role identities while they are being socialized into the profession during their first years in the job. As Varghese, Morgan, Johnston, and Johnson (2005: 37) have noted, the socialization process during the first years of teaching includes "a process of identification – that is, of acquiring an identity, of becoming someone or something." When early career TESOL teachers enter the workplace for the first time after qualifying, they must negotiate contextual factors that, as Miller (2009: 175) has noted, are far from their experiences on "their pre-service education courses" and as such may be outside their control. The contextual factors ESL teachers in their first years must negotiate include workplace conditions, curriculum policy, bilingual policy, cultural differences, and the social demographics of the students and the school. Negotiating these challenges, as Miller (2009: 175) has observed, "forms part of their dynamic of professional development."

Thus, as early career TESOL teachers are being challenged from the moment they enter the classroom in their first year, they inevitably encounter issues and events that make them reflect on the various roles they take on or are given at the time. When early career TESOL teachers consciously reflect on the various roles that they take on or are given to them by their institutions, colleagues, or others, they can start the process of trying to figure out who they are and who they want to become as they continue their teaching careers.

REFLECTIVE BREAK

- Farrell (2012b) identified thirteen professional identity roles divided into three main clusters: *teacher as manager*, *teacher as "acculturator"*, and *teacher as professional*, as outlined by a group of novice TESOL teachers. Reflect on the list below.
    - What is your understanding of each of these roles and how would you rank them in order of importance for you as an early career TESOL teacher?
    - What other professional identity roles do you envisage you will have in your early career years?

Category	Role
Teacher as manager	Attempts to control classroom
Communication controller	Attempts to control communication and interaction
Arbitrator	Offers feedback (positive and negative) in classroom
Motivator	Motivates students to learn; keeps students on task
Presenter	Delivers information
Teacher as "acculturator"	Helps students to get accustomed to life outside class
Volunteer	Gives time outside class to organized activities
Friend	Befriends students (offering advice and support)
Care provider	Plays a role of care provider for students
Teacher as professional	Dedicated to work
Novice	*New* to teaching
Follower	Follows expectations of the administration
Unique	Is unique (differs from other teachers)

Reading and Discussion Task

John Trent and Jenny Lim (2010) explored the experiences of two groups of secondary school English language teachers as they participated in school–university partnerships in Hong Kong. The authors highlighted how teacher identity formation shaped and was shaped by participation in such a partnership.

- Read and summarize the authors' notion of identity development and its implications for developing a critical perspective on school–university partnerships.
- Discuss your findings with a colleague.

[Trent, J., and Lim, J. (2010). Teacher identity construction in school–university partnerships: Discourse and practice. *Teaching and Teacher Education, 26,* 1609-18]

EARLY CAREER YEARS: TEACHER AS RESEARCHER

In their early career years, learner TESOL teachers will work in many different contexts that can both nurture but also limit their development and thus, as the above discussion points out, they will need to be supported as they develop their professional identity as TESOL teachers. As was also pointed out above, the support they receive can unfortunately be hit or miss, and as a result they will have to depend on themselves a lot of the time when responding to the ecological conditions of the specific environment and classrooms (Bullough, 1989). Indeed, depending on such work contexts, learner TESOL teachers will discover that the ecology of their particular classrooms may have language learners from all age ranges, from children and teenagers to adults, and from a variety of different social, economic, cultural, and educational backgrounds. In addition, as Richards and Farrell (2005) point out, the learner TESOL teacher's own experience of schooling will play a role in how context is interpreted; consequently, this experience must also be examined in some detail.

Thus, the 'crucible of the classroom' will present different notions of the processes of teaching for early career TESOL teachers, as well as the norms of practice expected of teachers in that context. The crucible of the classroom is the place where innovations are tested, adapted, resisted, embraced, and/or ignored. In addition, it is there, as Stronach, Corbin, McNamara, Stark, and Warne (2002: 124) point out, that "a sense of the vocational commitment and reward of the teacher [is] most vividly expressed." This suggests that during their early career years learner TESOL teachers should continue using the mediational tools of reflective practice that they used in their TESOL teacher education programs (see Chapter 3), as they attempt to understand the crucible of their own classrooms in their own contexts of teaching.

REFLECTIVE BREAK

- Reflect on this example of how one early career TESOL teacher noticed that she was going to have to teach adult students in mixed ability ESL classes and how she prepared to use the mediational tools of reflective practice that she had learned in her TESOL teacher education program. What do you think of her approach? Would you do the same or would you have a different approach?

    One of the challenges I have faced in my teaching is catering to the disparate abilities of adult students in mixed level classes. A major priority, therefore, has been finding methods of teaching course content in ways that challenge, motivate and engage all students, regardless of ability. Group work is a strategy I have often employed, and in an effort to encourage as much variety of interaction as possible, I have always grouped students at random. Although students seem to work well in this way, I am aware that new students sometimes feel intimidated by the more able learners. As this can potentially impact student motivation and participation, I wish to investigate groupings further focusing on two questions:

- How do learners feel about homogeneous grouping (being grouped with classmates of similar levels) compared to heterogeneous grouping (being grouped with classmates of different levels)?
- Do these different groupings affect the degree of student participation?

This investigation would help me improve students' learning by enabling me to group them in ways that are most beneficial to them. It would also make me more aware of the dynamics of different groupings and their effects on the way students participate. This, in turn would influence the types of activities I choose for my lessons and the way I ask my students to interact.

Wider reading on the topic has revealed that, although much research exists on the pros and cons of homogeneous and heterogeneous grouping in mainstream schooling, there is a paucity of literature comparing the impact of these groupings on adult EFL learners. Much of the general research supporting heterogeneous grouping is based on the 'Zone of Proximal Development', which asserts that learners learn through interactions with others more knowledgeable than themselves. It has been observed that high level learners placed in groups with learners of lower ability can improve group interaction, assist understanding, provide encouragement and extend groupmates' learning. However, it has also been argued that heterogeneous grouping can result in less able students feeling intimidated by their more able peers and students of all levels becoming frustrated through lack of appropriate challenge. I believe that the benefits of heterogeneous grouping can outweigh the disadvantages. However, as my classroom observations to date have provided evidence both for and against heterogeneous grouping, I feel deeper investigation is necessary.

The investigation would be conducted in one of my smaller classes; a class of eight consisting of four beginner and four pre-intermediate students. This would allow me to create two groups which I can observe simultaneously and unobtrusively. Data would be collected through observation and student questionnaires. I would monitor student interaction over the course of two lessons; one using heterogeneous groupings and the other homogeneous. The observations would focus on students' communication and participation, any issues that arise, and how the students react to such issues. I would make written notes both as I observe and after each lesson in a reflective diary. Additionally, I would make audio recordings and transcripts of the group interactions to assist me in analyzing the content of students' communication, and to determine their degree of participation. It is also important to listen to the voices of the students themselves. Questionnaires with a mixture of closed (Likert-scale) and open-ended questions would be used at the end of each lesson to garner feedback on group dynamics and student participation [see "Appendix: Group Work Questionnaire" at the end of this reflective break].

The observation notes would be used to examine general patterns of student interaction and participation. The recordings would be analyzed using a SCORE [seating chart observation record] chart to determine the frequency of utterances of all group members and hence the degree of each student's participation. Furthermore, students' language would be analyzed from the transcript by classifying the types of utterances made (e.g. question, explanation, suggestion, prompt etc.). This would help determine whether groupings affect the nature of students' participation, for example, whether low-level students are more likely to ask questions when working in a heterogeneous group or in a homogeneous group. The answers to the Likert questionnaire items would be tabulated and mean scores calculated. These scores would be analyzed both separately and summed to ascertain students' feelings about each grouping. Finally, the answers to the open-ended questions would provide more detailed information to complement the Likert data. The data results from the two lessons would then be compared and contrasted in order to determine the differences in student participation, interaction and response to the two types of grouping.

Several constraints are foreseeable in this study. Firstly, as the students are well known to me, I may not notice as much as an impartial observer. It may therefore be useful to enlist the help of another teacher to assist with observations in order to provide a differing viewpoint which could be compared against my own. Secondly, although recordings may assist with data collection, variables such as sound quality, background noise levels, and students being distracted or made nervous by the recording equipment may affect their usefulness. The use of tablets or smartphones as recording devices may be the solution; they are ubiquitous enough to cause minimum distraction to the students and their quality is such that voices can be clearly distinguished. Thirdly, the groupings themselves may cause difficulties. Factors such as seniority or friendship may influence participation and must therefore be considered when examining the data. Finally, to guarantee accurate data, it would be necessary to ensure that, apart from the groupings themselves, all other factors affecting group work such as task difficulty and available resources are the same.

Studying the effects of different groupings on my students would help me create a learning environment in which my students can be comfortable, motivated and productive. As many of my classes are multi-level, I could take the results of the study on this small group into consideration when planning for other classes. This would help me to make my classes even more student-centered, enabling me to align my teaching more closely with my philosophy and principles of practice.

Appendix: Group Work Questionnaire
This survey asks you to discuss your feelings about group work in
English classes. Please answer the following questions in as much detail as
you can.
1.   Think about how you worked in your group today. Please rank your
     feelings about each aspect of today's group.

     1. Strongly disagree; 2. Disagree; 3. Neither agree nor disagree; 4. Agree;
     5. Strongly agree

I felt comfortable working with the members of today's group.	1	2	3	4	5
I am happy with my participation in today's group.	1	2	3	4	5
I found it easy to work in today's group.	1	2	3	4	5
Communication in today's group was good.	1	2	3	4	5
Working in today's group helped my learning.	1	2	3	4	5
I felt adequately challenged working in today's group.	1	2	3	4	5
I was comfortable with the pace that my group worked at.	1	2	3	4	5
My group members respected my opinion.	1	2	3	4	5
I was able to share my ideas with the group.	1	2	3	4	5

2.   Did you enjoy working in today's group? Why or why not?
3.   Did you have any problems working in today's group? If so, explain.

The above account of an early career TESOL teacher's approach to conducting her own research about mixed ability classes shows how she decided to try to
take more control and responsibility for her practice and development during her
early career years. This account sets us up for an approach to early career TESOL
teachers' development where they begin to take control of their own future careers
by engaging in teacher research. However, in a novice-service approach to teacher
education as outlined in Chapter 2, learner TESOL teachers should not just be told
to 'engage in teacher research' when they begin teaching in a real classroom. Rather,
they should be made aware of how the various mediational reflective tools and collaborative techniques (see Chapter 3) they have been exposed to in their TESOL
teacher education program can be further utilized during their early career teaching
years.

Encouraging learner TESOL teachers to engage in research during their early
teaching years emphasizes that the crucible of the classroom is not only a place
where the teacher performs but also a place where the teacher learns. This approach
also enhances the idea of shared teaching evaluation (outlined in Chapter 4), where
learner TESOL teachers engage in self-appraisal and continue such approaches to
investigate personal issues relevant to their lives as TESOL teachers for their continuous self-education and development. In short, they will engage in praxis.

Teacher research is defined as "all forms of practitioner enquiry that involve systematic, intentional, and self-critical inquiry about one's work" (Cochran-Smith and
Lytle, 1999: 22), and when early career TESOL teachers engage in such research

collaboratively, it can not only stimulate them to reflect on their practice but also enhance the quality of their students' learning. As Sachs (1999: 41) argues: "teacher research has the potential to act as a significant source of teacher and academic professional renewal and development because learning stands at the core of this renewal through the production and circulation of new knowledge about practice." However, some may ask why early career TESOL teachers need to or should do any research, and if so, what type of research and for what reason. After all, the reasoning goes, teachers are usually told what to do by outside experts and their work is often studied by others (i.e. these experts), so some may wonder "do they need to study it themselves?" as Stenhouse (1975: 144) asked many years ago.

There is still some disagreement within TESOL as to the nature of a TESOL teacher's job in terms of research; teaching and researching are two different jobs. Indeed, TESOL teachers can still be effective teachers without undertaking any form of research, as many effective, experienced TESOL teachers have known for years. Some TESOL scholars go as far as suggesting that doing research is not good in itself and may even be considered detrimental to 'good' teaching. One of the major arguments, for example, against teacher research is that although some say it is research 'driven by teachers', one could also say that it is driven *at* teachers by ivory-tower academics/teacher educators who know nothing much about the classrooms, outside their university settings, where TESOL teachers must survive.

In addition, when the word 'research' (as in 'teacher research') is used in any publication, readers, no matter who they are, have particular expectations about what they will read in terms of the type of language that is used in the publication. In most cases such publications in education are written with a particular audience in mind, and for the most part are aimed at academics rather than practicing teachers. Academics usually author such publications for many reasons, such as their own academic advancement and dissemination of the results of their research. Moreover, many of these academic-style publications related to teaching are filled with studies and reports of why language teachers teach in the way they do, or how they should be doing something in the classroom; in other words, these are research reports *on* teachers *by* academics *for* academic audiences. (Yes, I admit that this book is written in somewhat of an academic style but I believe that the writing style is still accessible to all readers.)

Such reports are fine in themselves, as they may advance the 'knowledge base' of the profession and the career of the academics that author such reports. However, many times these same reports criticize practicing teachers for some lack of knowledge or engagement in such 'research'. The teachers themselves remark that in many cases these same publications are not really accessible in the academic forms that they are presented in. In other words, from the teachers' perspective, what is missing from the literature is research reports that are accessible to teachers, or reports about what language teachers themselves think about what they do: research *with* teachers, *by* teachers, and *for* teachers. As Farrell (2016d: 353) discovered in his review of language teacher research, not all TESOL teachers are in favor of being 'encouraged' by academics to do research. One early career TESOL teacher reflected after his research was completed under the 'supervision' of an academic:

Practitioners outside of the academia have their own knowledge of what is good learning, what is a good teacher, what they understand by education, and so on, and it is very important that they (we) reflect on what they know and what they do, share their questions, try to find answers to them and share their partial understandings with their students, other practitioners and the public in general. The academia has created rules that suit their academics. Teachers outside of the academia have other times and responsibilities. Thus it is unfair to ask teachers to adapt themselves to the academic's lifestyle when it comes to doing research. Teachers are capable of researching their own practice which should be done in a way that fits the nature of their work.

Reading and Discussion Task

Jim McKinley (2019) observed that TESOL research was traditionally led by researcher-practitioners, who acknowledged real-world English language teaching problems as the basis for research inquiries. Over time, however, he noted that the focus has moved away from anecdotes on teaching English toward empirical TESOL research, grounded in educational, linguistic, or psychological principles. These changes have contributed to a teaching and research bifurcation, where studies conducted by researchers who are removed from teaching tend to be more highly valued by the TESOL research community than many of the practical, classroom-based, teaching-led work done by researcher-practitioners. He maintains that this results in de-contextualized research publications, which do not always reflect the messiness of the real world, or the complex issues that teachers deal with in their daily practices. In this article he calls for the research to be more grounded in classroom contexts, and for methods to be more transparent about the messiness of doing real-world classroom research.

- Read the paper and explain your understanding of teacher research as outlined by the author and your opinion of his views.
- Discuss your findings with a colleague.

[McKinley, J. (2019). Evolving the TESOL teaching–research nexus. *TESOL Quarterly, 53*, 3, 875-84]

TESOL teacher education from a reflective, collaborative point of view includes the development of learner TESOL teachers to become researchers of the crucible of their own classrooms. Some scholars may separate teacher research (some also call this the small 'r') from academic research (which some call the big 'R'), with the latter being viewed as more important (of course by academics). It is the belief of this author that there is room for all kinds of research and that teacher research (the so-called small 'r'), subsumed under the reflective practice umbrella, is as important as any other type of research, given that it is driven by TESOL teachers on topics and issues related to *their* practice. As Fueyo and Koorland, (1997: 339) note:

Teachers as researchers ask questions and systematically find answers. They observe and monitor themselves and their students while participating in the teaching and learning process. They question instructional practices and student outcomes. They make data-based decisions, validating their practice. They implement change. Teachers as researchers are professionals.

In fact, the concept of teachers as researchers can be embedded in the TESOL teacher education program and teaching practice when learner TESOL teachers are exposed to the tools of reflective practice, encouraged to collaborate as they investigate all aspects of their practice, and see classrooms as centers of inquiry as well as places of learning on both sides of the desk.

Borg (2013) reports the following benefits for teachers of conducting their own research: promotes teacher autonomy (e.g. by boosting teachers' criticality so they depend less on educators and/or 'external' authorities); develops teacher empowerment (e.g. by getting involved in processes of social change); and improves teacher well-being (e.g. reducing feelings of professional inadequacy). To these Farrell (2016d) adds the following benefits, stating that TESOL teachers can: learn about, with, and from their learners; improve classroom dynamics via collaboration on research with their learners (e.g. by involving learners in various stages of the research project); and positively influence other TESOL teachers' practices by sharing their own work.

A novice-service approach to TESOL teacher education includes the concept of learner TESOL teachers engaging in teacher research in whatever format, because it has the possibility of enriching TESOL teachers' practical knowledge in their particular context so that they can obtain new understanding of their practice. As Freeman (1998: 6) has pointed out, TESOL teachers are best suited to carry out research in their own classrooms because they are "more insiders to their settings than researchers whose work lives are elsewhere." TESOL teacher research can be weaved into courses, teaching practice, and the early career years where teacher research strategies such as action research projects are incorporated into the program (see also Chapter 4).

Thus, action research projects can be encouraged throughout the TESOL teacher education program. For example, during teaching practice the collaborative nature of teacher supervision and teaching evaluation outlined in previous chapters are interconnected with action research, given that both require observation and decision making as well as problem-identification and problem-solving. The introduction of action research projects during teaching practice has been shown to increase learner TESOL teachers' self-efficacy as well as equip them to face future teaching challenges during the early career years and beyond. Indeed, action research has a reflexive relationship with reflection, and as Wallace (1991: 56-7) has noted, action research is "an extension of the normal reflective practice of many teachers, but it is slightly more rigorous and might conceivably lead to more effective outcomes." Indeed, reflective practitioners are ideally placed to investigate, articulate, and uncover the complexities of the classroom through the mediational tool of action research (Mann and Walsh, 2017).

TESOL teachers can also collaborate with TESOL teacher educator-mentors, who can create opportunities for teachers to reflect during and after their TESOL teacher education courses and feed the results back into these courses, as noted above. This type of collaborative research may go some way to alleviate some of the problems associated with the theory/practice divide in many teacher education programs, because the research will be relevant to all practicing teachers as well as those in training. Indeed, as Cochran-Smith and Lytle (1993: 15) have noted, "The unique feature of questions that prompt teacher research is that they emanate from neither theory nor practice alone but from critical reflection on the two."

Thankfully, as Wright (2010: 288) pointed out, "there is a growing and healthy 'practitioner research' culture in SLTE [second language teacher education], in which teacher educators are examining the effect of the learning experiences they initiate." The appendix that follows Chapter 8 outlines various examples of TESOL professional organizations, such as the teacher research initiative of the International Association of Teachers of English as a Foreign Language (IATEFL) and the TESOL International Association's Language Teacher Research series (of which I had the honor of being series editor). Learner TESOL teachers and early career TESOL teachers can be encouraged to go through these and engage in whatever research they feel is most appropriate for them.

REFLECTIVE BREAK

- What does the concept 'teacher as researcher' mean to you?
- Do you think you or other TESOL teachers should engage in teacher research once they begin their teaching careers? Why or why not?
- Do you think that doing research can be detrimental to 'good' teaching?

Reading and Discussion Task

Vivian Fueyo and Mark A. Koorland (1997) state that teachers as researchers "analyze their plans and actions and their subsequent impact on the students they teach. By understanding both their own and their students' classroom behaviors, teachers as researchers make informed decisions about what to change and what not to change" (1997: 337-8).

- Read and summarize the authors' notion of teachers as researchers. Do you agree or disagree with their ideas? What is the link to teachers as reflective practitioners?
- Discuss your findings with a colleague.

[Fueyo, V., and Koorland, M. (1997). Teacher as researcher: A synonym for professionalism. *Journal of Teacher Education, 48,* 5, 336-44]

CONCLUSION

As the contents of this book suggest, when a novice-service framework is applied to educate learner TESOL teachers, it begins in the TESOL teacher education program, where a reflective, collaborative disposition is embedded in all the candidates throughout its courses as well as teaching practice, and continues well into the early career teaching years, when the mentoring process is continued. As this chapter has pointed out, during these important early career years, learner TESOL teachers will still require a lot of support from TESOL teacher educator-supervisors, who will now act as mentors, as well as support from within the school placement, through a formal induction program and/or a school-appointed teacher mentor who will guide early career teachers to successfully navigate their negotiation of their identity as they develop during these years. In addition, this chapter has suggested that as early career TESOL teachers progress through their early teaching years and beyond, they can take more responsibility for their own development by becoming teacher researchers.

8

CONCLUSIONS

PREAMBLE

In this final chapter I share some comments from practicing teachers of different subjects about their reflections on their identity as a teacher. All are from the website Reddit. They begin in the first year of teaching and end with reflections by a teacher in her fifteenth year. Where possible I include the subject area the teacher was teaching.

I'm a first-year teacher in my second semester and I almost always feel like I'm playing teacher.

Yeah, I'm in my second year and totally still feel it sometimes. I tried to talk to my head of department about it (she's 24 years deep) and she had no idea what I was trying to get at.

I'm a second-year teacher and feel the same way this year.

Third year and I feel this a lot. Lately Ive felt like I'm just a big strict mean lady but today at open house people kept telling me how patient I am and that my students love me. I rarely feel like I'm being as patient or nice as I should be so I'm glad I'm at least perceived the way I wish to be. (K-1, US)

I feel ya! I'm in my sixth year, but I got a student teacher this year and imposter syndrome hit HARD. Like I barely know what I'm doing but I guess I'll pretend I do for your benefit?? Maybe when we stop feeling like an imposter is when we need to worry? That's what I'll tell myself!

4 years in, been feeling a lot of this the past week over disagreements in pedagogy from my colleague who has been teaching 19 years.

I thought I was the only one who felt like this . . . I'm in the middle of my 6th year, and I legit feel like a phony so much of the time. My colleagues look like they have it all together. I'm so glad to see I'm not alone in this!! (8th grade Language Arts, US)

155

7th year teaching. I still have no idea what I'm doing.

I'm nearly 10 years in and STILL feel this.

13 years and SAME. (8th grade History US)

Here I am at year 15 and I keep thinking this will fade with time. Just making sure I get better each day, put in as much effort as I can, and doing everything I can to make sure that central admin doesn't get in the way of children learning.

All of the above comments have one common theme and that is that all of the teachers, regardless of how many years they have been teaching, seem to be suffering from a kind of professional identity crisis that involves each feeling he or she is an imposter as a teacher. Many reveal that they are 'playing the role' of teacher but do not really feel that they are real teachers. This is sometimes called the "imposter phenomenon" in general psychology or the "imposter syndrome" in teaching. People who experience the imposter phenomenon generally worry that they may be exposed as a fraud at any time and, as a result, feel distressed and that any achievements they may have acquired are largely undeserved (Clance, 1985). Indeed, it's estimated that some 70 percent of the general public experience such episodes of the imposter phenomenon in their lives (Gravois, 2007). For teachers, as in all the cases outlined in the preamble above, such imposter-type feelings never really go away, and I suspect a lot more teachers also 'suffer' in silence and possibly without being aware of why they have such a debilitating feeling of being inadequate as a teacher. However, such feelings as an imposter can be very debilitating for learner TESOL teachers and novice TESOL teachers in their early years, especially if these feelings are not addressed in some manner during the initial teacher education program. In this final chapter I address the imposter syndrome as it impacts novice TESOL teachers and show how it can be overcome through reflective practice, which after all is a summary of the main contents of this book.

INTRODUCTION

We may be surprised perhaps to learn that famous and influential people we are familiar with as public icons have experienced feelings of inadequacy even though they are famous and fully established. Shorten (2013) notes the following:

- Maya Angelou, award-winning author: "I have written eleven books, but each time I think, 'Uh oh, they're going to find out now. I've run a game on everybody, and they're going to find me out.'"
- Kate Winslet, Academy award winner: "Sometimes I wake up in the morning before going off to a shoot, and I think, I can't do this. I'm a fraud."
- Darren Lockyer, Australian rugby league champion: "Every time I go to a game I always have that fear of losing or a sense of failure."

- Dr Margaret Chan, chief of the World Health Organization: "There are an awful lot of people out there who think I'm an expert. How do these people believe all this about me? I'm so much aware of all the things I don't know."
- Alan Dye, vice president of Apple: "I'm scared to death that at some point I'm going to get found out. You know, Tim [Cook] is going to realize the truth about me, which is I'm terrible."

Perhaps we all suffer from feelings of being inadequate at different times in our lives, but when these become more frequent, we can feel, like those famous people above, that we are going to get found out in some way at some time. In other words, we will always be looking over our shoulders. When we experience such feelings as teachers, and we similarly always feel that we are looking over our shoulders, then tensions between our philosophy, principles, and theories and our teaching practices will erupt and our students, if they do not pick up on these, will suffer from not having the optimal opportunities to learn. Because teachers of all experience levels are sometimes vulnerable and as a result may be prone to the imposter syndrome, the reflective approach that the contents of this book take become even more important for learner TESOL teachers, novice TESOL teachers, TESOL teacher educators, and all others involved with the successful integration of novice teachers into the profession. Such a reflective approach to TESOL teacher education and early career TESOL teacher development provides these teachers and teacher educators with the tools and strategies that allow them to identify their practices and the beliefs behind those practices, and thus help reduce the sense of being an imposter that is most frequent in these important early years. In this chapter I outline what the imposter syndrome is and how it can be overcome by using such reflective strategies as are detailed in all of the previous chapters of this book. In such a manner, we can better ensure our learner TESOL teachers in their early career years can become competent professionals, because they know they have the resourcefulness and resilience required from such an education to face future challenges and changes throughout their careers.

IMPOSTER SYNDROME

"Imposterism" and "imposter fears" (Thompson, Davis, and Davidson, 1998; Thompson, Foreman, and Martin, 2000) generally describe the psychological state of people who think of themselves as intellectual frauds and, as a result, have a fear of being exposed as such. The imposter phenomenon in psychology, defined as "internal experience of intellectual phoniness" (Matthews and Clance, 1985: 71), generally 'strikes' successful people unable to handle and internalize their success (Bernard, Dollinger, and Ramaniah, 2002; Clance, 1985). Although this imposter phenomenon is not "a pathological disease that is inherently self-damaging or self-destructive" (Clance, 1985: 23), it disrupts the psychological well-being of the individual who suffers from it because they always feel they need to be special or the very best, and as a result experience fearful feelings of failure because they will deny their own competence. If they experience any success, they will probably deny it, and/or feel guilty about it, and discount any praise they may receive. As Clance (1985) pointed out, feelings of such self-doubt and inadequacy, the most typical traits of the imposter syndrome, can cause lots of distress and result in some maladaptive behavior. When it comes to TESOL teaching, then, because research has indicated such a clear relationship between beliefs teachers have about themselves (their philosophy, principles, and theories) and their practice (Farrell and Bennis, 2013; Farrell and Mom, 2015; Farrell and Ives, 2015; Farrell and Yang, 2018; Farrell and Vos, 2018), those learner TESOL teachers and early career TESOL teaches with any feelings of self-doubt or inadequacy often turn out to be weaker teachers (Brems, Baldwin, Davis, and Namyniuk, 1994). Thus a greater awareness of the imposter syndrome through self-reflection with others, as the contents of this book attest to, can help learner TESOL teachers and early career TESOL teachers better minimize any feelings of inadequacy or failure throughout their teaching careers, and thus prepare them better for how to deal with these feelings.

TESOL TEACHER EDUCATION: A REFLECTIVE APPROACH

I first entered a classroom over forty years ago as a teacher and I have been teaching in classrooms ever since. I have learned a lot from my students and my colleagues over these years and although I too suffer occasionally from imposter syndrome, I always try to base my professional decisions on reflective evidence, and this has always helped me overcome any such feelings of doubt about my practice or how I have advised learner TESOL teachers over all these years. Yes, I have self-cited many times throughout this book, but not out of any arrogance; rather it is to show that I am basing all of the contents of this book on much of the hard, evidence-based research I have carried out over those years, working closely with wonderful TESOL teacher educators and TESOL teachers at all levels of experience.

I have written this book with the intention of providing learner TESOL teachers and their TESOL teacher educators with a way forward so that they too can overcome any feelings of 'impostership'. The book outlines a collaborative, reflective, novice-service approach (Chapter 2) to TESOL teacher education, which includes the years of initial teacher education and all of the early career years, and in which learner TESOL teachers, novice TESOL teachers, mentor teachers, cooperating teachers, and all others involved can come together and assist each other as colleagues, while all the time learning from each other along the way. Learner TESOL teachers are especially vulnerable when making the challenging transition from their initial teacher education programs to the first years of teaching, and thus it is necessary to help them build their confidence through such a transition by providing them with the tools of reflective practice, as outlined in this book, as they enter the community of practice of the TESOL profession.

The framework for reflecting on practice (Chapter 3) can help learner TESOL teachers, early career TESOL teachers, and teacher educators, supervisors, and mentor-teachers better examine the relationship between principles and practices and how this impacts their daily lives as TESOL professionals. Such collaborations (Chapter 4) can be facilitated in TESOL teacher education programs and the early years of teaching in different contexts through mentoring and the use of critical friends groups, team teaching, and peer coaching, along with providing such reflective tools as writing, dialogue, engaging in action research, and making use of whatever technology is available to help develop a reflective stance during teaching practice (Chapter 5) and teaching evaluation (Chapter 6), and throughout the early career years (Chapter 7).

WHAT NEXT?

For sure, learner TESOL teachers will face adjustment challenges as they transition from their TESOL teacher education program to become early career teachers (Kang and Cheng, 2014). During this transition there is bound to be some kind of evolution of their beliefs and practice as they adjust to their new environments. Inevitably some learner TESOL teachers may ignore, abandon, or completely reject some or all of the foundations and concepts they were presented with in their TESOL teacher education programs as they adapt to their new workplace and new colleagues. As they enter these early career years, and as pointed out in this chapter and throughout this book, a 'novice-service' framework is most suited to help in mentoring them to achieve realistic expectations about their new realities of teaching, and ultimately to succeed and grow as TESOL professionals throughout their careers (Kang and Cheng, 2014).

REFLECTIVE BREAK

- Will you hold true to your visions of teaching regardless of the obstacles you will inevitably face during your early careers?
- If yes, how will you negotiate in order to realize these visions?
- Will you keep, ignore, or abandon the principles you learned in your TESOL teacher education program?
- Will you continue to reflect and innovate on your practice during your early career years and beyond?

Reading and Discussion Task

Yan Kang and Xiaotang Cheng (2014) report on a detailed case study of a novice middle-school EFL teacher's learning to teach in the workplace. They were especially interested in examining whether the teacher changed her beliefs and/or classroom practices as a result of making adjustments to her new workplace and, if so, what were the various factors that may have influenced her to make these changes.

- Read and summarize how the teacher changed her beliefs and/or classroom practices and the factors that influenced these.
- As you embark on your early career teaching years, what did you learn from reading about the adjustments of this EFL teacher during her first year?
- Discuss your findings with a colleague.

[Kang, Y., and Cheng, X. (2014). Teacher learning in the workplace: A study of the relationship between a novice EFL teacher's classroom practices and cognition development. *Language Teaching Research*, *18*, 2, 169–86]

CONCLUSION

By way of conclusion I offer you the opportunity of listening to a podcast I gave, at the invitation of Ross Thornburn, that sums up many of the ideas I have expressed in this book: https://www.youtube.com/watch?v=8JA44WOf3e0&feature=youtu.be.

Happy teaching and reflecting!

APPENDIX

TESOL TEACHER RESEARCH

Conducting teacher research in the early career years can be done alone or in collaboration with other TESOL teachers. There are many different papers and books already published about how TESOL teachers should engage in research and how they should read up about it before they engage in such research. However, following Mann and Walsh's (2017) advice, it is better that early career TESOL teachers avoid too much reading of these publications (especially given time constraints) because they may be offputting. Mann and Walsh (2017) suggest that TESOL teachers jump in at the deep end and just get on with doing the research. As Mann and Walsh (2017: 226) point out, "It is hard to conceive of practitioner research that is not based on the elements of observation, reflection, planning, action, but there is no necessary 'right order'." I outline IATEFL teacher research initiatives first and invite readers to examine each of the collections listed below, all freely available to download from the IATEFL Research Special Interest Group (SIG): http://resig.weebly.com/books.htm.

IATEFL

A wide range of terms is used in these publications to cover research conducted by teachers: practitioner research, teacher research, integrated teacher research, action research, informal action research, collaborative action research, small research, exploratory practice, exploratory practice study, and exploratory action research, to name but a few. *Teacher-Researchers in Action* (Dikilitaş, Smith, and Trotman, 2015: 3), succinctly explains the aim of IATEFL's wonderful initiative when they developed all of these books: "To inspire other teachers across the world" to engage in their own form of teacher research.

- *Horizontes 1: ELT Teacher-Research in Latin America*, edited by Darío Luis Banegas, Magdalena De Stefani, Paula Rebolledo, Carlos Rico Troncoso, and Richard Smith (2020)
- *ELT Research in Action: Bringing Together Two Communities of Practice*, edited by Jessica Mackay, Marilisa Birello, and Daniel Xerri (2020)
- *Creating Quiet Reflective Spaces: Language Teacher Research as Professional Development*, edited by Loreto Aliaga Salas and Elena Ončevska Ager (2020)
- *Energizing Teacher Research*, edited by Kenan Dikilitaş, Mark Wyatt, Anne Burns, and Gary Barkhuizen (2019)

- *Stories by Teacher Researchers in an Online Research Community*, edited by Aslı Lidice Göktürk Sağlam and Kenan Dikilitaş (2019)
- *Empowering Teacher-Researchers, Empowering Learners*, edited by Gary Barkhuizen, Anne Burns, Kenan Dikilitaş, and Mark Wyatt (2018)
- *ELT Research in Action: Bridging the Gap between Research and Classroom Practice*, edited by Jessica Mackay, Marilisa Birello and Daniel Xerri (2018)
- *Developing Insights into Teacher-Research*, edited by Anne Burns, Kenan Dikilitaş, Richard Smith, and Mark Wyatt (2017)
- *Developing as an EFL Researcher: Stories from the Field*, edited by Siân Etherington and Mark Daubney (2017)
- *Teachers Engaging in Research*, edited by Kenan Dikilitaş, Mark Wyatt, Judith Hanks, and Deborah Bullock (2016)
- *Teacher-Researchers in Action*, edited by Kenan Dikilitaş, Richard Smith, and Wayne Trotman (2015)
- *Teachers Research!*, edited by Deborah Bullock and Richard Smith (2015)

Many of the topics that are covered in the above excellent collection of edited books will be of interest to most learner TESOL teachers as well as early career TESOL teachers and, indeed, more experienced TESOL teachers who are looking to refresh their practice. For example, in the collection *Teachers Research!* (Bullock and Smith, 2015), topics include: students' use of technology; balancing exam-oriented activities with meaning-learning activities; dealing with student cliques in a writing class; student perceptions of reasons for success and failure in learning English; preparing students to deliver successful presentations; getting EAP students to take responsibility for learning outside the classroom and addressing student use of offensive nicknames. I praise the IATEFL Research SIG for all the work they do in encouraging teachers to reflect on their practice, as without these edited collections, many TESOL teachers would be left again to survive on their own.

TESOL INTERNATIONAL ASSOCIATION

As series editor and developer of language teacher research in the TESOL International Association's US organization some years ago, I was honored to be able to launch the Association's Language Teacher Research series of six volumes that outlined how practicing TESOL teachers conducted teacher research in six different areas of the world: Europe, the Americas, Asia, the Middle East, Australia and New Zealand, and Africa. What is distinctive about the series is that all the sixty-seven studies reported document how TESOL teachers systematically reflected on their own practice.

- *Language Teacher Research in Europe*, edited by Simon Borg (2006)
- *Language Teacher Research in the Americas*, edited by Hedy M. McGarrell (2007)
- *Language Teacher Research in Asia*, edited by Thomas S. C. Farrell (2006)
- *Language Teacher Research in the Middle East*, edited by Christine Coombe and Lisa Barlow (2007)

- *Language Teacher Research in Australia and New Zealand,* edited by Anne Burns and Jill Burton (2008)
- *Language Teacher Research in Africa,* edited by Leketi Makalela (2009)

Because the range of topics in language teaching that TESOL teacher researchers can focus on is practically unlimited, all sixty-seven chapters across the six areas were organized on a template to help authors and readers compare across chapters and volumes, by looking at aspects such as the research issue, background literature, procedures, results, and reflection. I now outline each of the volumes so that learner TESOL teachers and early career TESOL teachers can be encouraged to not only read these accounts but also perhaps replicate some of the studies that may resonate for them currently in their particular context. For each volume, a table below summarizes the topics, the methods used in each study, the results of the studies, the authors' reflections, and the type of setting.

LANGUAGE TEACHER RESEARCH IN EUROPE

Borg (2006) presents TESOL research conducted by TESOL teachers at different levels, many in a university setting (66 percent of participants) and others in a secondary/high school setting (33 percent of participants), covering twelve issues/topics, only three of which were related to language teacher education. All the other nine were very different in focus. See Table 1.

Table 1 *Language Teacher Research in Europe*

Topic/Issue	Method	Result	Reflection	Setting
Professional development for primary EFL teachers	Field notes, journals	Teachers were motivated to do classroom research	Teachers' heavy workloads and lack of time were obstacles to teacher research	University
Ethnic minority students' writing skills at university	Formative and summative data, phone interviews	Improvements to student writing were noted	There were problems with attention to detail of the research design	University
Secondary school learners' reflections about learning	Interviews, written narratives, learner self-assessment	Learners had a positive attitude toward learning English	There were differences between views of success and the importance of learning a foreign language	High school

Table 1 (*continued*)

Topic/Issue	Method	Result	Reflection	Setting
Designing and implementing an effective literature-based English course	Questionnaires, observations, test scores	Literature-based learning improved the autonomy and motivation of students	The level of student interest in literature was important for student success	High school
Research methods for learner teachers	Questionnaires, interviews, students' written/ oral work	Student teachers developed a research identity	Developing a researcher identity was challenging	University
Improving speaking and listening skills	Mini-projects, pre- and post-test scores, students' written/oral work	Proficiency levels in speaking and listening improved	Engaging in teacher research was rewarding but time-consuming	University
Local and national action research implementation	Intrapersonal journal writing, group discussions with teachers	National and local methods were combined	Action research methodology and teacher collaboration were important	University
Support for linguistically weaker students' mixed-level ESP course	Study groups, performance and evaluation data	The participation of all students improved	Collegial collaboration was important	University
Language teachers use when setting up tasks	Audio recordings of language lessons	Teacher language had three functions: teaching, structuring, and rapport-enhancing	Analyzing samples of teacher language helps	University
Active vs. passive participants in class discussions	Questionnaires, learners' self-assessments, teaching journal	Awareness of 'other' perspectives on oral participation increased	Sharing between teacher and students was very important	High school
Pre-service course based on multiple intelligence (MI) theory	Observations, trainees' work, end-of-course evaluations	MI theory can be productively applied in teacher education contexts	It takes time for students to adjust to MI	University

Table 1 (*continued*)

Topic/Issue	Method	Result	Reflection	Setting
Intercultural communicative competence	Interaction journals, emails	Interaction journals stimulate intercultural learning	Teachers are important in role managing and monitoring learning environments	High school

Most research issues in Europe centered on improving student learning in some way, such as finding ways of improving both the motivation and the speaking and listening skills of the engineering students on a language course, while one TESOL teacher education issue focused on better preparing learner TESOL teachers for how to do research. The most common research methods used by the participants were qualitative in nature, such as journals, questionnaires, observations, and samples of student work.

LANGUAGE TEACHER RESEARCH IN THE AMERICAS

McGarrell (2007) presents TESOL research from both North (Canada and the USA) and South America (e.g. Brazil, Colombia, and Jamaica), with most conducted in a university setting and only two studies conducted by practicing classroom teachers. See Table 2.

Table 2   *Language Teacher Research in the Americas*

Topic/Issue	Method	Result	Reflection	Setting
Raising test scores in reading and writing	Survey, questionnaires, interviews	Drafts were not seen as a necessity in writing tasks	There was not enough critical thinking .	University
Training pre-service teachers in teacher feedback	Survey, open-ended questions	There were inappropriate comments on content	With training, pre-service teachers could learn how to comment on more than surface errors	University
Films for language learning	Student questionnaires	Students appreciate cultural aspects of learning from films	Films stimulated discussion best when students could identify with the themes	University

Table 2 (*continued*)

Topic/Issue	Method	Result	Reflection	Setting
Preparing ESL students for interactions in university	Observation of students' oral discourse, interviews, teacher journal	Students valued opportunities for critical inquiry	Teacher collaboration with ESL students was important	University
Students' problems on tests	Student responses, two tests	Students discovered the overall purpose of articles read	Tests should engage students in activities that allow them to show what they know	University
Listening to stories to increase vocabulary	Testing and scores of ESL students after listening to a story	Reading aloud assists vocabulary gains	Developing the curriculum to suit students' needs was important	Elementary school
Communicative techniques and writing development	Observations, collaborative research sessions	Students' writing improved	Reflective collaboration was helpful for innovative teaching approaches	University
Pre-service teachers' resistance to using English outside class	Attitude survey, focus group	Students feared a loss of self-identity when using English outside class	Continue to a bilingual approach to teaching	University
Pre-service teachers' awareness of sociocultural aspects of TEFL	Teaching journals, critical incident reports, videotaped classes, questionnaires	Pre-service teachers began to critique beliefs about sociocultural factors	The approach helped teacher educators become more informed about teaching	University
Teaching vocabulary to middle school ESL students	Sustained silent reading in class, group discussion	Spanish L1 (first language) students had the most trouble with English words of Germanic origin	Collecting and analyzing data about one's own students was important	Middle school
Use of discourse markers	Corpus linguistics (frequency counts, posterior analysis)	Non-native speakers use far fewer discourse markers and conversational hedges	The value of research was realized	University

Table 2 (*continued*)

Topic/Issue	Method	Result	Reflection	Setting
Metacognition to improve English learning	Exam scores, discussions, self-evaluations	There was no significant score increase between those trained in metacognition and those not	The training process may be a longer-term investment	University

As in Europe, most of the research topics in the Americas focused on improving student learning of some sort, covering such issues as improving writing, vocabulary, listening, and better use of strategies. The researchers tended to use qualitative methods exclusively, such as survey examples of their students' work and questionnaires as well as teacher and student journals, and only one study utilized both quantitative and qualitative methods.

LANGUAGE TEACHER RESEARCH IN ASIA

Farrell (2006c) presents TESOL research that was conducted by TESOL teachers at all levels, but mostly in a university setting and with only one study from a high school and one from a private language school. The countries represented cover both north and south Asia. See Table 3.

Table 3   *Language Teacher Research in Asia*

Topic/Issue	Method	Results	Reflection	Setting
Improving writing	Teaching genre	Students' writing improved	Teachers should continue using genre	University
Expert and non-expert teachers learning teaching methodology	Diaries, lesson plans, observations, interviews	Non-expert teachers used surface approaches, experts applied concepts beyond the course	Teachers needed regular opportunities to reflect	University
Learner autonomy English classes	Observations, interviews	Independent work does not always mean independent learning	Teachers should 'step back' during independent work	University
What do student teachers learn?	Pre-course and post-course concept maps	Students showed more detail in answers, but lacked complexity	Reflection with concept maps was useful	University

Table 3 (*continued*)

Topic/Issue	Method	Results	Reflection	Setting
Teacher-dependent students	Interviews	The exam-oriented was curriculum largely to blame for dependence	The role of teacher was critically assessed	University
Impact of self-access language learning centers	Questionnaires, implementation of self-access center	Hours spent voluntarily at the center indicate the usefulness of the program	Diverse learning preferences and needs were served in the centers	High school
Improving ESL students' listening	Questionnaires, implementation of process-oriented lessons	Students used more cognitive and metacognitive strategies	Students developed greater self-awareness as learners	University
Conflict between language and content	Analysis of lectures, student evaluations	Students' differing language abilities caused the instructor to re-evaluate their methods	The most appropriate methodology is the one that best suits students' abilities	University
Balance between language learning and testing	Student survey, curriculum revision	Students wanted more TOEFL (test of English as a foreign language) instruction	Curriculum review and consulting stakeholders were important	University
Teacher's and students' impressions of lessons	Learning logs, teacher reflections, course evaluations	Students focused on process and content	The teacher learned about impressions students develop of lessons	University
Implementing project-based learning	Project-based learning program, class discussions, observations	Success depended on appropriate planning, implementation, and assessment	Materials appropriate to the linguistic abilities and interests of students should be used	University
Willingness to communicate in L2	Teaching journal, tape-recorded lessons, peer observation	Comprehension and participation were better when content was familiar	There was a need to increase student extrinsic motivation	Private school

The topics in Asia tended to focus on the learner, learning, and how learning can become more autonomous; understanding student dependence on the teacher; creating a self-access language learning center in a high school; and developing project-based learning. Only two chapters were devoted to research on TESOL teacher education. The researchers tended to use interviews, observations, and questionnaires as their preferred mode of data collection, as in the other volumes.

LANGUAGE TEACHER RESEARCH IN THE MIDDLE EAST

Coombe and Barlow (2007) presents TESOL research that was conducted mostly by TESOL teacher educators in a university setting and by just one high school teacher and one language training development officer. See Table 4.

Table 4   *Language Teacher Research in the Middle East*

Topic/Issue	Method	Results	Reflection	Setting
Language-learning anxiety	Questionnaires, interviews, statistical analysis	Causes of anxiety were peers, the language teacher, and instructional materials	Language listening labs should reduce anxiety	High school
Course evaluations	Evaluation forms, statistical analysis	Not many students were able to comprehend all the questions on the evaluation form	The evaluation form should be translated into students' native language	University
Spelling errors	Spelling activity scores	One in five words were misspelled at intermediate level	Learners' awareness of graphological differences between Arabic and English should be raised	University
Native English speakers and non-native speaker teachers	Student essays	Students had a definite preference for native speaker teachers	Students should be made aware of the qualities of all teachers	University
Male and female students inside and outside class	Survey, analysis	Students saw the benefits of working in mixed groups, as it prepared them for workplace dynamics	Students should be given more opportunities to work with the opposite gender	University

Table 4 (*continued*)

Topic/Issue	Method	Results	Reflection	Setting
Exam-driven curriculum	Questionnaires, interviews	The exam-driven curriculum was not good for facilitated learning	Students wanted to communicate in English in an authentic, occupational context	Language development office
Learning contracts	Questionnaires, learning contracts	Students took more responsibility for learning	Learning contracts positively affect motivation	University
Improving students' thinking	Six-lesson model to reframe thinking	The model helped students plan and organize their thoughts better	Teachers need to promote thinking time	University
Best practices in teaching	Interviews, analysis	Good teaching includes effective organization, with a link between theory and practice	There should be some improvisation in addition to well-planned lessons	University
Peer feedback on students' writing	Pre- and post-tests, writing samples	Students' writing improved	Peer feedback was good	University
Students repeating same level of English class	Class observation, group and individual interviews, questionnaire	Seventy percent of multiple repeaters passed the course during the research project	Understanding of the linguistic needs of failing students was crucial	University
Computer assisted learning (CAL)	Online surveys	Students enjoyed CAL and found it useful	CAL activities needed to be integrated into class content	University

The focus of most of the research in the Middle East was on improving student performance in some way and especially in or around the writing class. Just as in the other volumes, the researchers tended to use qualitative methods such as interviews and questionnaires as their preferred mode of data collection, and two used both quantitative and qualitative methods.

LANGUAGE TEACHER RESEARCH IN AUSTRALIA AND NEW ZEALAND

Burns and Burton (2008) presents TESOL research that was conducted mostly by TESOL teacher educators in a university setting and by just one international consultancy. See Table 5.

Table 5 *Language Teacher Research in Australia and New Zealand*

Topic/Issue	Method	Results	Reflection	Setting
Immersion programs	Reflective writing, interviews	Most students had a positive response	Opportunity to talk to locals and host family should be provided	University
Authenticity of EAP texts	Recorded authentic lectures	Students wanted explicit written outlines with lectures	Students need to be taught how to adopt more reflective stances on course content	University
Authentic models for teaching ESL conversation skills	Pre- and post-tests, survey, reflective journal	Listening to home-made cassettes was helpful	Clear wording was needed in student surveys	University
Retaining new vocabulary items	Student reflections, interviews, video-recorded lessons	Repetition, focusing, and turn-taking all had positive effects on recall of new vocabulary	There was greater awareness of the role of interaction in lessons	University
Success in international exams	Questionnaires, interviews, statistical analysis	Higher-scoring students reported more frequent use of strategies related to all four skills	Teaching test strategies in addition to the regular curriculum were beneficial	International consultancy
Mixed-parentage students and non-English heritage languages	Forty-page survey	Those whose parental languages were non-English self-assessed their literacy skill at a third of the level of those with one English-speaking parent	Students should be asked more questions about their native languages and cultures	University
Multi-level, immigrant language classes	Implementation of new curriculum	Peer assistance met with unwillingness	The quality of personal reflective practice was enhanced	University

Table 5 (*continued*)

Topic/Issue	Method	Results	Reflection	Setting
EAP course for discipline-specific students	Implementation of EAP course, students' written work, survey	Students asked for more models of critical language in English	Reflection on and evaluation of the curriculum were important	Private
Reconciling researcher and practitioner identities	Reflections on practice, email correspondence	Teaching practice was far less valued than research in academia	Both identities were equally useful and important	University
Native speaker teachers' perceptions of non-native speakers	Interviews	The non-English native speaking teachers interviewed did not see themselves as victims	Cultural awakening of researcher	University
Improve literacy for deaf students	Implementation of an ESL course for deaf students	Creating maxims designed for deaf students helped to keep the course beneficial	It was important to make tacit understandings of teachers explicit	University
Teaching text comprehension strategies	Teaching strategy skills, student samples of work	Students became less teacher-dependent	Teachers must become more adaptable to classroom issues	University

Although the topics covered in research in Australia and New Zealand were diverse, they tended to focus on culture, the concept of authenticity, and the design of the curriculum for specific audiences such as a study of the responses of students of cross-cultural parentage who speak one or more non-English heritage language, the effect of local cultural norms on students' development of English as an additional language (EAL), and how students retain new vocabulary items. Again, like the all the other volumes, the Australia and New Zealand researchers tended to use qualitative research methods, such as action research, as their preferred mode of data collection, and one used a combination of qualitative and quantitative methods.

LANGUAGE TEACHER RESEARCH IN AFRICA

Makalela (2009) presents TESOL research that was conducted by a group of TESOL university professors. See Table 6.

Table 6   *Language Teacher Research in Africa*

Topic/Issue	Method	Result	Reflection	Setting
Difficulties with English academic writing conventions	Audio recording, writing protocols, focused group discussions, interviews	Neither code-translation of academic concepts nor reliance on dictionary is helpful for students	Teachers should directly intervene in compositions	University
Debate to develop oral English proficiency	Self-reflective inquiry	Teacher's and peers' feedback and assessment were successfully built into the assessment of the debates	Teachers should look at the practical constraints of learner communication preferences	University
Corrective feedback in L2 student writing	Quasi-experimental, pre-during and post-feedback writing	Comparison of pre- and post-intervention feedback writing favored post-feedback writing	There should be a focus on the immediate writing needs of the learners	University
Spelling errors in the writing of university students	Writing tests, dictation test, questionnaires	More errors were seen in a de-contextualized dictation test	Strategies of teaching spelling at secondary school levels are needed	University
Acquisition of English vocabulary	COBUILD Grammar Patterns series	There were challenges with students recalling lexical items for use due to inadequate lexical knowledge and failure to make use of lexical information	Lexical information and shifts in meaning should be precisely presented	University
Text genre and process writing drills	Ethnography and quasi-experimental design	The level of uptake on process writing was very low	Assumptions of process writing were not met in a culture that had a different orientation for the organization of ideas	University

Table 6 (*continued*)

Topic/Issue	Method	Result	Reflection	Setting
Local language as resource in teaching English pronunciation	Corrective feedback, post-feedback pronunciation task	Pronunciation skills improved and there were and positive attitudes toward English pronunciation	Teachers should decide what to concentrate on	University

Topics covered in research in Africa ranged from research on the challenges faced by English communication students with an isiXhosa language background to the use of debate to afford students autonomy and the critical thinking skills required at a university level; how a local language can be used as a resource, not an impediment, in teaching English pronunciation; and naturalized spelling errors in the writing of university students. Although the majority of researchers in this volume tended to use qualitative research methods as their preferred mode of data collection, three out of the seven studies used a combination of qualitative and quantitative methods.

SUMMARY

A common theme across the six areas and sixty-seven studies is how TESOL teachers can improve student performance in various aspects of language learning, with the majority of TESOL researchers using some kind of qualitative research methods as their preferred mode of data collection, and only seven out of sixty-seven studies (or less than 10 percent) using some form of quantitative research methods. Most of the research seems to have been conducted in university settings in each region. This result could likely be because people working in university settings are given more time and funding, and are also expected to complete research regularly, whereas secondary or middle school teachers are not. Given the result of this cross-analysis – that is, that across all six areas practicing TESOL teachers seem to be grossly under-represented – it may be necessary for international organizations such as the TESOL International Association and IATEFL to provide more support for these TESOL teachers to systematically reflect on their own practices.

Task

The TESOL International Association's Language Teacher Research series used the chapter template outlined below to conduct TESOL teacher research in six different areas:

- *Statement of the issue.* This includes a brief description of the context and the participants. Why was this issue (this does not have to be a problem) important to you? Identify and express what you see as important to the situated nature of your work.

- *Brief review of the literature relating to the issue researched.* Please only include previous research considered directly relevant to the issue.
- *Procedures or responses the researcher made to the issue.* What was the procedure or response taken, why this procedure or response, and where did it come from? How was it implemented? For example, if interviews were used, were they structured or unstructured? What were the questions asked? Please give as many details as possible here as other teachers may want to replicate your research in different contexts.
- *Result.* What was the outcome? Give details and discuss the results.
- *Reflection.* A statement that articulates answers to the question, "So what?" What will you do now and in the future? What action will you take as a result of your findings? If you have already acted on your findings, what did you do? What have you learned as a result of the whole process? For example, what have you learned about your teaching? What have you learned about doing research? Also, at this point, the issue of the situated nature of the work should be revisited: why you think the issue is specific to your context.

- Following the chapter template outlined above, conduct your own TESOL teacher research, either replicating some of the studies above or conducting research on your own topic
- Discuss your TESOL teacher research plans with a colleague.

[For source details, see the list above under 'TESOL INTERNATIONAL ASSOCIATION'.]

REFERENCES

Abednia, A. (2012). Teachers' professional identity: Contributions of a critical EFL teacher education course in Iran. *Teaching and Teacher Education, 28*, 5, 706-17.

Abramson, L. V., Seligman, M. E. P., and Teasdale, J. D. (1978). Learned helplessness in humans: Critique and reformulation. *Journal of Abnormal Psychology, 87*, 49–74.

Achugar, M. (2009). Constructing a bilingual professional identity in a graduate classroom. *Journal of Language, Identity, and Education, 8*, 65–87.

Ahmadi, P., Samad, A. A., and Noordin, N. (2013). Identity formation of TEFL graduate students through oral discourse socialization. *Theory and Practice in Language Studies, 3*, 10, 1764-9.

Akbari, R. (2007). Reflections on reflection: A critical appraisal of reflective practices in L2 teacher education. *System, 35*, 2, 192–207.

Aliakbari, M., and Nejad, A. M. (2013). On the effectiveness of team teaching in promoting learners' grammatical proficiency. *Canadian Journal of Education, 36*, 3, 5-22.

Anderson, J. (2020). Key concepts in ELT: Reflection. *ELT Journal*, ccaa039. Available from: https://doi.org/10.1093/elt/ccaa039. https://academic.oup.com/eltj/advance-article/doi/10.1093/elt/ccaa039/5891444.

Andrews, S. P., Gilbert, L. S., and Martin, E. P. (2007). The first years of teaching: Disparities in perceptions of support. *Action in Teacher Education, 28*, 4–13.

Anhorn, R. (2008). The profession that eats its young. *Delta Kappa Gamma Bulletin, 74*, 3, 15-26.

Arslan, F. Y., and Ilin, G. (2013). Effects of peer coaching for the classroom management skills of teachers. *Journal of Theory and Practice in Education, 9*, 1, 43-59.

Artigliere, M., and Baecher, L. (2017). Sink or swim: aligning training with classroom reality in ESL co-teaching. In T. S. C. Farrell (ed.) *Preservice Teacher Education* (pp. 43-50). Alexandria, VA: TESOL Press.

Ashcraft, N. (2014). *Lesson Planning*. Alexandria, VA: TESOL Press.

Baecher, L. (2012). Feedback from the field: What novice preK-12 ESL teachers want to tell TESOL teacher educators. *TESOL Quarterly, 46*, 3, 578-88.

Bailey, K., Curtis, A., and Nunan, D. (2001). *Pursuing Professional Development: The Self as Source*. Boston, MA: Heinle and Heinle.

Banegas, D. L., De Stefani, M., Rebolledo, P., Troncoso, C. R., and Smith, R. (eds.). (2020). *Horizontes 1: ELT Teacher-Research in Latin America*. IATEFL. Available from: http://resig.weebly.com/uploads/2/6/3/6/26368747/horizontes_ebook.pdf.

Barkhuizen, G., Burns, A., Dikilitaş, K., and Wyatt, M. (eds.). (2018). *Empowering Teacher-Researchers, Empowering Learners*. IATEFL. Available from: http://resig.weebly.com/uploads/2/6/3/6/26368747/kenan_d_hoca_k%C4%B0tap_online.pdf.

Beijaard, D., Meijer, P. C., and Verloop, N. (2004). Reconsidering research on teachers' professional identity. *Teaching and Teacher Education, 20*, 2, 107–28.

Berliner, D. (1990). If the metaphor fits why not wear it? The teacher as executive. *Theory into Practice, 29*, 85-93.

Bernard, N. S., Dollinger, S. J., and Ramaniah, N. V. (2002). Applying the big five personality factors to the impostor phenomenon. *Journal of Personality Assessment, 78*, 2, 321-33.

Bleakley, A. (1999). From reflective practice to holistic reflexivity. *Studies in Higher Education, 24*, 3, 315–30.

Block, D. (1992). Metaphors we teach and learn by. *Prospect, 7*, 42-55.

Boblett, N., and Waring, H. (2017). The corrective feedback assignment: Seeing error correction in slow motion. In T. S. C. Farrell (ed.) *Preservice Teacher Education* (pp. 93-100). Alexandria, VA: TESOL Press.

Borg, S. (ed.). (2006). *Language Teacher Research in Europe.* Alexandria, VA: TESOL Press.

Borg, S. (2013). *Teacher Research in Language Teaching: A Critical Review.* New York, NY: Cambridge University Press.

Brandt, S. L. (2005). A life preserver for the "sink or swim" years: An investigation of new teacher obstacles and the impact of a peer support group. Dissertation Abstracts International, 3443A. (UMI No. 3201434).

Brems, C., Baldwin, M., Davis, L., and Namyniuk, L. (1994). The imposter syndrome as related to teaching evaluations and advising relationships. *Journal of Higher Education, 65*, 2, 183-93.

Brody, C. M., and Davidson, N. (eds.). (1998). *Professional Development for Cooperative Learning: Issues and Approaches.* Albany, NY: State University of New York Press.

Brookfield, S. (1995). *Becoming a Critically Reflective Teacher.* San Francisco, CA: Jossey-Bass.

Brown, H. D. (2007). *Teaching by Principles: An Interactive Approach to Language Pedagogy* (5th edn). White Plains, NY: Pearson.

Bullock, D., and Smith, R. (eds.). (2015). *Teachers Research!.* IATEFL. Available from: http://resig.weebly.com/teachers-research.html.

Bullough, R. V. (1989). *First-Year Teacher: A Case Study.* New York, NY: Teachers College Press

Bullough, R. V. (1990). Teacher education and teacher reflectivity. *Journal of Teacher Education, 40*, 2, 15-21.

Bullough, R. V., and Baughman, K. (1993). Continuity and change in teacher development: A first year teacher after five years. *Journal of Teacher Education, 44*, 86-95.

Bullough, R. V., and Gitlin, A. D. (1991). Educative communities and the development of the reflective practitioner. In B. R. Tabachnick and K. M. Zeichner (eds.) *Issues and Practices in Inquiry-Oriented Teacher Education* (pp. 35-55). London: Falmer Press.

Burns, A. (2009). Action research in second language teacher education. In A. Burns and J. C. Richards (eds.) *The Cambridge Guide to Second Language Teacher Education* (pp. 289-97). New York, NY: Cambridge.

Burns, A., and Burton, J. (eds.). (2008). *Language Teacher Research in Australia and New Zealand.* Alexandria, VA: TESOL Press.

Burns, A., and Richards, J. C. (2009). *The Cambridge Guide to Second Language Teacher Education.* New York, NY: Cambridge University Press.

Burns, A., Dikilitaş, K., Smith, R., and Wyatt, M. (eds.). (2017). *Developing Insights into Teacher-Research.* IATEFL. Available from: http://resig.weebly.com/developing-insights-into-teacher-research-2017.html.

Cabaroglu, N. (2014). Professional development through action research: Impact on self-efficacy. *System, 44*, 10, 79-88.

Calderhead, J. (1992). Induction: A research perspective on the professional growth of the newly qualified teacher. In J. Calderhead and J. Lambert (eds.) *The Induction of Newly Appointed Teachers* (pp. 5-21). London: General Teaching Council.

Caspersen, J., and Raaen, D. (2014). Novice teachers and how they cope. *Teachers and Teaching: Theory and Practice, 20,* 2, 189-211.

Chick, M. (2015). The education of language teachers: Instruction or conversation? *ELT Journal, 69,* 3, 297-307.

Chik, A., and Breidbach, S. (2011). Online language learning histories exchange: Hong Kong and German perspectives. *TESOL Quarterly, 45,* 3, 553-64.

Cirocki, A., and Farrell, T. S. C. (2017). Reflective practice for professional development of TESOL practitioners. *The European Journal of Applied Linguistics and TEFL, 6,* 2, 5–22.

Cirocki, A., Madyarov, I., and Baecher, L. (2019). Contemporary perspectives on student teacher learning and the TESOL practicum. In A. Cirocki, I. Madyarov, and L. Baecher (eds.) *Current Perspectives on the TESOL Practicum: Cases from around the Globe* (pp. 1-20). Amsterdam: Springer.

Clance, P. (1985). *The Imposter Phenomenon: When Success Makes You Feel Like a Fake.* Toronto: Bantam.

Clandinin, D. J., et al. (2015). Early career teacher attrition: intentions of teachers beginning. *Teaching Education, 26,* 1, 1-16.

Clarke, M. A. (1994). The dysfunctions of the theory/practice discourse. *TESOL Quarterly, 28,* 1, 9–26.

Cochran-Smith, M., and Lytle, S. L. (1993). *Inside/Outside Teacher Research and Knowledge.* New York, NY: Teachers College Press.

Cochran-Smith, M., and Lytle, S. L (1999). Relationships of knowledge and practice: Teacher learning in communities. *Review of Research in Education, 24,* 249-305.

Colombo, M., Brazil, K., and White, L. (2017). Reflections on service-learning. In T. S. C. Farrell (ed.) *Preservice Teacher Education* (pp. 51-8). Alexandria, VA: TESOL Press.

Coombe, C., and Barlow, L. (eds.). (2007). *Language Teacher Research in the Middle East.* Alexandria, VA: TESOL Press.

Copland, F. (2011). Legitimate talk in feedback conferences. *Applied Linguistics, 33,* 1–20.

Crookes, G. (2013). *Critical ELT in Action: Foundations, Promises, Praxis.* New York, NY: Routledge.

Danielson, C., and McGreal, T. (2000). *Teacher Evaluation: To Enhance Professional Practice.* Alexandria, VA: ASCD.

Darling-Hammond, L. (1997). *Doing What Matters Most: Investing in Quality Teaching.* New York, NY: National Commission on Teaching and America's Future.

Darling-Hammond, L., Chung, R., and Frelow, F. (2002). Variation in teacher preparation: How well do different pathways prepare teachers to teach? *Journal of Teacher Education, 53,* 286-302.

DeAngelis, K. J., Wall, A. F., and Che, J. (2013). The impact of preservice preparation and early career support on novice teachers' career intentions and decisions. *Journal of Teacher Education, 64,* 4, 338-55.

DelliCarpini, M., and Alonso, O. B. (2015). Teaching everything to no one and nothing to everyone: Addressing the content in content based instruction. In T. S. C. Farrell (ed.) *International Perspectives on English Language Teacher Education: Innovations from the Field* (pp. 51–73). Basingstoke: Palgrave Macmillan.

Deng, L., and Yuen, A. H. K. (2011). Towards a framework for educational affordances of blogs. *Computers & Education, 56,* 2, 441-51.

Dewey, J. (1920, reprint 1962). *Reconstruction and Philosophy.* Boston, MA: Beacon.

Dewey, J. (1933). *How We Think*. Madison, WI: University of Wisconsin Press.

Dikilitaş, K., Smith, R., and Trotman, W. (eds.). (2015). *Teacher-Researchers in Action*. IATEFL. Available from: http://resig.weebly.com/teacher-researchers-in-action.html.

Dikilitaş, K., Wyatt, M., Burns, A., and Barkhuizen, G. (eds.). (2019). *Energizing Teacher Research*. IATEFL. Available from: http://resig.weebly.com/uploads/2/6/3/6/26368747/energizing_teacher_research.pdf.

Dikilitaş, K., Wyatt, M., Hanks, J., and Bullock, D. (eds.). (2016). *Teachers Engaging in Research*. IATEFL. Available from: http://resig.weebly.com/teachers-engaging-in-research-2016.html.

Edge, J. (2006). *(Re-)Locating TESOL in an Age of Empire*. New York, NY: Palgrave Macmillan.

Edge, J. (2011). *The Reflexive Teacher Educator in TESOL*. New York, NY: Routledge.

Edge, J., and Richards, K. (1998). Why best practice is not good enough. *TESOL Quarterly*, *32*, 3, 569-76.

Edwards-Groves, C. J. (2014). Learning teaching practices: The role of critical mentoring conversations in teacher education. *Journal of Education and Training Studies*, *2*, 2, 151–66.

Eisen, M. J., and Tisdell, E. J. (2000). Editors' notes. In M.-J. Eisen and E. J. Tisdell (eds.) *Team Teaching and Learning in Adult Education* (vol. 87, pp. 1–3). San Francisco, CA: Jossey-Bass.

Eisenman, G., and Thornton, H. (1999). Telementoring: Helping new teachers through the first year. *T.H.E. Journal*, *26*, 9, 79-82.

Eröz-Tuğa, B. (2012). Reflective feedback sessions using video recordings. *ELT Journal*, *67*, 2, 175-83.

Erwing, R. A., and Smith, D. L. (2003). Retaining quality beginning teachers in the profession. *English Teaching: Practice and Critique*, *2*, 1, 15-32. Available at: http://education.waikato.ac.nz/research/files/etpe/2003v2nlart2.pdf.

Etherington, S., and Daubney, M. (eds.). (2017). *Developing as an EFL Researcher: Stories from the Field*. IATEFL. Available from: http://resig.weebly.com/developing-as-an-efl-researcher-2017.html.

Faez, F., and Valeo, A. (2012). TESOL teacher education: Novice teacher perceptions of their preparedness and efficacy in the classroom. *TESOL Quarterly*, *46*, 3, 450-71.

Faez, F., Cooke, S., Karas, M., and Vidwans, M. (2017). Examining the effectiveness of online discussion forums for teacher development. In T. S. C. Farrell (ed.) *Preservice Teacher Education* (pp. 7-12). Alexandria, VA: TESOL Press.

Fanselow, J. F. (1988). "Let's see": Contrasting conversations about teaching. *TESOL Quarterly*, *22*, 1, 113-30.

Fantilli, R. D., and McDougall, D. E. (2009). A study of novice teachers: Challenges and supports in the first years. *Teaching and Teacher Education*, *25*, 6, 814–25.

Farr, F. (2010). How can corpora be used in teacher education? In A. O'Keeffe and M. McCarthy (eds.) *The Routledge Handbook of Corpus Linguistics* (pp. 620-32). London and New York, NY: Routledge.

Farr, F. (2011). *The Discourse of Teaching Practice Feedback*. London: Routledge.

Farr, F. (2015). *Practice in TESOL*. Edinburgh: Edinburgh University Press.

Farr, F., and O'Riordan, E. (2017). Prospective and practising teachers discuss the theory–practice divide through blogs and E-portfolios. In T. S. C. Farrell (ed.) *Preservice Teacher Education* (pp. 13-28). Alexandria, VA: TESOL Press.

Farr, F., Farrell, A., and O'Riordan, E. (2019). *Social Interaction in Language Teacher Education*. Edinburgh: Edinburgh University Press.

Farrell, A. (2019). *Corpus Perspectives on the Spoken Models used by EFL Teachers*. New York: Routledge.

Farrell, T. S. C. (1999). The reflective assignment: Unlocking pre-service English teachers' beliefs on grammar teaching. *RELC Journal*, *30*, 2, 1-17.

Farrell, T. S. C. (2001a). Tailoring reflection to individual needs: A TESOL case study. *Journal of Education for Teaching, 21,* 23–38.

Farrell, T. S. C. (2001b). Critical friendships: Colleagues helping each other develop. *ELT Journal, 52,* 368-74.

Farrell, T. S. C. (2001c). English language teacher socialization during the practicum. *Prospect, 16,* 1, 49–62.

Farrell, T. S. C. (2003). Learning to teach English language during the first year: Personal influences and challenges. *Teaching and Teacher Education, 19,* 95-111.

Farrell, T. S. C. (2006a). "The teacher is an octopus": Uncovering preservice English language teachers' prior beliefs through metaphor analysis. *RELC Journal, 37,* 239-51.

Farrell, T. S. C. (2006b). The first year of language teaching: Imposing order. *System,* 34, 2, 211-21.

Farrell, T. S. C. (ed.). (2006c). *Language Teacher Research in Asia.* Alexandria, VA: TESOL Press.

Farrell, T. S. C. (2007a). Failing the practicum: Narrowing the gap between expectation and reality with reflective practice. *TESOL Quarterly, 41,* 193-201.

Farrell, T. S. C. (2007b). *Reflective Language Teaching: From Research to Practice.* London: Continuum Press.

Farrell, T. S. C. (2008). Here's the book, go teach the class: ELT practicum support. *RELC Journal, 39,* 2, 226–41.

Farrell, T. S. C. (2009). *Talking, Listening and Teaching: A Guide to Classroom Communication.* Thousand Oaks, CA: Corwin Press.

Farrell, T. S. C. (2012a). Novice-service language teacher development: Bridging the gap between preservice and in-service education and development. *TESOL Quarterly, 46,* 3, 435-49.

Farrell, T. S. C. (2012b). Exploring the professional role identities of novice ESL teachers through reflective practice. *The European Journal of Applied Linguistics and TESOL, 1,* 1, 2-14.

Farrell, T. S. C. (2012c). Reflecting on reflective practice: (Re) visiting Dewey and Schön. *TESOL Journal, 3,* 1, 7–16.

Farrell, T. S. C. (2013). *Reflective Writing for Language Teachers.* London: Equinox.

Farrell, T. S. C. (2014). *Reflective Practice in ESL Teacher Development Groups: From Practices to Principles.* Basingstoke: Palgrave Macmillan.

Farrell, T. S. C. (ed.). (2015a). *International Perspectives on English Language Teacher Education: Innovations from the Field.* Basingstoke: Palgrave Macmillan.

Farrell, T. S. C. (2015b). *Promoting teacher Reflection in Second Language Education: A Framework for TESOL Professionals.* New York, NY: Routledge.

Farrell, T. S. C. (2015c). It's not who you are! It's how you teach! Critical competencies associated with effective teaching. *RELC Journal, 46,* 1, 79-88.

Farrell, T. S. C. (2016a). From Trainee to Teacher: Reflective Practice for Novice Teachers. London: Equinox.

Farrell, T. S. C. (2016b). The teacher is a facilitator: Reflecting on ESL teacher beliefs through metaphor analysis. *IJLTR, 4,* 1, 1-10. Available from: https://files.eric.ed.gov/fulltext/EJ1127419.pdf.

Farrell, T. S. C. (2016c). TESOL, a profession that eats its young: The importance of reflective practice in teacher education. *IJLTR, 4,* 3, 97-107.

Farrell, T. S. C. (2016d). Teacher-researchers in action: Teachers research! *ELT Journal, 70,* 3, 352–5.

Farrell, T. S. C. (ed.). (2017). *Preservice Teacher Education.* Alexandria, VA: TESOL Press.

Farrell, T. S. C. (2018). *Research in Reflective Practice in TESOL*. New York, NY: Routledge.

Farrell, T. S. C. (2019a). *Reflection as Action in ELT*. Alexandria, VA: TESOL Press.

Farrell, T. S. C. (2019b). *Reflective Practice in ELT*. London: Equinox.

Farrell, T. S. C. (2020). *Reflective Teaching* (rev. edn). Alexandria, VA: TESOL Press.

Farrell, T. S. C., and Baecher, L. (2017). *Reflecting on Critical Incidents in Language Education*. London: Bloomsbury.

Farrell, T. S. C., and Bennis, K. (2013). Reflecting on ESL teacher beliefs and classroom practices: A case study. *RELC Journal, 44*, 163-76.

Farrell, T. S. C., and Ives, J. (2015). Exploring teacher beliefs and classroom practices through reflective practice: A case study. *Language Teaching Research, 19*, 5, 594-610.

Farrell, T. S. C., and Jacobs, G. (2011). *Essentials in Language Teaching*. London: Continuum Press.

Farrell, T. S. C., and Jacobs, G. (2020). *Essentials in Language Teaching*. London: Bloomsbury.

Farrell, T. S. C., and Mom, V. (2015). Exploring teacher questions through reflective practice. *Reflective Practice, 16*, 6, 849-66.

Farrell, T. S. C., and Vos, R. (2018). Exploring the principles and practices of teaching L2 speaking: Importance of reflective practice. *IJLTR, 4*, 3, 97-107.

Farrell, T. S. C., and Yang, D. (2018). Exploring an EAP teacher's beliefs and practices teaching L2 speaking: A case study. *RELC Journal, 50*, 1, 104-17.

Feiman-Nemser, S. (2001a). Helping novices learn to teach: Lessons from an exemplary support teacher. *Journal of Teacher Education, 52*, 1, 17-30.

Feiman-Nemser, S. (2001b). From preparation to practice: Designing a continuum to strengthen and sustain teaching. *Teachers College Record, 103*, 6, 1013–55.

Fenwick, A. (2011). The first three years: Experiences of early career teachers. *Teachers and Teaching: Theory and Practice, 17*, 3, 325–43.

Fradd, S. H., and Lee, O. (1997). Teachers' voices in program evaluation and improvement: A case study of a TESOL program. *Teaching and Teacher Education, 13*, 6, 563-77.

Franzak, J. K. (2002). Developing a teacher identity: The impact of critical friends practice on the student teacher. *English Education, 34*, 4, 258-80.

Freeman, D. (1998). *Doing Teacher-Research: From Inquiry to Understanding*. New York, NY: Heinle and Heinle.

Freeman, D. (2001). Second language teacher education. In R. Carter and D. Nunan (eds.) *The Cambridge Guide to Teaching English to Speakers of Other Languages* (pp. 72–80). Cambridge: Cambridge University Press.

Freeman, D. (2016). *Educating Second Language Teachers*. Oxford: Oxford University Press.

Friedman, I. A. (2004). Directions in teacher training for low-burnout teaching. In E. Frydenberg (ed.) *Thriving, Surviving, or Going Under: Coping with Everyday Lives* (pp. 305–26). Greenwich, CT: Information Age.

Fueyo, V., and Koorland, M. (1997). Teacher as researcher: A synonym for professionalism. *Journal of Teacher Education, 48*, 5, 336-44.

Fuller, F. F., and Brown, O. H. (1975). Becoming a teacher. In K. Ryan (ed.) *Teacher Education: The Seventy-Fourth Yearbook of the National Society for the Study of Education* (pp. 25-51). Chicago, IL: National Society for the Study of Education.

Furlong, J., and Maynard, T. (1995). *Mentoring Student Teachers The Growth of Professional Knowledge*. London and New York, NY: Routledge.

Gallant, A., and Riley, P. (2017). Early career teacher attrition in Australia: Inconvenient truths about new public management. *Teachers and Teaching, 23*, 8, 896-913.

Gan, Z. (2014). Learning from interpersonal interactions during the practicum: A case study of non-native ESL student teachers. *Journal of Education for Teaching, 40*, 2, 128-39.

Gándara, P., Maxwell-Jolly, J., and Driscoll, A. (2005). *Listening to Teachers of English Language Learners: A Survey of California Teachers' Challenges, Experiences, and Professional Development Needs*. Berkeley, CA: Policy Analysis for California Education.

Genc, Z. S. (2010). Teacher autonomy through reflective journals among teachers of English as a foreign language in Turkey. *Teacher Development, 14*, 3, 397-409.

Gladman, A. (2014). Team teaching is not just for teachers! Student perspectives on the collaborative classroom. *TESOL Journal, 6*, 1, 130-48.

Goker, S. D. (2006). Impact of peer coaching on self-efficacy and instructional skills in TEFL teacher education. *System, 34*, 239–54.

Golombek, P. (2015). Redrawing the boundaries of language teacher cognition: Language teacher educators' emotion, cognition, and activity. *Modern Language Journal, 99*, 3, 470-84.

Golombek, P., and Doran, M. (2014). Unifying cognition, emotion, and activity in language teacher professional development. *Teaching and Teacher Education, 39*, 102-11.

Goodson, I. F. (2000). Professional knowledge and the teacher's life and work. In: C. Day, A. Fernandez, T. E. Hauge, and J. Møller (eds.) *The Life and Work of Teachers: International Perspectives in Changing Times* (pp. 13–25). London and New York, NY: Falmer Press.

Gordon, R., Kane, T., and Staiger, D. (2006). *Identifying Effective Teachers Using Performance on the Job*. Hamilton Project discussion paper. Brookings Institution.

Graves, K. (2009). The curriculum of second language teacher education. In A. Burns and J. C. Richards (eds.) *The Cambridge Guide to Second Language Teacher Education* (pp. 115-24). New York, NY: Cambridge University Press.

Gravois, J. (2007). You're not fooling anyone. *The Chronicle of Higher Education, 54*, 11, A1. Available from: http://chronicle.com.

Guerrero-Nieto, C. H., and Meadows, B. (2015). Global professional identity in deterritorialized spaces: A case study of a critical dialogue between expert and novice nonnative English speaker teachers [Identidad profesional global en espacios desterritorializados: Un estudio de caso de los diálogos críticos entre profesores de inglés no nativos]. *PROFILE: Issues in Teachers' Professional Development, 17*, 2, 13-27.

Gun, B. (2010). Quality self-reflection through reflection training. *ELT Journal, 65*, 2, 126-35.

Halford, J. (1998). Easing the way for new teachers. *Educational Leadership, 55*, 5, 33–6.

Hammond, M., and Cartwright, V. (2003). "Three up": A case study of teachers of information and communications technology in their third year of teaching. *Teacher Development, 7*, 2, 211-27.

Hanington, L., and Pillai, A. (2017). Bridging the theory–practice gap in teaching writing in pre-service teacher education. In T. S. C. Farrell (ed.) *Preservice Teacher Education* (pp. 37-42). Alexandria, VA: TESOL Press.

Hao, X. (2017). Seeing trees in the forest: Using focused observation in preservice TESOL teacher education. In T. S. C. Farrell (ed.) *Preservice Teacher Education* (pp. 77-84). Alexandria, VA: TESOL Press.

Hatton, N., and Smith, D. (1995). Reflection in teacher education: Towards definition and implementation. *Teaching and Teacher Education, 11*, 33-9.

Hennerby-Leung, M., Gayton, A., Hu, X., and Chen, X, (2019). Transitioning from Master's studies to the classroom: From theory to practice. *TESOL Quarterly, 53*, 3, 685-711.

Hernandez, L. J. (2015). Making sense of SLA theories through reflection. *Lenguaje, 43*, 1, 137-58.

Higginbotham, C. (2019). Professional development: Life or death after pre-service training? *ELT Journal, 73*, 4, 396-408.

Hoban, G. F. (2005). *The Missing Links in Teacher Education Design: Developing a Multi-Linked Conceptual Framework*. Dordrecht: Springer.

Hobson, A. J., Ashby, P., Malderez, A., and Tomlinson, P. D. (2009). Mentoring beginning teachers: What we know and what we don't. *Teaching and Teacher Education, 25,* 1, 207–16.

Hopper, D., and Snyder, W. (2017). Becoming a "real" teacher: A case study of professional development in *eikaiwa. The European Journal of Applied Linguistics and TEFL, 6,* 2, 183-201.

Houston, C. R. (2016). Do scaffolding tools improve reflective writing in professional portfolios? A content analysis of reflective writing in an advanced preparation program. *Action in Teacher Education, 38,* 4, 399–409.

Howe, E. R. (2006). Exemplary teacher induction: An international review. *Educational Philosophy and Theory, 38,* 3, 287-97.

Hung, H., and Yeh, H. (2013). Forming a change environment to encourage professional development through a teacher study group. *Teaching and Teacher Education, 36,* 153-65.

Hunt, K., Gurvitch, R., and Lund, J. L. (2016). Teacher evaluation: Done to you or with you? *JOPERD: The Journal of Physical Education, Recreation & Dance, 87,* 9, 21-7.

Ingersoll, R. (2012). Beginning teacher induction: What the data tell us. *Phi Delta Kappan, 93,* 8, 47-51.

Ingersoll, R., and Smith, T. (2003). The wrong solution to the teacher shortage. *Educational Leadership, 60,* 8, 30-3.

Ingersoll, R. M., Merrill, L., and May, H. (2014). *What Are the Effects of Teacher Education and Preparation on Beginning Teacher Attrition?* CPRE Research Reports. Philadelphia, PA: Consortium for Policy Research in Education. Available from: http://repository.upenn.edu/cgi/viewcontent.cgi?article=1002&context=cpre_research reports.

Ji Hong. (2010). Pre-service and beginning teachers' professional identity and its relation to dropping out of the profession. *Teaching and Teacher Education, 26,* 8, 1530-43.

Johnson, K. E. (1992). The relationship between teachers' beliefs and practices during literacy instruction for non-native speakers of English. *Journal of Reading Behavior, 24,* 1, 83-108.

Johnson, K. E. (2006). The sociocultural turn and its challenges for L2 teacher education. *TESOL Quarterly, 40,* 1, 235-57.

Johnson, K. E. (2009). *Second Language Teacher Education: A Sociocultural Perspective.* New York, NY: Routledge.

Johnson, K. E. (2013). Innovation through teacher education programs. In K. Hyland and L. C. Wong (eds.) *Innovation and Change in English Language Education* (pp. 13–27). New York, NY: Routledge.

Johnson, K. R., Harrold, L. M., Cochran, D. J., Brannan, D., and Bleistein, T. (2014). An examination of the first years: Novice ESOL teachers' experiences with loneliness and stress. *Pure Insights, 3,* 1–10.

Johnston, B., and Madejski B. (2004). A fresh look at team teaching. *The Language Teacher, 29,* 2–7.

Joram, E., and Gabriele, A. (1998). Pre-service teachers' prior beliefs: Transforming obstacles into opportunities. *Teaching and Teacher Education 14,* 2, 175-91.

Kagan, D. M. (1992). Professional growth among pre-service and beginning teachers. *Review of Educational Research, 64,* 129-69.

Kang, Y., and Cheng, X. (2014). Teacher learning in the workplace: A study of the relationship between a novice EFL teacher's classroom practices and cognition development. *Language Teaching Research, 18,* 2, 169–86.

Kardos, S. M., Johnson, S. M., Peske, H. G., Kauffman, D., and Liu, E. (2001). Counting on colleagues: New teachers encounter the professional cultures of their schools. *Educational Administration Quarterly, 37,* 2, 250-90.

Kelly, N., and Antonio, A. (2016). Teacher peer support in social network sites. *Teaching and Teacher Education, 56*, 138-49.

Knezedivc, B. (2001). Action research. *IATEFL Teacher Development SIG Newsletter, 1*, 10-12.

Kömür, Ş., and Çepik, H. (2015). Diaries as a reflective tool in pre-service language teacher education. *Educational Research and Reviews, 10*, 12, 1593-8.

Korthagen, F. (2004). In search of the essence of a good teacher: Towards a more holistic approach in teacher education. *Teaching and Teacher Education, 20*, 77–97.

Kwan, T., and López-Real, F. (2010). Identity formation of teacher-mentors: An analysis of contrasting experiences using a Wengerian matrix framework. *Teaching and Teacher Education, 26*, 3, 722–31.

Laats, E. (2020). Novice teachers' satisfaction with teacher preparation and recommendations for improving teacher training. In *Proceedings of the 3rd International Conference on Research in Education, Teaching and Learning*, 1-12. Available from: https://www.dpublication.com/wp-content/uploads/2020/02/33-488.pdf.

Lacey, C. (1977). *The Socialisation of Teachers*. London: Methuen.

Lakshmi, B. S. (2014). Reflective practice through journal writing and peer observation: A case study. *Turkish Online Journal of Distance Education, 15*, 4, 189-204.

Lave, J., and Wenger, E. (1991). *Situated Learning*. Cambridge: Cambridge University Press.

Leshem, S., and Bar-Hama, R. (2008). Evaluating teaching practice *ELT Journal, 62*, 257-65.

Lindqvist, P., Nordänger, U. K., and Carlsson, R. (2014). Teacher attrition the first five years: A multifaceted image. *Teaching and Teacher Education, 40*, 94–103.

Lortie, D. C. (1975). *Schoolteacher: A Sociological Study*. Chicago, IL: University of Chicago Press.

McCarthy, M. J. (ed.). (2016). *The Cambridge Guide to Blended Learning in Language Teaching*. Cambridge: Cambridge University Press.

McCormack, B. (2017). Reflective writing feedback: Thinking beyond the constraints of research-driven recommendations. In T. S. C. Farrell (ed.), *Preservice Teacher Education* (pp. 85-92). Alexandria, VA: TESOL Press.

McCormack, B., Baecher, L., and Cuenca, A. (2019). University-based teacher supervisors: Their voices, their dilemmas. *Journal of Educational Supervision, 2*, 1, 22-37.

McGarrell, H. M. (ed.). (2007). *Language Teacher Research in the Americas*. Alexandria, VA: TESOL Press.

Mackay, J., Birello, M., and Xerri, D. (eds.). (2018). *ELT Research in Action: Bridging the Gap between Research and Classroom Practice*. IATEFL. Available from: http://resig.weebly.com/uploads/2/6/3/6/26368747/elt_final[2].pdf.

Mackay, J., Birello, M., and Xerri, D. (eds.). (2020). *ELT Research in Action: Bringing Together Two Communities of Practice*. IATEFL. Available from: http://resig.weebly.com/uploads/2/6/3/6/26368747/eltria2019formattedfinal2.pdf.

McKinley, J. (2019). Evolving the TESOL teaching–research nexus. *TESOL Quarterly, 53*, 3, 875-84.

Macknish, C., Porter-Szucs, I., Tomaš, Z., Scholze, A., Slucter, C., and Kavetsky, A. (2017). Voices from an MA-TESOL program: Bridging theory and practice from the ground up. In T. S. C. Farrell (ed.) *Voices from the TESOL Classroom: Participant Inquiries in Pre-Service Teacher Education Classes* (pp. 29-36). Alexandria, VA: TESOL Press.

Mak, B., and Pun, S. (2015). Cultivating a teacher community of practice for sustainable professional development: Beyond planned efforts. *Teachers and Teaching: Theory and Practice, 21*, 1, 4-21.

Makalela, L. (ed.). (2009). *Language Teacher Research in Africa*. Alexandria, VA: TESOL Press.

Malderez, A., and Bodoczky, C. (1999). *Mentor Courses: A Resource Book for Teacher-Trainers.* Cambridge: Cambridge University Press.

Mann, S. (2015). Using screen capture software to improve the value of feedback on academic assignments in teacher education. In T. S. C. Farrell (ed.) *International Perspectives on English Language Teacher Education* (pp 160-80). Basingstoke: Palgrave Macmillan.

Mann, S., and Walsh, S. (2017). *Reflective Practice in English Language Teaching.* New York, NY: Routledge.

Manuel, J., and Carter, D. (2016). Sustaining hope and possibility: Early-career English teachers' perspectives on their first years of teaching. *English in Australia, 51,* 1, 91-103.

Manuel, J., Dutton, J., and Carter, D. (2018). "As much as I love being in the classroom . . . ": Understanding secondary English teachers' workload. *English in Australia, 53,* 3, 5-22.

Mattheoudakis, M. (2007). Tracking changes in EFL teachers' beliefs in Greece. *Teaching and Teacher Education, 23,* 1272-88.

Matthews, G., and Clance, P. (1985). Treatment of the impostor phenomenon in psychotherapy clients. *Psychotherapy in Private Practice, 3,* 1, 71-81.

Mattsson, M., Eilertsen, T. V., and Rorrison, D. (2011). What is practice in teacher education? In M. Mattsson, T. V. Eilertsen, and D. Rorrison (eds.) *A Practicum Turn in Teacher Education* (pp. 1–15). Rotterdam: Sense.

Melnick, S. A., and Meister, D. G. (2008). A comparison of beginning and experienced teachers' concerns. *Educational Research Quarterly, 31,* 3, 39-56.

Mercado, L., and Baecher, L. (2014). Video-based self-observation as a component of developmental teacher evaluation. *Global Education Review, 1,* 3, 63-77.

Mercado, L., and Mann, S. (2014). Mentoring for teacher evaluation and development. In A. Howard and H. Donaghue (eds.) *Teacher Evaluation in Second Language Education* (pp. 43-65). London: Bloomsbury.

Mikulec, E., and Hamann, K. (2020). "My eyes have been opened": Pre-service secondary teachers exploring behavior management through a microteaching project. *Action in Teacher Education, 42,* 2, 102-19.

Miller, J. (2009). Teacher identity. In A. Burns and J. Richards (eds.) *The Cambridge Guide to Second Language Teacher Education* (pp. 171-81). New York, NY: Cambridge University Press.

Mirici, I. H., and Hergüner, S. (2015). A digital European self-assessment tool for student teachers of foreign languages: The EPOSTL. *Turkish Online Journal of Educational Technology, 14,* 1, 1-10.

Murray, D. E., and Christison, M. (2018). *Online Language Teacher Education: A Review of the Literature.* Norwich: Aqueduto.

OECD (Organisation for Economic Co-operation and Development) (2018a). *Teachers Matter: Attracting, Developing and Retaining Effective Teachers: Pointers for Policy Development.* Paris: OECD.

OECD (Organisation for Economic Co-operation and Development) (2018b). *Early Career Teachers: Pioneers Triggering Innovation or Compliant Professionals?* Paris: OECD.

Olsen, B., and Anderson, L. (2007). Courses of action: A qualitative investigation into urban teacher retention and career development. *Urban Education, 42,* 5–29.

Ong, W. A., Swanto, S., and Alsaqqaf, A. (2020). Engaging in reflective practice via vlogs: Experience of Malaysian ESL pre-service teachers. *Indonesian Journal of Applied Linguistics, 9,* 716-24.

Ong'ondo, C. O., and Borg, S. (2011). "We teach plastic lessons to please them": The influence of supervision on the practice of English language student teachers in Kenya. *Language Teaching Research, 15,* 4, 509–28.

O'Riordan, E. (2018). *TESOL Student Teacher Discourse: A Corpus-Based Analysis of Online and Face-to-Face Interactions*. London and New York: Routledge.

O'Riordan, E., and Murray, L. (2010). A corpus-based analysis of online synchronous and asynchronous modes of communication within language teacher education. *Classroom Discourse*, 1, 2, 181-98.

O'Riordan, E., and Murray, L. (2012). Sharing and collaborating between an online community of novice teachers: CMC in language teacher education. *Journal of e-Learning and Knowledge Society*, 8, 3, 91-103.

Orland-Barak, L. (2005). Portfolios as evidence of reflective practice: What remains untold. *Educational Research*, 47, 25-44.

Oxford, R. L., Tomlinson, S., Barcelos, A., Harrington, C., Lavine, R. Z., Saleh, A., and Longhini, A. (1998). Clashing metaphors about classroom teachers: Toward a systematic typology for the language teaching field. *System*, 26, 3-50.

Palmer, P. J. (1998). *The Courage to Teach*. San Francisco, CA: Jossey-Bass.

Parks, S. (2010). Using a WebCT discussion forum during the TESL practicum: Reflection as social practice. *Canadian Journal of Applied Linguistics*, 13, 1, 52-70.

Payant, C., and Murphy, J. (2012). Cooperating teachers' roles and responsibilities in a MATESOL practicum. *TESL Canada Journal*, 29, 2, 1-23.

Peercy, M. M. (2012). Problematizing the theory–practice gap: How ESL teachers make sense of their preservice teacher education. *Journal of Theory and Practice in Education*, 8, 1, 20-40.

Pennington, M., and Richards, J. C. (2016). Teacher identity in language teaching: Integrating personal, contextual, and professional factors. *RELC Journal*, 1, 5-23.

Pennington, M., and Urmston, A. (1998). The teaching orientation of graduating students on a BATESL course in Hong Kong: A comparison with first-year students. *Hong Kong Journal of Applied Linguistics*, 3, 2, 17-45.

Phillips, O. (2015). Revolving door of teachers costs schools billions every year. *nprEd*, March 30.

Rebolledo, P., Smith, R., and Bullock, D. (eds.). (2016). *Champion Teachers: Stories of Exploratory Action Research*. Available from: https://englishagenda.britishcouncil.org/sites/default/files/attachments/british_council_champion_teachers_1.pdf.

Renard, L. (2003). Setting new teachers up for failure . . . or success. *Educational Leadership*, 60, 8, 62-6.

Richards, J. C. (1998). *Beyond Training*. New York, NY: Cambridge University Press.

Richards, J. C. (2014). *Key Issues in Language Teaching*. New York, NY: Cambridge University Press.

Richards, J. C., and Farrell, T. S. C. (2005). *Professional Development for Language Teachers*. New York, NY: Cambridge University Press.

Richards, J. C., and Farrell, T. S. C. (2011). *Teaching Practice: A Reflective Approach*. New York, NY: Cambridge University Press.

Richards, J. C., and Lockhart, C. (1994). *Reflective Teaching*. New York, NY: Cambridge University Press.

Richards, J. C., Gallo, P., and Renandya, W. (2001). Exploring teachers' beliefs and the processes of change. *The PAC Journal*, 1, 1, 41-62.

Richards, J. C., Platt, J., and Platt, H. (1992). *Longman Dictionary of Language Teaching and Applied Linguistics* (2nd edn). London: Longman.

Roberts, J. (1998). *Language Teacher Education*. London: Arnold.

Sachs, J. (1999). Using teacher research as a basis for professional renewal. *Journal of Inservice Education*, 25, 1, 39–53.

Sağlam, A. L. G., and Dikilitaş, K. (eds.). (2019). *Stories by Teacher Researchers in an Online Research Community*. IATEFL. Available from: http://resig.weebly.com/stories-by-teacher-researchers-in-an-online-research-community-2019.html.

Salas, L. A., and Ager, E. O. (eds.). (2020). *Creating Quiet Reflective Spaces: Language Teacher Research as Professional Development*. IATEFL. Available from: http://resig.weebly.com/uploads/2/6/3/6/26368747/creating_quiet_reflective_spaces.pdf.

Schlechty, P. C. (1990). *Reform in Teacher Education: A Sociological View*. ERIC Document Reproduction Service No. 332981.

Schön, D. A. (1983). *The Reflective Practitioner: How Professionals Think in Action*. New York, NY: Basic Books.

Schön, D. A. (1987). *Educating the Reflective Practitioner: Towards a New Design for Teaching and Learning in the Profession*. San Francisco, CA: Jossey-Bass.

Schwille, J., Dembele, M., and Schubert, J. (2007). *Global Perspectives on Teacher Learning: Improving Policy and Practice*. Paris: UNESCO.

Senior, R. M. (2006). *The Experience of Language Teaching*. New York, NY: Cambridge University Press.

Shi, L., and Yang, L. (2014). A community of practice of teaching English writing in a Chinese university. *System*, *42*, 133-42.

Shorten, K. (2013, 10 December). High-achievers suffering from "impostor syndrome." Available from: http://www.news.com.au/finance/highachievers-suffering-from-imposter-syndrome/newsstory/9e2708a0d0b7590994be28bb6f47b9bc.

Shulman, J. (ed.). (1992). *Case Methods in Teacher Education*. New York, NY: Teachers College Press.

Smith, M. G. (2019). A video-mediated critical friendship reflection framework for ESL teacher education. *TESL-EJ*, *23*, 1. Available from: http://tesl-ej.org/pdf/ej89/a7.pdf.

Smith, R., and Rebolledo, P. (2018). *A Handbook for Exploratory Action Research*. Available from: https://www.teachingenglish.org.uk/sites/teacheng/files/pub_30510_BC%20Explore%20Actions%20Handbook%20ONLINE%20AW.pdf.

Sowa, P. A. (2009). Understanding our learners and developing reflective practice: Conducting action research with English language learners. *Teaching and Teacher Education*, *25*, 8, 1026-32.

Stanley, C. (1998). A framework for teacher reflectivity. *TESOL Quarterly*, *32*, 584–91.

Stenhouse, L. (1975). *An Introduction to Curriculum Research and Development*. London: Heinemann.

Stewart, T. (2001). The value of action research in exploring methodology: A case of instruction on questioning in debate. *PAC Journal*, *1*, 79-92.

Stoynoff, S. (1999). The TESOL practicum: An integrated model in the US. *TESOL Quarterly*, *33*, 1, 145-51.

Stronach, I., Corbin, B., McNamara, O., Stark, S., and Warne, T. (2002). *Towards an uncertain politics of professionalism: Teacher and nurse identities in flux. Journal of Education Policy*, *17*, 1, 109-38.

Sydnor, J. (2017). "I didn't realize how hard it would be!" Tensions and transformations in becoming a teacher. *Action in Teacher Education*, *39*, 2, 218-36.

Taggart, G., and Wilson, A. P. (1998). *Promoting Reflective Thinking in Teachers*. Thousand Oaks, CA: Corwin Press.

Tang, E. (2009). Introduction and development of a blog-based teaching portfolio: A case study in a pre-service teacher education program. *The International Journal of Learning*, *16*, 8, 89-100.

Tarone, E. (2007). Equipping teachers to be language explorers: Exploring language in the classroom. Paper presented at the Language Teacher Education conference, Minneapolis, MN. Available from: https://apps.cla.umn.edu/directory/items/publica tion/297452.pdf.

Thomas, L. (2017). Learning to learn about the practicum: A self-study of learning to support student learning in the field. *Studying Teacher Education, 13*, 2, 165–78.

Thompson, T., Davis, H., and Davidson, J. (1998). Attributional and affective responses of impostors to academic success and failure outcomes. *Personality and Individual Differences, 25*, 2, 381-96.

Thompson, T., Foreman, P., and Martin, F. (2000). Impostor fears and perfectionistic concern over mistakes. *Personality and Individual Differences, 29*, 4, 629-47.

Thornbury, S. (1991). Metaphors we work by: EFL and it metaphors. *ELT Journal, 45*, 3, 193–200.

Thornbury, S. (1996). Teachers research teacher talk. *ELT Journal, 50*, 4, 279-89.

Tomaš, Z., Moger, N., Park, A., and Specht, K. (2017). Enriching graduate TESOL methods and materials courses with academic service-learning pedagogy. In T. S. C. Farrell (ed.) *Preservice Teacher Education* (pp. 59-66). Alexandria, VA: TESOL Press.

Tomlinson, P. (1995). *Understanding Mentoring: Reflective Strategies for School-Based Teacher Preparation.* Buckingham: Open University Press.

Trent, J. (2010). "My two masters": Conflict, contestation, and identity construction within a teaching practicum. *Australian Journal of Teacher Education, 35*, 7, 1-14.

Trent, J., and Lim, J. (2010). Teacher identity construction in school–university partnerships: Discourse and practice. *Teaching and Teacher Education, 26*, 1609-18.

Ussher, B. and Earl, K. (2010). Summative and formative: Confused by the assessment terms? *New Zealand Journal of Teachers' Work, 7*(1), 53–63

Valencia, S. W., and Killion, J. P. (1988). Overcoming obstacles to teacher change: Direction from school-based efforts. *Journal of Staff Development, 9*, 2-8.

Varghese, M., Morgan, B., Johnston, B., and Johnson, K. (2005). Theorizing language teacher identity: Three perspectives and beyond. *Journal of Language, Identity, and Education, 4*, 1, 21–44.

Vaughan, E. (2007). "I think we should just accept . . . our horrible lowly status": Analysing teacher–teacher talk within the context of community of practice. *Language Awareness, 16*, 3, 173-89.

Vo, L. T., and Nguyen, H. T. M. (2010). Critical friends group for EFL teacher professional development. *ELT Journal, 64*, 2, 205-13.

Vonk, J. (1989). Beginning teachers' professional development and its implication for teacher education and training. *The Irish Journal of Education, 23*, 1, 5-21.

Wach, A. (2015). Promoting pre-service teachers' reflections through a cross-cultural keypal project. *Language Learning and Technology, 19*, 1, 34-45.

Wallace, M. J. (1991). *Teacher training: a reflective approach.* Cambridge: Cambridge University Press.

Waring, H. Z. (2013). Two mentor practices that generate teacher reflection without explicit solicitations: Some preliminary considerations. *RELC Journal, 44*, 1, 103-19.

Waring, H. Z. (2014). Mentor invitations for reflection in post-observation conferences: Some preliminary considerations. *Applied Linguistics Review, 5*, 1, 99-123.

Wenger, E. (1998). *Communities of Practice.* Cambridge: Cambridge University Press.

Wexler, L. J. (2020). How feedback from mentor teachers sustained student teachers through their first year of teaching. *Action in Teacher Education, 42*, 2, 167–85.

Widdowson, H. G. (1984). The incentive value of theory in teacher education. *ELT Journal, 38*, 86-90.

Widdowson, H. (2012). Closing the gap, changing the subject. In J. Hüttner, B. Mehlmauer-Larcher, S. Reichl, and B. Schiftner (eds.), *Theory and Practice in EFL Teacher Education: Bridging the Gap* (pp. 3-15). Bristol: Multilingual Matters.

Wideen, M., Mayer-Smith, J., and Moon, B. (1998). A critical analysis of the research on learning to teach: Making the case for an ecological perspective on inquiry. *Review of Educational Research, 68,* 130–78.

Wright, T. (2010). Second language teacher education: Review of recent research on practice. *Language Teaching, 43,* 3, 259-96.

Yan, C., and He, C. (2010). Transforming the existing model of teaching practicum: A study of Chinese EFL student teachers' perceptions. *Journal of Education for Teaching, 36,* 1, 57–73.

Yang, P. (2013). Two heads are better than one: Team teaching in TESOL internship. *Kalbų Studijos, 23,* 113-25.

Yang, S. (2009). Using blogs to enhance critical reflection and community of practice. *Educational Technology & Society, 12,* 2, 11-21.

Yazan, B. (2015). "You learn best when you're in there": ESOL teacher learning in the practicum. *The CATESOL Journal, 27,* 2, 171-99.

Yost, D. S. (2006). Reflection and self-efficacy: Enhancing the retention of qualified teachers from a teacher education perspective. *Teacher Education Quarterly, 33,* 4, 59-74.

Zeichner, K., and Grant, C. (1981). Biography and social structure in the socialization of student teachers. *Journal of Education for Teaching, 1,* 298–314.

INDEX

CPSIA information can be obtained
at www.ICGtesting.com
Printed in the USA
JSHW030215080521
14506JS00001B/1